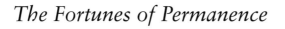

The Fortunes of Permanence

ROGER KIMBALL

The Fortunes of Permanence

CULTURE AND ANARCHY
IN AN AGE OF AMNESIA

South Bend, Indiana

ST. AUGUSTINE'S PRESS

2012

Manufactured in the United States and printed on
acid-free paper. The paper used in this publication meets
the minimum requirements of ANSI/NISO Z39.48 1992
(R 1997) (*Permanence of Paper*).

2 3 4 5 6 18 17 16 15 14 13 12

Library of Congress Cataloging-in-Publication Data

Kimball, Roger, 1953–
The fortunes of permanence: culture and anarchy in an age of amnesia/
Roger Kimball.
p. cm.
Includes bibliographical references and index.
ISBN 978-1-58731-256-4 (hardcover: alk. paper)
1. Social values—United States. 2. Social change—United States.
3. Cultural relativism. 4. United States—Civilization—
21st century. 5. Civilization, Western—21st century.
6. Civilization, Modern—21st century.
I. Title. II. Title: Culture and anarchy in an age of amnesia.
HN90.M6K56 2012
303.4—dc23

2011053476

St. Augustine's Press
www.staugustine.net

For Michael *&* Marilyn Fedak

Contents

Acknowledgments

"WHAT'S IT ABOUT?" That's the question I usually fielded after telling someone the title of this book. "*The Fortunes of Permanence*" is bad enough: I mean, in what sense do permanent things have fortunes? Aren't fortunes—those "slings and arrows" that so arrested the melancholy Dane—aren't they a liability of the impermanent? And then we move on to the subtitle: "Culture and Anarchy in an Age of Amnesia." Doesn't Matthew Arnold, who wrote an entire book called *Culture and Anarchy*, have enough to worry about without the prospect of wholesale forgetfulness? I sometimes say that this is a book about memory, sometimes that it is a defense of permanent things at a time when they are conspicuously under seige. True enough. There is a sense, though, in which the British writer John Buchan got to the core of what this book is about when he observed in his memoir *Pilgrim's Way* that "The world must remain an oyster for youth to open. If not, youth will cease to be young, and that will be the end of everything." Buchan speculated that "the challenge with which we are now faced may restore us to that manly humility which alone gives power." If that seems elliptical, well, so be it. Though *The Fortunes of Permanence* ranges over a wide swathe of cultural and political history, both bits of Buchan's reflection—the part about youth and innocence and wonder as well as the part about manly humilty and power (see below, "Rereading John Buchan")—are at the heart of my concern in what follows.

One thing of which youth tends to have an imperfect appreciation is the extent to which its achievements bear witness to the accumulated benefactions of others. Maturity has no excuse: it well knows what it owes to others, even if it is often reticent about saying so. A complete list of my intellectual and moral creditors would be long indeed. Here let me acknowledge the help and inspiration, not to mention the conversation, admonition, and correction, of Conrad Black, Robert H. Bork, Peter Collier, James Franklin, Robert P. George, the late John Gross, Joseph Hartmann, Daniel Kelly, Henry A. Kissinger, Andrew C. McCarthy, Robert L. Paquette, James F. Penrose, Peter Pettus, James Piereson, Andrew Roberts, Dianne Sehler, John Silber, and Harry Stein.

Special thanks go to my splendid colleagues at *The New Criterion* and Encounter Books: Cricket Farnsworth, Rebecca Litt, Lauren Miklos, Heather Ohle, James Panero, Sam Schneider, Emily Smith, Nola Tully, and David Yezzi. I could not have gotten outside the technical aspects of putting this book together without the patient ministrations of InDesign maestros Jeffrey Greggs and Lesley Rock. To Hilton Kramer, dear friend and founding editor of *The New Criterion*, who died, age 84, in March 2012, I owe an unpayable debt. Into that same category belongs Alexandra Kimball, whose compilation of the book's index is but a minor item on an unsurveyable roster of gratitude. Finally, it gives me great pleasure to dedicate this book to Michael and Marilyn Fedak, stalwart friends who have done an immense amount to bolster the fortunes of permanence. I am deeply grateful to them all.

RK   *March 2012*

Preface: Mostly About Relativism

As a rule, only very learned and clever men deny what is obviously true. Common men have less brains, but more sense.
—William T. Stace

IT WASN'T *that* long ago that a responsible educated person in the West was someone who entertained firm moral and political principles. When those principles were challenged, he would typically rise to defend them. The more serious the challenge, the more concerted the defense.

Today, as the Canadian writer William Gairdner reminds us in *The Book of Absolutes* (2008), his little-noticed but excellent study of relativism, the equivalent educated person is likely to have a very different attitude towards whatever moral and political ideas—"principles" is no longer the right word—he lives by. When those ideas are challenged, deference to the challenger rather than defense of the principles is the order of the day. "While perhaps more broadly learned" than his less forgiving predecessor, such a person, Gairdner writes,

> is more likely to think of him or herself as proudly distinguished by the *absence* of "rigid" opinions and moral values,

to be someone "tolerant" and "open." Such a person will generally profess some variation of relativism, or "you do your thing and I'll do mine," as a personal philosophy. Many in this frame of mind privately consider themselves exemplars of an enlightened modern attitude that civilization has worked hard to attain, and if pushed, they would admit to feeling just a little superior to all those sorry souls of prior generations forced to bend under moral and religious constraints.

The institutionalization of this amalgam of attitudes—blasé tolerance shading into moral indifference underwritten by that giddy sense of self-righteousness and superiority—has precipitated what Cardinal Joseph Ratzinger (now Pope Benedict XVI) called "the dictatorship of relativism."

I understand that, for those enthralled by this dictatorship, the fact that an orthodox Catholic provided a rubric for the servitude is reason enough to dispute its relevance. But considered simply as a sociological datum, the triumph (if that is a less opprobrious word than "dictatorship") of relativism describes, in Anthony Trollope's phrase, "the way we live now"—"we" being the beneficiaries of that "enlightened modern attitude" that Gairdner described in the passage just quoted.

Not that the attitude itself is exclusively modern. One could go back at least to Aristotle's dissection of Protagoras's "man-is-the-measure-of-all-things" philosophy to find a warning flag about the species of intellectual incontinence concentrated in the doctrine of relativism. What Gairdner is talking about is the metastasis of an abstract human possibility into a commonly shared assumption about the world and our place in it. The English historian Paul Johnson located the modernity of modern times in its embrace of relativism. In *Modern Times* (rev. ed. 1991), his magisterial procession through the political and moral history of the

2

twentieth century, Johnson even announced the exact birthday of the era he set out to describe. The Modern World, Johnson wrote in his opening flourish, began on May 29, 1919. That was the day Einstein's theory of relativity was experimentally confirmed, thus shattering the complacent confidence of the Newtonian world view.

Granted, the theory of relativity is not the same thing as relativism. Johnson acknowledges this. And yet . . . As with the second law of thermodynamics (which popularized the term "entropy") or Heisenberg's "Uncertainty Principle," the theory of relativity was a piece of science that cast a large metaphorical shadow. Was it misunderstood—even un-understood? It didn't matter. Johnson was right that the popular appropriation of Einstein's theory provided a good illustration of the "dual impact" of scientific innovators: Their theories change our understanding of the physical world, "but they also change our ideas. The second effect is often more radical than the first."

The embrace of relativism was a harbinger, a symptom of a seismic shift in the way people view the world. People? Well, those educated people, anyway, of which Gairdner spoke. Of them we have a greater and greater supply. (I say "educated"; I mean "schooled"—a difference that makes all the difference.) More and more, however, relativism has assumed the role of civil religion in the West. There are, of course, pockets of resistance. There are even some indications that the confident spread of relativism may be faltering. Part of the task of this book is to identify and champion some of those pockets of resistance. But there can be little doubt that the values and assumptions of relativism, e.g., multiculturalism, have made great inroads, penetrating from elite to demotic culture.

This is a fact that Madison Avenue has recognized and sought to capitalize on. Consider the popular campaign undertaken by the HSBC bank. At many large airports these days, one cannot process down the gangway to one's plane without confronting their clever, insinuating series of ads dedicated to encouraging travelers to congratulate themselves on their lack of principle. After the original barrage, the campaign opened a new beachhead on trains, buses, and other venues.

IT'S A CATCHY, if semantically troubling, promotion. In the original series, each ad consisted of two pairs of identical pictures boldly labeled with opposite one-word descriptors. For example, an image of a serious-looking young businessman in suit and tie bears the label "Leader" while next to it is an image of legs in ratty jeans and scuffed boots bearing the legend "Follower." The same images are then repeated with the words reversed: the leader becomes the follower and vice versa. Other image-pairs come labeled "Good/Bad," "Trendy/Traditional," "Pain/Pleasure," "Perfect/Imperfect," etc. And in case you are slow on the uptake, the Aesop behind the ad includes a helpful moral: "If everyone thought the same, nothing would ever change," for example, or "An open mind is the best way to look at the world," or "Isn't it better to be open to other people's points of view?"

The question, of course, is meant to be rhetorical, what Latinists call a *nonne* question, i.e., one that expects the answer "Yes." Indeed, the series later dispensed with the question mark and moved from two to three alternatives. Thus we might see a cordon of power-generating windmills. Whether we think "Nature," "Future," or "Eyesore," we are meant to agree with the declarative assertion: "Different values make the world a richer place." (Do they? Doesn't it depend on the values being promulgated?)

What HSBC proudly calls its "yourpointofview.com" campaign is doubtless a successful bit of huckstering. But it is

4

also a wearisome bit of propaganda. Propaganda for what? There's an irony here. The whole rhetorical machinery of the ads communicates the presumption that we are dealing with the spirit of bold openness (a talismanic word, "openness") and a healthy tolerance for diversity. The incidental beneficiary of that happy thought is HSBC. But the reality of the message is simply the biggest unexamined cliché of our time: that differences among people are simply so many "points of view" and therefore (note the logic) that discriminating among those points of view with an eye to favoring one over another is to be guilty of an intellectual incapacity that is at the same time a moral failing (narrowness, intolerance, elitism, ethnocentrism—the whole menu of politically incorrect vices).

It is often said that an anthropologist is someone who respects the distinctive values of every culture but his own. We in the West are all anthropologists now. It is curious, though, that proponents of relativism and multiculturalism should use ethnocentrism as a stick with which to beat the West. As I argued in my book *Tenured Radicals* (rev. ed. 2008), both the idea and the critique of ethnocentrism are quintessentially Western. There has never in history been a society more open to other cultures than our own; nor has any tradition been more committed to self-criticism than the Western tradition: the figure of Socrates endlessly inviting self-scrutiny and rational explanation is a definitive image of the Western spirit. Moreover, "Western" science is not exclusively Western: it is science plain and simple. It was, to be sure, invented and developed in the West, but it is as true for the inhabitants of the Nile Valley as it is for the denizens of New York. That is why, outside the precincts of the humanities departments of Western universities, there is a mad dash to acquire Western science and technology. The deepest foolishness of multiculturalism shows itself in the puerile attacks it mounts on the cogency of scientific rationality, epitomized poignantly by the Afrocentrist who flips on his word processor to write books decrying the parochial nature of Western science and extolling the virtues of the "African way."

In part, HSBC's campaign is a certification of how far the assumptions of cultural relativism have penetrated. But what makes the ad campaign a significant emblem of the Zeitgeist is the way it insinuates a consistent prejudice into its brief against prejudice. The smartly attired young chap and the slob in jeans are not so much equals as competitors. The moral burden of the campaign (as distinct from its aim of benefiting its client) is not to encourage us to think more carefully about what it means to be a leader or follower, to be good or bad, to be trendy or traditional, but rather to blur the distinction between those contraries altogether. The aim is to short-circuit, not refine, our powers of discrimination. And the goal of that disruption is always at the expense of one side of the equation. (Yet another irony: were the transvaluation implicit in the "point-of-view" campaign really to succeed, one of the first casualties would be competitive enterprises like HSBC.) The ostensible tenet of this catechism is that all cultures are equally valuable and, therefore, that preferring one culture, intellectual heritage, or moral and social order to another is to be guilty of ethnocentrism. It's actually not quite as egalitarian as it looks, however, for you soon realize that the doctrine of cultural relativism is always a weighted relativism: Preferring Western culture or intellectual heritage is culpable in a way that preferring other traditions is not.

It is often said that relativism is the conviction that, when it comes to morals, there are no such things as absolute values and, when it comes to knowledge, there is no such thing as absolute truth. It is worth meditating on the use of the word "absolute" here. If there were a law against abusing innocent words, we would be justified in contacting OSHA about this unfair exploitation of "absolute."

What a relativist really believes (or believes he believes) is that 1) there is no such thing as value (as distinct from mere preference) and 2) there is no such thing as truth. The word "absolute" is merely an emollient, a verbal sedative intended to forestall unhappiness. What after all is the difference between saying "There is no such thing as absolute truth" and saying "There is no such thing as truth"? Take your time.

Relativism is a Cole Porter view of the world: "The world has gone mad today/And good's bad today,/And black's white today. . . . Anything Goes." The first upsurge of relativism can seem like fun. It's a Cole Porterish, jazz-age tipsiness: a moral and epistemological holiday from the stuffy concerns of . . . well, of everything that has nailed things down and inhibited one.

THE UNPLEASANT HANGOVER is not long in coming, however. What at first seemed like a welcome liberation soon reveals itself as a vertiginous exile. Which is to say that, at bottom, relativism is a religious problem. "God is dead," Nietzsche proclaimed in the 1880s. What he observed was an emotional, not an historical, fact. The unspoken allegiance to something transcending the vicissitudes of human desire had been (among the elites, anyway) shattered. "If there is no God," Dostoevsky said, "everything is permissible." Meaning what? Paul Johnson's long book is in part an illustration of and a commentary on those pronouncements of Nietzsche and Dostoyevsky. "Among the advanced races," Johnson notes, "the decline and ultimately the collapse of the religious impulse would leave a huge vacuum. The history of modern times is in great part the history of how that vacuum has been filled."

Relativism is the theme of *Modern Times*; the moral might be indexed thus: "Utopianism, dangers of. See Communism, ideology, professional politicians, socialism." And, indeed, that list could well be part of the card-catalogue entry for *The Fortunes of Permanence*, especially the third section. It is a sobering thought that Lenin (for example) was a committed humanitarian—a "friend of humanity," as I put it below. Johnson speaks of his "burning humanitarianism, akin to the love of the saints for God." Yes, and here's the rub: "But his humanitarianism was a very abstract passion. It embraced humanity in general but he seems to have little love for, or even interest in, humanity in particular. He saw the people with whom he dealt, his comrades, not as individuals but as receptacles for his ideas."

The paterfamilias of this brand of sentimental humanitarianism was Jean-Jacques Rousseau: "I think I know man," Rousseau said mournfully toward the end of his life, "but as for men, I know them not." (Nor, come to that, did he know any of his five illegitimate children, all of whom he abandoned to the orphanage.) It's a short step from Rousseau and his celebration of the emotion (as distinct from the reality) of virtue to Robespierre and his candid talk about "virtue and its emanation, terror." Lenin was a utopian. Hitler was a utopian. Ditto Stalin, Pol Pot, and . . . you can extend the list. All were adept practitioners of what Johnson calls the twentieth century's "most radical vice: social engineering—the notion that human beings can be shovelled around like bags of cement."

In a memorable passage at the beginning of the *Critique of Pure Reason*, Kant evokes a soaring dove that, "cleaving the air in her free flight," feels the resistance of the wind and imagines that its flight "would be easier still in empty space." A fond thought, of course, since absent that aeolian pressure the dove would simply plummet to the ground.

How regularly the friction of reality works that way: making possible our endeavors even as it circumscribes and limits their extent. And how often, like Kant's dove, we are tempted to imagine that our freedoms would be grander and more extravagant absent the countervailing forces that make them possible.

Such fantasies are as perennial as they are vain. They insinuate themselves everywhere in the economy of human desire, not least in our political arrangements. Noticing the imperfection of our societies, we may be tempted into thinking that the problem is with the limiting structures we have inherited. If only we could dispense with them, we might imagine, beating our wings, how much better things might be.

What a cunning, devilish word, "might." For here as elsewhere, possibility is cheap. Scrap our current political accommodations and things *might* be better. Then again, they might be a whole lot worse. Think again of Rousseau. "Man was born free," he declaimed, "but is everywhere in chains": two startling untruths in a single famous utterance. But such beguiling mendacity licensed the totalitarian goal of (as Rousseau himself put it) "forcing men to be free." Or think about that other acolyte of possibility, Karl Marx. How much misery have his theories underwritten, always promising paradise but instead delivering tyranny, oppression, poverty, and death?

It wasn't so long ago that I had hopes that the Marxist-socialist rot—outside the insulated purlieus of humanities departments at Western universities, anyway—was on the fast track to oblivion. Has any "philosophy" ever been so graphically refuted by events (or number of corpses)?

Maybe not, but refutation plays a much more modest role in human affairs than we might imagine. In fact, the socialist-inspired utopian chorus is alive and well, playing to full houses at an anti-democratic redoubt near you. Consider the apparently unkillable dream of "world government." It is as fatuous now as it was when H. G. Wells infused it with literary drama towards the beginning of the last century.

Every human child needs to learn to walk by itself; so, it seems, every generation needs to wean itself from the blandishments of various utopian schemes. In 2005, the political philosopher Jeremy Rabkin published a fine book called *Law Without Nations? Why Constitutional Government Requires Sovereign States.* Rabkin ably fleshes out the promise of his subtitle, but it would be folly to think this labor will not have to be repeated. As the English philosopher Roger Scruton argues in *A Political Philosophy* (2007), "Democracies owe their existence to national loyalties— the loyalties that are supposedly shared by government and opposition." Confusing national loyalty with nationalism, many utopians argue that the former is a threat to peace. After all, wasn't it national loyalty that sparked two world wars? No, it was that perverted offspring, national*ism*, which was defeated at great cost only by the successful mobilization of national loyalty. Scruton quotes Chesterton on this point: to condemn patriotism because people go to war for patriotic reasons, he said, is like condemning love because some loves lead to murder.

It is one of the great mysteries—or perhaps I should say it is one of the reliable reminders of human imperfection— that higher education often fosters a particular form of political stupidity. Scruton anatomizes that stupidity, noting "the educated derision that has been directed at our national loyalty by those whose freedom to criticize would have been extinguished years ago, had the English not been prepared to die for their country." This peculiar mental deformation, Scruton observes, involves "the repudiation of inheritance and home." It is a stage, he writes, through which the adolescent mind normally passes. But it is a stage in which intellectuals tend to become arrested. As George Orwell pointed out, intellectuals on the Left are especially prone to it, and this has often made them willing agents of foreign powers. The Cambridge spies [Guy Burgess, Kim Philby, et al.] offer a telling illustration of what [this tendency] has meant for our country.

It is also telling that this *déformation professionelle* of intellectuals encourages them to repudiate patriotism as an atavistic passion and favor transnational institutions over national governments, rule by committee or the courts over democratic rule.

AND THIS BRINGS US to yet another irony: that relativism and tyranny, far from being in opposition, are in fact regular collaborators. (See below, "What's Wrong with Benevolence.") This surprises many people, for it seems at first blush that relativism, by loosening the sway of dogma, should be the friend of liberty. In fact, as Mussolini saw clearly, in its "contempt for fixed categories" and "objective truth," "there is nothing more relativistic" than fascism. And it is not only fascism that habitually makes use of relativism as a moral softening-up agent. Modern liberal democracies champion reason in the form of a commitment to science and technology, but there, too, relativism shows itself as the friend of various strains of dehumanization. As Gairdner notes,

> wherever the materialist attitude of modern science is combined with relativism, we can predict that moral and political statements will soon emerge about the worthlessness of some forms of human life and how we ought to be eliminating certain classes of unworthy people such as "unwanted"

children by abortion, or the very old, or Jews, or the infirm by outright genocide or euthanasia.

Why does relativism, which begins with a beckoning promise of liberation from "oppressive" moral constraints, so often end in the embrace of immoral constraints that are politically obnoxious? Part of the answer lies in the hypertrophy or perversion of relativism's conceptual enablers—terms like "pluralism," "diversity," "tolerance," "openness," and the like. They all name classic liberal virtues, but it turns out that their beneficence depends on their place in a constellation of fixed values. Absent that hierarchy, they rapidly degenerate into epithets in the armory of political suasion. They retain the aura, the emotional charge, of positive values. But in reality they act as moral solvents, as what Gairdner calls "value-dispersing terms that serve as an official warning to accept all behaviours of others without judgment and, most important, to keep all moral opinions private." In this sense, the rise of relativism encourages an ideology of non-judgmentalism only as a prelude to ever more strident discriminations. "Where conditions permit," Gairdner writes, the strong step in,

> either to impose a new regime or, as in the Western democracies, where overt totalitarianism is still unthinkable, to further permeate ordinary life with the state's quietly overbearing, regulating role. Relativism is the natural public philosophy of such regimes because it repudiates all natural moral or social binding power, replacing these with legal decrees and sanction of the state.

Tocqueville did not, I believe, use the term "relativism," but he vividly delineated its political progeny in his description of democratic despotism, another leitmotif in the reflections of *The Fortunes of Permanence.*

"PERMANENCE": It is curious how hollow that stately word sounds to modern ears. Are we moderns not on the side of innovation, the untested, the new? In the preface to a collection of essays called *Giants and Dwarfs*, Allan Bloom, the author of *The Closing of the American Mind*, insisted that "the essence of education is the experience of greatness." Almost everything that Bloom wrote about the university flowed from this fundamental conviction. And it was just this, of course, that branded him an "elitist." In fact, Bloom's commitment to greatness was profoundly democratic. But this is not to say that it was egalitarian. The true democrat wishes to share the great works of culture with all who are able to appreciate them; the egalitarian, recognizing that genuine excellence is rare, declares greatness a fraud and sets about obliterating distinctions.

As Bloom recognized, the fruits of egalitarianism are ignorance, the habit of intellectual conformity, and the systematic subjection of cultural achievement to political criteria. In the university, this means classes devoted to pop novels, rock videos, and third-rate works chosen simply because their authors are members of the requisite sex, ethnic group, or social minority. It involves an attack on permanent things for the sake of the trendy and ephemeral. It means students who are graduated not having read Milton or Dante or Shakespeare—or, what is in some ways even worse, who have been taught to regard the works of such authors chiefly as hunting grounds for examples of patriarchy, homophobia, imperialism, or some other politically correct vice. It means faculty and students who regard education as an exercise in disillusionment and who look to the past only to corroborate their sense of superiority and self-satisfaction. *The Fortunes of Permanence* aims to disturb that complacency and reaffirm the tradition that made both the experience of and the striving for greatness possible.

Part One

The Fortunes of Permanence

*Do not be proud of the fact that your grandmother was
shocked at something which you are accustomed to seeing
or hearing without being shocked. . . . It may be that your
grandmother was an extremely lively and vital animal, and
that you are a paralytic.*
—G. K. Chesterton, *As I Was Saying*

*How but in custom and in ceremony
Are innocence and beauty born?
Ceremony's a name for the rich horn,
And custom the spreading laurel tree.*
—W. B. Yeats, "A Prayer For My Daughter"

*"Seven and a half hours of mild, unexhausting labour,
and then the soma ration and games and unrestricted
copulation and the feelies. What more can they ask for?"*
—Mustapha Mond in Huxley's *Brave New World*

I REMEMBER the first time I noticed the legend "cultural
instructions" on the brochure that accompanied some
seedlings. "How quaint," I thought, as I pursued the advisory: this much water and that much sun, certain tips about

fertilizer, soil, and drainage. Planting one sort of flower nearby keeps the bugs away but proximity to another sort makes bad things happen. Young shoots might need stakes, and watch out for beetles, weeds, and unseasonable frosts . . .

The more I pondered it, the less quaint, the more profound, those cultural instructions seemed. I suppose I had once known that the word "culture" comes from the capacious Latin verb *colo*, which means everything from "live, dwell, inhabit," to "observe a religious rite" (whence our word "cult"), "care, tend, nurture," and "promote the growth or advancement of." I never thought much about it.

I should have. There is a lot of wisdom in etymology. The noun *cultura* (which derives from *colo*) means first of all "the tilling or cultivation of land" and "the care or cultivation of plants." But it, too, has ambitious tentacles: "the observance of a religious rite," "well groomed" (of hair), "smart" (of someone's appearance), "chic, polished, sophisticated" (of a literary or intellectual style).

It was Cicero, in a famous passage of the *Tusculan Disputations*, who gave currency to the metaphor of culture as a specifically intellectual pursuit. "Just as a field, however good the ground, cannot be productive without cultivation, so the soul cannot be productive without education." Philosophy, he said, is a sort of "*cultura animi*," a cultivation of the mind or spirit: "it pulls out vices by the roots," "makes souls fit for the reception of seed," and sows in order to bring forth "the richest fruit." But even the best care, he warned, does not inevitably bring good results: the influence of education, of *cultura animi*, "cannot be the same for all: its effect is great when it has secured a hold upon a character suited to it." The results of cultivation depend not only on the quality of the care but the inherent nature of the thing being cultivated. How much of what Cicero said do we still understand?

In current parlance, "culture" (in addition to its use as a biological term) has both a descriptive and an evaluative meaning. In its anthropological sense, "culture" is neutral. It describes the habits and customs of a particular population: what its members do, not what they should do. Its task is to inventory, to docket, not judge.

But we also speak of "high culture," meaning not just social practices but a world of artistic, intellectual, and moral endeavor in which the notion of hierarchy, of a rank-ordering of accomplishment, is integral. (More etymology: "hierarchy" derives from words meaning "sacred order." Egalitarians are opposed to hierarchies in principle; what does that tell us about egalitarianism?) Culture in the evaluative sense does not merely admit, it requires judgment as a kind of coefficient or auxiliary: comparison, discrimination, evaluation are its lifeblood. "We never really get near a book," Henry James remarked in an essay on American letters, "save on the question of its being good or bad, of its really treating, that is, or not treating, its subject." It was for the sake of culture in this sense that Matthew Arnold extolled criticism as "the disinterested endeavour to learn and propagate the best that is known and thought in the world."

It is of course culture in the Arnoldian sense that we have primarily in view when we speak of "the survival of culture." And it is the fate of culture in this sense that I will be chiefly concerned with in this essay. But it would be foolish to draw too firm a distinction between the realms of culture. There is much confluence and interchange between them. Ultimately, they exist symbiotically, nurturing, supplementing, contending with each other. The manners, habits, rituals, institutions, and patterns of behavior that define culture for the anthropologist provide the sediment, the ground out of which culture in the Arnoldian sense takes root—or fails to take root. Failure or degradation in one area instigates failure or degradation in the other. (Some people regard the astonishing collapse of manners and civility in our society as a superficial event. They are wrong. The fate of decorum expresses the fate of a culture's dignity, its attitude toward its animating values.)

The problem with metaphors is not that they are false but that they do not tell the whole truth. The organic image of culture we have inherited from Cicero is illuminating. Among other things, it reminds us that we do not exist as self-sufficient atoms but have our place in a continuum that stretches before and after us in time. Like other metaphors, however, it can be elevated into an absurdity if it is pushed too far. Oswald Spengler's sprawling, two-volume lament, *The Decline of the West*, is a good illustration of what happens when genius is captivated by a metaphor. Spengler's book, published in the immediate aftermath of World War I, epitomized the end-of-everything mood of the times and was hailed as the brilliant key to understanding—well, just about everything. And Spengler really is brilliant. For example, his remarks about how the triumph of scepticism breeds a "second religiousness" in which "men dispense with proof, desire only to believe and not to dissect," have great pertinence to an age, like ours, that is awash in new-age spiritual counterfeits. Nevertheless, Spengler's deterministic allegiance to the analogy between civilizations and organisms ultimately infuses his discussion with an air of unreality. One is reminded, reading Spengler, of T. S. Eliot's definition of a heretic: "a person who seizes upon a truth and pushes it to the point at which it becomes a falsehood."

That said, for anyone who is concerned about the survival of culture, there are some important lessons in the armory of cultural instructions accompanying a humble tomato plant. Perhaps the chief lesson has to do with time and continuity, the evolving permanence that *cultura animi* no less than agricultural cultivation requires if it is to be successful. All those tips, habits, prohibitions, and necessities that have been accumulated from time out of mind and passed down, generation after generation: How much in our society militates against such antidotes to anarchy and decay!

Culture survives and develops under the aegis of permanence. And yet instantaneity—the enemy of permanence—is one of the chief imperatives of our time. It renders anything lasting, anything inherited, suspicious by definition. As Kenneth Minogue observed in an essay for *The New Criterion* called "The New Epicureans" (September 2001), "The idea is that one not only lives for the present, but also *ought* to live thus." We want what is faster, newer, less encumbered by the past. If we also cultivate a nostalgia for a simpler, slower time, that just shows the extent to which we are separated from what, in our efforts to decorate our lives, we long for. Nostalgia (Greek for "homesickness") is a version of sentimentality—a predilection, that is to say, to distort rather than acknowledge reality.

The political philosopher Hannah Arendt dilated on one essential aspect of the problem when she argued against taking an instrumental, "self-help" approach to culture. "What is at stake here," Arendt observed in "The Crisis in Culture,"

> is the objective status of the cultural world, which, insofar as it contains tangible things—books and paintings, statues, buildings, and music—comprehends, and gives testimony to, the entire recorded past of countries, nations, and ultimately mankind. As such, the only nonsocial and authentic criterion for judging these specifically cultural things is their relative permanence and even eventual immortality. Only what will last through the centuries can ultimately claim to be a cultural object. The point of the matter is that, as soon as the immortal works of the past became the

object of social and individual refinement and the status accorded to it, they lost their most important and elemental quality, which is to grasp and move the reader or the spectator over the centuries.

The "objective status" of the cultural world to which Arendt appeals is precisely the aspect of culture we find hardest to accommodate. If there is a "nonsocial and authentic criterion" for judging cultural achievements, then what happens to the ideology of equivalence that has become such a powerful force in Western societies? Are we not committed to the proposition that *all* values are social? Isn't this part of what social constructionists like Richard Rorty mean when they say language goes "all the way down"? That there is no self, no value, no achievement, no criteria independent of the twitterings of fashion, which in turn are ultimately the twitterings of social power?

The attack on permanence comes in many guises. When trendy literary critics declare that "there is no such thing as intrinsic meaning," they are denying permanent values that transcend the prerogatives of their lucubrations. When a deconstructionist tells us that truth is relative to language, or to power, or to certain social arrangements, he seeks to trump the unanswerable claims of permanent realities with the vacillations of his ingenuity. When the multiculturalist celebrates the fundamental equality of all cultures—excepting, of course, the culture of the West, which he reflexively disparages—he substitutes ephemeral political passions for the recognition of objective cultural achievement. "A pair of boots," a nineteenth-century Russian slogan tells us, "is worth more than Shakespeare." We have here a process of leveling that turns out to be a revolution in values. The implication, as the French philosopher Alain Finkielkraut observed, is that the footballer and the choreographer, the painter and the couturier, the writer and the ad-man, the musician and the rock-and-roller, are all the same: creators. We must scrap the prejudice which restricts that title to certain people and regards others as sub-cultural.

But what seems at first to be an effort to establish cultural parity turns out to be a campaign for cultural reversal. When Sir Elton John is put on the same level as Bach, the effect is not cultural equality but cultural insurrection. (If it seems farfetched to compare Elton John and Bach, recall the literary critic Richard Poirier's remark, in *Partisan Review* in 1967, that "sometimes [the Beatles] are like Monteverdi and sometimes their songs are even better than Schumann's.") It might also be worth asking what had to happen in English society for there to be such a thing as "Sir Elton John." What does *that* tell us about the survival of culture? But some subjects are too painful. Let us draw a veil . . .

"The history of philosophy," Jean-François Revel observed in *The Flight from Truth* (1991), "can be divided into two different periods. During the first, philosophers sought the truth; during the second, they fought against it." That fight has escaped from the parlors of professional sceptics and has increasingly become the moral coin of the realm. As Anthony Daniels wrote in "The Felicific Calculus of Modern Medicine," it is now routine for academics and intellectuals to use "all the instruments of an exaggerated scepticism . . . not to find truth but to destroy traditions, customs, institutions, and confidence in the worth of civilization itself." The most basic suppositions and distinctions suddenly crumble, like the acidic pages of a poorly made book, eaten away from within. "*A rebours*" becomes the rallying cry of the anti-cultural cultural elite. Culture degenerates from being a *cultura animi* to a *corruptio animi*.

ALDOUS HUXLEY'S *Brave New World* may be a second-rate novel—its characters wooden, its narrative overly didactic—but it has turned out to have been first-rate prognostication. Published in 1932, it touches everywhere on twenty-first-century anxieties. Perhaps the aspect of Huxley's dystopian—what to call it: fable? prophecy? admonition?—that is most frequently adduced is its vision of a society that has perfected what we have come to call genetic engineering. Among other things, it is a world in which reproduction has been entirely handed over to the experts. The word "parents" no longer describes a loving moral commitment but only an attenuated biological datum. Babies are not born but designed according to exacting specifications and "decanted" at sanitary depots like The Central London Hatchery and Conditioning Centre with which the book opens.

As with all efforts to picture future technology, Huxley's description of the equipment and procedures employed at the hatchery seems almost charmingly antiquated, like a space ship imagined by Jules Verne. But Huxley's portrait of the human toll of human ingenuity is very up-to-date. Indeed, we have not—not quite, not yet—caught up with the situation he describes. We do not—not quite, not yet—inhabit a world in which "mother" and "monogamy" are blasphemous terms from which people have been conditioned to recoil in visceral revulsion. Maybe it will never come to that. (Though monogamy, of course, has long been high on the social and sexual revolutionary's list of hated institutions.) Still, it is a nice question whether developments in reproductive technology will not soon make other aspects of Huxley's fantasy a reality. Thinkers as different as Michel Foucault and Francis Fukuyama have pondered the advent of a "posthuman" future, eagerly or with dismay, as the case may be. Scientists busily manipulating DNA may give substance to their speculations. It is often suggested that what is most disturbing about *Brave New World* is its portrait of eugenics in action: its vision of humanity deliberately divided into genetically ordered castes, a few supersmart Alpha-pluses down through a multitude of drone-like Epsilons who do the heavy lifting. Such deliberately instituted inequality offends our democratic sensibilities.

What is sometimes overlooked or downplayed is the possibility that the most disturbing aspect of the future Huxley pictured has less to do with eugenics than genetics. That is to say, perhaps what is centrally repellent about Huxley's hatcheries is not that they codify inequality—nature already does that more effectively than our politically correct sensibilities like to acknowledge—but that they exist at all. Are they not a textbook example of Promethean hubris in action? It is worth stepping back to ponder that possibility.

In the seventeenth century, Descartes predicted that his scientific method would make man "the master and possessor of nature": Are we not fast closing in on the technology that proves him right? And this raises another question. Is there a point at which scientific development can no longer be described, humanly, as progress? We know the benisons of technology. Consider only electricity, the automobile, modern medicine. They have transformed the world and underscored the old observation that art, that *techne*, is man's nature. Nevertheless, the question remains whether, after two hundred years of breathtaking progress, we are about to become more closely acquainted with the depredations of technology. It would take a brave man, or a rash one, to venture a confident prediction either way. For example, if, as in *Brave New World*, we manage to bypass the "inconvenience" of human pregnancy altogether, ought we to do it? (Note the moral adumbration of the word "ought.") If—or rather when—that is possible (as it certainly will be, and soon), will it also be desirable? If not, why not? Why should a woman go through the discomfort and danger of pregnancy if a fetus could be safely incubated, or cloned, elsewhere? Wouldn't motherhood by proxy be a good thing—the ultimate labor-saving device? Most readers, I think, will hesitate about saying yes. What does that hesitation tell us? Some readers will have no hesitation about saying yes; what does *that* tell us?*

As Huxley saw, a world in which reproduction was "rationalized" and emancipated from love was also a world in which culture in the Arnoldian sense was not only otiose but dangerous, and hence severely policed. This suspicion of culture is also a sub-theme of that other great dystopian novel, George Orwell's *1984*, which ends with the work of "various writers, such as Shakespeare, Milton, Swift, Byron, Dickens," being vandalized by being translated into Newspeak. When that laborious propaganda effort is finally complete, the "original writings, with all else that survived of the literature of the past, would be destroyed." The point is that culture has roots. It limns the future through its implications with the past. Moving the reader or spectator over the centuries, in Arendt's phrase, the monuments of culture transcend the local imperatives of the present. They escape the obsolescence that fashion demands, the predictability that planning requires. They speak of love and hatred, honor and shame, beauty and courage and cowardice—permanent realities of the human situation insofar as it remains human.

---

* Item: an article in *The Wall Street Journal* reported on the new popularity of using continuous birth-control pills or other methods to suppress women's menstrual cycles. The article quoted one obstetrician-gynecologist who, noting that most women in primitive societies had many more pregnancies than women today, argued that stopping monthly periods "gets women to a more natural state." Really?

The denizens of Huxley's brave new world are designed and educated—perhaps his word, "conditioned," is more accurate—to be rootless, without culture. Ditto the denizens of Orwell's nightmare totalitarian society. In *Brave New World*, when a relic of the old order of civilization—a savage who had been born, not decanted—is brought from a reservation into the brave new world, he is surprised to discover that the literary past is forbidden to most of the population.

> "But why is it prohibited?" asked the Savage. In the excitement of meeting a man who had read Shakespeare he had momentarily forgotten everything else.
>
> The Controller shrugged his shoulders. "Because it's old; that's the chief reason. We haven't any use for old things here."
>
> "Even when they're beautiful?"
>
> "Particularly when they're beautiful. Beauty's attractive, and we don't want people to be attracted by old things. We want them to like the new ones."

Huxley's brave new world is above all a superficial world. People are encouraged to like what is new, to live in the moment, because that makes them less complicated and more pliable. Emotional commitments are even more strictly rationed than Shakespeare. (The same, again, is true in *1984*.) In the place of emotional commitments, sensations—thrilling, mind-numbing sensations—are available on demand through drugs and motion pictures that neurologically stimulate viewers to experience certain emotions and feelings. The fact that they are artificially produced is not considered a drawback but their very point. Which is to say that the brave new world is a virtual world: experience is increasingly vivid but decreasingly real. The question of meaning is deliberately short-circuited. "You've got to choose," the Resident World Controller for Western Europe patiently explains to the Savage,

> "between happiness and what people used to call high art. We've sacrificed the high art. We have the feelies and the scent organ instead."
>
> "But they don't mean anything."
>
> "They mean themselves; they mean a lot of agreeable sensations to the audience."

If this seems like a prescription for arrested development, that, too, is part of the point: "It is their duty to be infantile," the Controller explains, "even against their inclination." Promiscuity is encouraged because it is a prophylactic against emotional depth. The question of meaning is never pursued beyond the instrumental question of what produces the most pleasure. Socrates told us that the unexamined life is not worth living. Huxley (yet again like Orwell) pictures a world in which the unexamined life is the only one available.

Huxley's imagination failed him in one area. He understood that in a world in which reproduction was emancipated from the body, sexual congress for many people would degenerate into a purely recreational activity, an amusement not inherently different from one's soma ration or the tactile movies. He pictured a world of casual, indeed mandatory, promiscuity. But he thought it would develop along completely conventional lines. He ought to have known that the quest for "agreeable sensations" would issue in a pansexual carnival. In this area, anyway, we seem to have proceeded a good deal further than the characters who inhabit Huxley's dystopia.

In part, the attack on permanence is an attack on the idea that anything possesses inherent value. Absolute fungibility—the substitution of anything for anything—is the ideal. In one sense, this is a product of what the philosopher Michael Oakeshott criticized as "rationalism." "To the Rationalist," Oakeshott wrote in the late 1940s, "nothing is of value merely because it exists (and certainly not because it has existed for many generations), familiarity has no worth and nothing is to be left standing for want of scrutiny." The realm of sexuality is one area where the effects of such rationalism are dramatically evident. It was not so long ago that the description from Genesis—"male and female created he them"—was taken as a basic existential fact. True, the obstinacy of sexual difference has always been a thorn in the side of utopian rationalism. But it is only in recent decades that the engines of judicial meddlesomeness, on the one hand, and surgical know-how, on the other, have effectively assaulted that once permanent-seeming reality.

For an illustration of how sexual politics has been enlisted in the attack on permanence, consider the recently acquired habit of using the term "gender" when what we mean is "sex." This may seem an innocent, nearly a euphemistic, innovation. But it is not innocent. It issues not from any residual sense of modesty about sexual matters but from a hubristic effort to reduce sex to gender. The term "gender" has its home in grammar: it names a certain linguistic convention. Sex describes a basic biological division. As the columnist George Will noted, the substitution of "gender" for "sex" is so widespread because it suggests that sexual differences are themselves a matter of convention—"socially constructed" and therefore susceptible to social deconstruction: susceptible to being "erased by sufficiently determined social engineers." A powerful legal tool in the campaign to substitute gender for sex is Title IX, which celebrated its fortieth anniversary in May 2012. Written to prohibit discrimination on the basis of sex, it has, in the hands of what Will calls

"Title IX fanatics," become a legal bludgeon that is wielded to deny the reality of sexual differences. It has already been used to gut the athletic programs of hundreds of schools and colleges across the country; the next target, as Will foresaw, was the curriculum: if a college has an engineering department, it must also have proportional representation of the sexes—sorry, the genders—in that department. Anything less would be an insult to the ideal of equality.

A more florid example of sexual fungibility at work is the explosion of interest in—indeed, the incipient normalization of—"gender reassignment surgery" and other adventures in sexual plasticity. (Though a friend reminds me of another alternative: that transsexuals are not apostles of sexual plasticity but rebels against the tyranny of anatomy. "They don't want to be transgressive," he observes, "they want to be as normal members as possible of the sex they take themselves to be." Perhaps.) A glance at the personal ads of any "alternative" newspaper—to say nothing of internet sex sites—will reveal a burgeoning sexual demi-monde where the "transsexual," "pansexual," and "virtually sexual" heartily compete with more traditional promiscuities.

Nor are such phenomena confined to such "help wanted" venues. Headline from a California newspaper: "San Francisco is about to embark on another first in the nation: providing health care benefits for city workers undergoing sex-change procedures." "Oh, well," you say: "It's California, what do you expect?" Here's another headline: "Britain's free health care service should provide sex-change operations for transsexuals because they suffer from a legitimate illness, a court has ruled." Not to be left behind, *The New York Times Sunday Magazine* not so long ago ran a long and sympathetic cover story about a "transgendered" thirteen-year-old who, though born as a girl, has lived for the last several years as a boy. And *The New Republic*, in a cover story from July 2011, described the situation of "transgendered" people as "America's next great civil rights struggle."

Real-life transsexuals are what we might call the objective correlative of an increasingly prominent strand in our culture's fantasy life. Consider, to take just one example, the British artists Dinos and Jake Chapman. Their signature works are pubescent female mannequins studded with erect penises, vaginas, and anuses, fused together in various postures of sexual congress. The thing to notice is not how outrageous but how common such items are. The Chapman brothers are not a back-alley, plain-brown-wrapper phenomenon. Their works are exhibited in major, once staid, galleries like the Royal Academy in London and the Brooklyn Museum in New York. They are "transgressive," all right. But the point is that the transgressions they announce have been to a large extent domesticated and welcomed into the mainstream. It would be bootless to multiply examples—readers will doubtless have lists of their own. Hardly anyone is shocked anymore, but that is a testament not to public enlightenment but to widespread moral anaesthesia. (The question of aesthetics, of distinctively artistic achievement, does not even enter the calculation: what does that tell us?)

What we are seeing in sexual life is the fulfillment, in some segments of society, of the radical emancipatory vision enunciated in the 1960s by such gurus as Herbert Marcuse and Norman O. Brown. In *Eros and Civilization* Marcuse looked forward to the establishment of a "non-repressive reality principle" in which "the body in its entirety would become . . . an instrument of pleasure." The sexual liberation Marcuse hailed was not a fecund liberation. As in *Brave New World*, children do not enter into the equation. The issue is pleasure, not progeny. Marcuse speaks glowingly of "a resurgence of pregenital polymorphous sexuality" that

"protests against the repressive order of procreative sexuality." A look at the alarmingly low birth rates of most affluent
nations today suggests that the protest has been effective.
When Tocqueville warned about the peculiar form of despotism that threatened democracy, he noted that instead of
tyrannizing men, as past despotisms had done, it tended to
infantilize them, keeping "them fixed irrevocably in childhood." What Tocqueville warned about, Marcuse celebrated, extolling the benefits of returning to a state of "primary
narcissism" in which one will find "the redemption of pleasure, the halt of time, the absorption of death; silence, sleep,
night, paradise—the Nirvana principle not as death but as
life." What Marcuse encouraged, in other words, is solip-
sism, not as a philosophical principle but as a moral indulgence, a way of life.

IT IS OFTEN SAID that we are entering the "information
age." There is doubtless some truth in that. But what does
it mean? The shocking bulletins appear with clocklike regularity: students seem to know less and less history, less and
less mathematics, less and less literature, less and less geog-
raphy. In one of her reflections on the state of education,
Diane Ravitch bemoaned the "truly abysmal scores" high-
school seniors made in an American history examination:
only one in ten did well enough to be considered proficient
in the subject. You won't have to look far to find corroborative reports carrying bad news about other students and
other subjects. A look in the papers today will reveal yet
another depressing finding about the failure of education.

Welcome to the information age. Data, data everywhere,
but no one knows a thing. In the West, at least, practically
everybody has instant access to huge databases and news-
retrieval services, to say nothing of television and other media. With a few clicks of the mouse we can bring up every

line of Shakespeare that contains the word "darkling" or the complete texts of Aeschylus in Greek or in translation. Information about contract law in ancient Rome or yesterday's developments in microchip technology in Japan is at our fingertips. If we are traveling to Paris, we can book our airline ticket and hotel reservation online, check the local weather, and find out the best place to have dinner near the Place des Vosges. We can correspond and exchange documents with friends on the other side of the globe in the twinkling of an eye. Our command of information is staggering.

And yet with that command comes a great temptation. Partly, it is the temptation to confuse an excellent means of communication with communications that are excellent. We confuse, that is to say, process with product. As the critic David Guaspari memorably put it, "comparing information and knowledge is like asking whether the fatness of a pig is more or less green than the designated hitter's rule." Oops.

That is not the only confusion. There is also a tendency to confuse propinquity with possession. The fact that some text is available online or on CD-ROM does not mean that one has read and absorbed its contents. When I was in graduate school, there were always students who devoted countless hours to copying articles on the library's Xerox machines. They somehow supposed that by making a copy of some document they had also read, or half-read, or at least looked into it. Today that same tendency is exacerbated by high-speed internet access. We can download a veritable library of material to our computer in a few minutes; that does not mean we have mastered its riches. Information is not synonymous with knowledge, let alone wisdom.

This is not a new insight. At the end of the *Phaedrus*, Plato has Socrates tell the story of the god Theuth, who, legend has it, invented the art of writing. When Theuth presented his new invention to the king of Egypt, he promised

33

the king that it would make his people "wiser and improve their memories." But the king disagreed, claiming that the habit of writing, far from improving memories, would "implant forgetfulness" by encouraging people to rely on external marks rather than "the living speech graven in the soul."

Well, none of us would wish to do without writing—or computers, come to that. Nor, I think, would Plato have wanted us to. (Though he would probably have taken a dim view of television. That bane of intelligence could have been ordered up specially to illustrate Plato's idea that most people inhabit a kind of existential "cave" in which they mistake flickering images for realities.) Plato's indirect comments—through the mouth of Socrates recounting an old story he picked up somewhere—have less to do with writing (an art, after all, in which Plato excelled) than with the priority of immediate experience: the "living speech graven in the soul." Plato may have been an idealist. But here as elsewhere he appears as an apostle of vital, first-hand experience: a realist in the deepest sense of the term.

The problem with computers is not the worlds they give us instant access to but the world they encourage us to neglect. Everyone knows about the studies showing the bad effects on children and teenagers of too much time in cyberspace (or, indeed, in front of the television set). It cuts them off from their family and friends, fosters asocial behavior, disrupts their ability to concentrate, and makes it harder for them to distinguish between fantasy and reality. I suspect, however, that the real problem is not so much the sorry cases that make headlines but a more generally disseminated attitude toward the world.

When I entered the phrase "virtual reality," the Google search engine returned 1,260,000 hits in .12 seconds. There are many, many organizations like the Virtual Reality Society, "an international society dedicated to the discussion and advancement of virtual reality and synthetic environments." Computer simulations, video games, special effects: in some areas of life, virtual reality seems to be crowding out the other variety. It gives a whole new significance to Villiers de L'Isle-Adam's world-weary mot: *Vivre? Les serviteurs feront cela pour nous.*

THE ISSUE IS NOT, or not only, the digital revolution—the protracted tsunami of computers and e-mail, "social media" and the internet. It is rather the effect of such developments on our moral and imaginative life, and even our cognitive and political life.

Why bother to get Shakespeare by heart when you can look it up in a nonce on the internet? One reason, of course, is that a passage memorized is a passage internalized: it becomes part of the mental sustenance of the soul. It's the difference between a living limb and a crutch. Former Secretary of State Henry Kissinger touched on this aspect of the issue when he observed that

> We have entered a time of total change in human consciousness of how people look at the world. Reading books requires you to form concepts, to train your mind to relationships. You have to come to grips with who you are. A leader needs these qualities. But now we learn from fragments of facts. A book is a large intellectual construction; you can't hold it all in mind easily or at once. You have to struggle mentally to internalize it. Now there is no need to internalize because each fact can instantly be called up on the computer. There is no context, no motive. Information is not knowledge. People are not readers but researchers, they float on the surface. This new thinking erases context. It disaggregates everything. All this makes strategic thinking about world order impossible to achieve.

Alexander the Great carried a copy of the *Iliad* with him on his Eastern conquests. What do you suppose Barack Obama, Vladimir Putin, or Wen Jiabao carry along on their travels?

It used to be said that in dreams begin responsibilities. What responsibilities does a virtual world inspire? Virtual responsibilities, perhaps: responsibilities undertaken on spec, as it were. Consider the horrifying story of the couple who, in 2010, let their baby starve while they were engaged in a marathon video game session nurturing a virtual baby. A virtual world is a world that can be created, manipulated, and dissolved at will. It is a world whose reverberations are subject to endless revision. The Delete key is always available. Whatever is done can be undone. Whatever is undone can be redone. Reality has no Reboot option.

Of course, as the meditations of Huxley in the 1930s and Marcuse in the 1960s suggest, computers and the internet do not create the temptations of virtual reality; they merely exacerbate those temptations. They magnify a perennial human possibility. Human beings do not need cyberspace to book a vacation from reality. The problem is not computers or indeed any particular technology but rather our disposition toward the common world that culture defines. When we ask about the survival of culture and the fortunes of permanence, we are asking about the fate of that common world. In many respects it is a political question—or, more precisely, a question regarding the limits of politics. When Susan Sontag, in the mid-1960s, championed the "new sensibility" she saw erupting across American society, she rightly observed that its representatives "have broken, whether they know it or not, with the Matthew Arnold notion of culture, finding it historically and humanly obsolescent."

What exactly is the "Matthew Arnold notion of culture" that Sontag and her cadre of hip intellectuals rejected as outmoded and irrelevant? For one thing, as we have seen, it is culture understood as a repository of mankind's noblest spiritual and intellectual aspirations: "the best," in Arnold's famous phrase, "that has been thought and said in the world." The "Matthew Arnold notion of culture" is thus a hierarchical idea of culture—a vision of culture as a "sacred order" whose majesty depends on its relevance to our deepest cares and concerns.

A second feature of the "Matthew Arnold notion of culture" is its independence—what Arnold summed up in the term "disinterestedness." Criticism achieves disinterestedness, Arnold said,

> by keeping aloof from what is called "the practical view of things"; by resolutely following the law of its own nature, which is to be a free play of the mind on all subjects which it touches. By steadily refusing to lend itself to any of those ulterior, political, practical considerations about ideas . . .

Understood in one way, Arnold's ideal of disinterestedness—with its emphasis on "a free play of the mind on all subjects"—might seem to be a prescription for moral quietism or frivolous aestheticism. What rescues it from that fundamental unseriousness is Arnold's unwavering commitment to truth and honesty. The business of criticism, he said, is to know and propagate the best, to "create a current of true and fresh ideas," and "to do this with inflexible honesty." It tells us a great deal about the state of culture that Arnold's demanding ideal of disinterestedness is not merely neglected but actively repudiated by many influential academics and intellectuals today.

A THIRD FEATURE of the "Matthew Arnold notion of culture" is its immediacy, its emphasis not on virtual but on first-hand experience. "Here," Arnold noted, "the great safeguard is never to let oneself become abstract, always to retain an intimate and lively consciousness of the truth of what one is saying, and, the moment this fails us, to be sure that something is wrong." The "Matthew Arnold notion of culture," then, comes armed with a sixth sense against the seductions of the spurious, the attractions of the ersatz.

Ultimately, what Sontag had against Arnold's view of culture was its earnestness, its seriousness. When she celebrated the Camp sensibility, she did so largely because in Camp she found a nimble ally in her effort "to dethrone the serious." Her praise of pop culture, pornography, and the pullulating ephemera of the counterculture must be understood as part of her battle against seriousness as traditionally defined. We have here that curious compact of moral levity and grim self-absorption that has characterized so many partisans of "advanced" opinion from Oscar Wilde on down to our own time. Redacted by the political passions of the 1960s, that strange compact resulted in the vertiginous relativisms that have overpopulated the academy, the art world, and other bastions of elite culture throughout Western society.

Part of what makes those relativisms vertiginous is their inconsistency. What we see in contemporary culture is relativism with a vengeance. It is a *directed*, an activist relativism, forgiving and nonjudgmental about anything hostile to the perpetuation of traditional Western culture, full of self-righteous retribution when it comes to individuals and institutions friendly to the West. It incubates what Mark Steyn has described as "the slyer virus": "the vague sense that the West's success must somehow be responsible for the rest's failure." It is in effect a sort of secularized Jansenism: we are always in the wrong, not in the eyes of God but in the eyes of the exotic Other as imagined by us.

It has long been obvious that "multiculturalism" is an ornate synonym for "anti-Americanism." It is anti-Americanism on a peculiar moralistic jag. I'll have more to say about multiculturalism in the next chapter. For now, it is enough to note that its effect has been to pervert institutions hitherto entrusted with the preservation and transmission of our spiritual, political, and intellectual heritage. The institutions persist, but their purpose is stymied. Wherever we look—at our schools and colleges, at our churches, museums, courts, and legislatures—we see well underway a process of abdication: a process whereby institutions created to protect certain values have been "deconstructed" and turned against the very things they were meant to preserve.

Consider what has happened to the judiciary. In any society that enjoys the rule of law, courts are a custodian of permanence. The task of judges is to uphold the laws that have been passed down to them, not make new ones. But as Judge Robert Bork has shown—and as we see all around us—the American judiciary has to an extraordinary extent become the "enemy of traditional culture." On issues from free speech and religion to sexuality, feminism, education, and race, the courts have acted less as defenders of the law than as an avant-garde establishing new beachheads to promulgate the gospel of left-liberal enlightenment. The attempt by the Ninth Circuit Court of Appeals in California to declare the Pledge of Allegiance unconstitutional because it includes the phrase "under God" is one of the more risible efforts in this campaign. The overall effect has been to inure society to rule by diktat, a situation in this country that is as novel as it is ominous. "It would," Judge Bork has observed, "have been unthinkable until recently that so many areas of our national life would be controlled by judges." One again recalls Tocqueville's warning about democratic despotism. Only now it is not the sovereign but the judiciary that

> extends its arms over society as a whole; it covers its surface with a network of small, complicated, painstaking, uniform rules through which the most original minds and the most vigorous souls cannot clear a way to surpass the crowd; it does not break wills, but it softens them, bends them, and directs them; it rarely forces one to act, but it constantly opposes itself to one's acting; it does not destroy, it prevents things from being born; it does not tyrannize, it hinders, compromises, enervates, extinguishes, dazes, and finally reduces each nation to being nothing more than a herd of timid and industrious animals of which the government is the shepherd.

The attack on permanence is a failure of principle that results in moral paralysis. Chesterton once defined madness as "using mental activity so as to reach mental helplessness." That is an apt description of a process we see at work in many segments of our social and intellectual life. It is not so much a version of Hamlet's disease—being sicklied o'er with the pale cast of thought—as an example of what happens when conscience is no longer animated by principle and belief.

Newspaper Item: "Hamas Founder Says Suicide Attacks Will Continue." Really? And what about us: what do we have to say about that abomination? Mostly, we wring our hands and mumble about restarting the "peace process." In one dissenting column, Linda Chavez reported on an episode of National Public Radio's "All Things Considered" in which a group of second- and third-generation Palestinian Americans living in Northern Virginia were interviewed. If you had been thinking of taking a holiday there, you may wish to reconsider, or at least be sure that your life insurance premiums are paid up. As Ms. Chavez noted, the sentiments expressed could have come from Hamas. "It doesn't matter who dies," said one young boy who idolizes the suicide bombers, "just as long as they're Israeli." His mother blames Israel: "They've made him violent and hate them." His father swells with paternal pride: "If his time has come, he will die, regardless of where he is. But at least he will die for a cause. I will live the rest of my life being proud of him." What about the rule of law? Forget it. American democratic values? Don't make me laugh. What we have here, Ms. Chavez observes, is "a reflection of our new multicultural America, where young people are taught that one's allegiance to one's ethnic group takes precedence over allegiance to the United States or adherence to democratic values." Thus it is, as the British historian David Pryce-Jones has observed, that "contempt for democratic institutions was translated into contempt for the moral values that had underpinned those institutions."

WHEN IMMIGRANTS become American citizens, they take an oath of allegiance. Among other things, they must "absolutely and entirely renounce and abjure all allegiance and fidelity to any foreign prince, potentate, state, or sovereignty of whom or which [they] have heretofore been a subject or citizen." But such promises are only so many words to a population cut adrift from the permanent values enshrined in America's political principles. The fault lies with the elites who no longer respect and stand up for those principles. "No taxation without representation" is a splendid demand. But so is "no immigration without assimilation." Where is the simple imperative that one live up to one's oaths or face the consequences? If one becomes an American citizen, then one must become an American citizen, with the rights *and duties* pertaining thereto. If that proves too onerous, perhaps citizenship should be revoked and a one-way ticket to elsewhere provided. Such drastic measures would not be a sign of excessive rigor but an example of beneficence in action. It is kindness to stymie the forces of anarchy. By supporting the permanent values that undergird society, such enforcement would be a vote for civilization against chaos.

Since the terror attacks of 9/11, questions about the survival of culture have naturally taken on a new urgency. The focus suddenly shifted away from the airier purlieus of cultural endeavor to survival in the most visceral sense. The murderous fanatics who destroyed the World Trade Center, smashed into the Pentagon, and killed thousands of innocent civilians took the issue of multiculturalism out of the fetid atmosphere of the graduate seminar and into the streets. Or, rather, they dramatized the fact that multiculturalism was never a merely academic matter. In a sense, the actions of those terrorists were less an attack on the United States than part of what Binyamin Netanyahu called "a war to reverse the triumph of the West." Even now, more than a decade on, we are very far from being in a position to assess the full significance of 9/11 for the simple reason that the detonations that began that day continue to reverberate and destroy. A battle of wills, a contest of values, was initiated or at least openly acknowledged on September 11, 2001. It is still, a decade later, too early to predict the course of that conflict.

September 11 precipitated a crisis the end of which we cannot see. Part of the task that faces us now is to acknowledge the depth of barbarism that challenges the survival of culture. And part of that acknowledgment lies in reaffirming the core values that are under attack. Ultimately, victory in the conflict that besieges us will be determined not by smart weapons but by smart heads. That is to say, the conflict is not so much—not only—a military conflict as a conflict of world views. It is convenient to command the carrier battle groups and cruise missiles; it is essential to possess the will to use them and the faith that our cause, the cause of culture, is the best hope for mankind. The critic Mark Steyn put it well: "If we are as ashamed as we insist we are—of ourselves, our culture and our history—then inevitably we will invite our own destruction." As I write, New Yorkers and indeed all Americans are about to commemorate the ten-year anniversary of 9/11. The horrifying slaughter of those terrorist attacks tempts us to draw a line around that day and treat it and its immediate consequences as an exceptional case. There is a deep sense, however, in which the terrorist attacks underscore not the fragility of normality but the normality of fragility. This is a point that C. S. Lewis made with great eloquence in a sermon he preached at Oxford in 1939. "I think it important," he said,

> to try to see the present calamity in a true perspective. The war creates no absolutely new situation: it simply aggravates the permanent human situation so that we can no longer ignore it. Human life has always been lived on the edge of a precipice. Human culture has always had to exist under the shadow of something infinitely more important than itself. If men had postponed the search for knowledge and beauty until they were secure, the search would never have begun.
>
> We are mistaken when we compare war with "normal life." Life has never been normal. Even those periods which we think most tranquil, like the nineteenth century, turn out, on closer inspection, to be full of crises, alarms, difficulties, emergencies. Plausible reasons have never been lacking for putting off all merely cultural activities until some imminent danger has been averted or some crying injustice put right. But humanity long ago chose to neglect those plausible reasons. They wanted knowledge and beauty now, and would

43

not wait for the suitable moment that never comes. Periclean Athens leaves us not only the Parthenon but, significantly, the Funeral Oration. The insects have chosen a different line: they have sought first the material welfare and security of the hive, and presumably they have their reward.

Men are different. They propound mathematical theorems in beleaguered cities, conduct metaphysical arguments in condemned cells, make jokes on scaffolds, discuss the latest new poem while advancing to the walls of Quebec, and comb their hair at Thermopylae. This is not panache: it is our nature.

Lewis's meditation is by turns cheering and sobering. On the one hand, it testifies to the heartiness of culture, which is the heartiness of the human spirit. Sonnets in Siberia, mathematical formulae in the besieged fortress. There is no time when cultural instructions are not pertinent. On the other hand, Lewis's meditation reminds us that culture, and the humanity that defines it, is constantly under threat. No achievement may be taken for granted; yesterday's gain may be tomorrow's loss; permanent values require permanent vigilance and permanent renewal.

WHAT LESSONS may we draw from these Janus-faced conclusions? One is that it is always later than you think. Another is that it is never too late to start anew. During the Bush years, the French sometimes disparaged the "*simplisme*" of America's foreign policy. In their subtlety they ignored the fact that most important truths are—I use the adverb advisedly—terribly simple. Our complexity is much more likely to lead us astray than any simplicity we may follow.

In *Notes Towards the Definition of Culture*, T. S. Eliot observed that "If any definite conclusions emerge from this study, one of them surely is this, that culture is the one thing that we cannot deliberately aim at. It is the product of a variety of more or less harmonious activities, each pursued for its own sake." "For its own sake." That is one simple idea that is everywhere imperiled today. When we plant a garden, it is bootless to strive directly for camellias. They are the natural product of our care, nurture, and time. We can manage that when it comes to agriculture. When we turn our hands to *cultura animi*, we seem to be considerably less successful. In 2002, the historian John Lukacs published a gloomy book called *At the End of an Age*. He argued that "we in the West are living near the end of an entire age," that the Modern Age, which began with the Renaissance, is jerking, crumbling irretrievably to its end. I believe Lukacs is precipitate. After all, prophecies of the end have been with us since the beginning. It seems especially odd that an historian of Lukacs's delicacy and insight would indulge in what amounts to a reprise of Spengler's thesis about the "decline of the West." How many times must historical "inevitabilities" be confounded before they lose their hold on our imaginations?

Where Lukacs is on to something, however, is in his meditations on the ideology of progress. Science does not deserve the scare quotes with which Lukacs adorns it, far from it. But it is true that much that we have taken for progress looks with the passage of time more and more dubious. Our stupendous power has accustomed us to say "yes" to every innovation, in manners and morals as well as the laboratory. We have yet to learn—even now, even at this late date— that promises of liberation often turn out to conceal new enchantments and novel forms of bondage. Our prejudice against prejudice tempts us to neglect the deep wisdom of tradition and time-sanctioned answers to the human predicament. The survival of culture is never a sure thing. No more is its defeat. Our acknowledgment of those twin facts, to the extent that we manage it, is one important sign of our strength.

Institutionalizing Our Demise: America vs. Multiculturalism

Here individuals of all nations are melted into a new race of men, whose labours and posterity will one day cause great changes in the world.
—J. H. St. John de Crèvecœur, *Letters from an American Farmer*, 1782

The one absolutely certain way of bringing this nation to ruin . . . would be to permit it to become a tangle of squabbling nationalities.
—Theodore Roosevelt, *Autobiography*, 1913

A FEW YEARS AGO, on a trip to Maryland, I stopped at Baltimore Harbor with my wife and five-year-old son to see Fort McHenry, the site, in September 1814, of the Battle of Baltimore, a decisive episode in the War of 1812. It was a glorious spring day: the sky was an infinite azure punctuated by a flotilla of stately white clouds.

Our first stop was a modern outbuilding adjacent to the eighteenth-century fort. We crowded into a small theater with about thirty fourth-graders and their teachers to watch a short film. Among other things, we learned about the origins of the war, about how the British took and burned Washington, about how at last a thousand U.S. troops under

George Armistead at Fort McHenry successfully defended their bastion against the British naval onslaught, saving Baltimore and turning the tide of the war.

It was (as the Duke of Wellington said of Waterloo) "a damn nice thing—the nearest run thing you ever saw." The British ships, anchored out of range of Armistead's cannons, pounded the fort with mortar and Congreve rocket fire over the course of twenty-five hours. Sitting on a truce ship behind the British fleet was a young American lawyer and amateur poet named Francis Scott Key. He watched as the battle raged, dappling the night sky with noisy coruscations.

Sometime before sunrise, the bombardment suddenly stopped. Key was uncertain of the battle's outcome until dawn broke and he saw the American flag fluttering boldly above Fort McHenry. (When he had taken command, Armistead asked for an extra large flag so that "the British would have no trouble seeing it from a distance.") There would be no surrender. The Brits abandoned their plans to invade Baltimore. The war would soon be over. As soon as he caught sight of Old Glory, Francis Scott Key began scribbling what would become "The Star-Spangled Banner" on the back of a letter. He finished it in a hotel in Baltimore a day or two later. The poem was an instant hit and was soon set to "The Anacreontic Song," an eighteenth-century English drinking tune. It became the official national anthem in 1931.

The film ended and strains of the song began floating out from the loudspeakers—softly at first, then louder and louder. Everyone in the room scrambled to his feet.

O say, does that star-spangled banner yet wave
O'er the land of the free and the home of the brave?

The schoolchildren stood reverently, each with his right hand over his heart. A floor-length curtain wheeled back, flooding the room with light. There was Fort McHenry. And there, rising above it, was the American flag, waving gently in the breeze. With the possible exception of our son, who was busy attacking The Enemy with his toy F14, there wasn't a dry eye in the house.

Of course, that calculated piece of theater was in part an exercise in sentimentality. Is that a bad thing? Wallace Stevens may have been right that, in general, "sentimentality is a failure of feeling"—a sign of counterfeit emotion rather than the real thing. Nevertheless, there is a place for a bit of affirmative sentimentality in the moral economy of our society. Among other things, it provides emotional glue for our shared identity as Americans. These days, perhaps more than ever before, that identity needs glue. As we contemplate the prospects for America and its institutions in the twenty-first century, it is not only particular cultural and social institutions that deserve scrutiny. What we might call the institution of American identity—of who we are as a people—also requires our attention.

It is often said that the terrorist attacks of September 11 precipitated a new resolve throughout the nation. There is some truth to that. Certainly, the extraordinary bravery of the firefighters and other rescue personnel in New York and Washington, D.C., provided an invigorating spectacle—as did Todd "Let's roll" Beamer and his fellow passengers on United Airlines Flight 93. Having learned from their cell phones what had happened at the World Trade Center and the Pentagon, they rushed and overpowered the terrorists who had hijacked their plane. As a result, the plane crashed on a remote Pennsylvania farm instead of on Pennsylvania Avenue. Who knows how many lives their sacrifice saved?

The widespread sense of condign outrage—of horror leavened by anger and elevated by resolve—testified to a renewed sense of national purpose and identity after 9/11.

Attacked, many Americans suddenly (if temporarily) redis-covered the virtue of patriotism. At the beginning of his re-markable book *Who Are We? The Challenges to America's National Identity*, the late Samuel Huntington tells about a certain block on Charles Street in Boston. At one time, American flags flew in front of a U.S. Post Office and a liquor store. At some point, the Post Office stopped displaying the flag, so on September 11, 2001, the flag flew only in front of the liquor store. Within two weeks, seventeen American flags decorated that block of Charles Street, in addition to a huge flag suspended over the street close by. "With their country under attack," Huntington notes, "Charles Street denizens rediscovered their nation and identified themselves with it."

Was that rediscovery anything more than a momentary passion? Huntington reports that within a few months, the flags on Charles Street began to disappear. By the time the first anniversary rolled around in September 2002, only four were left flying. True, that is four times more than were there on September 10, 2001, but it is less than a quarter of the number that populated Charles Street at the end of September 2001.

There are similar anecdotes from around the country—an access of flag-waving followed by a relapse into indiffer-ence. Does it mean that the sudden upsurge of patriotism in the weeks following 9/11 was only, as it were, skin deep? Or perhaps it merely testifies to the fact that a sense of per-manent emergency is difficult to maintain, especially in the absence of fresh attacks. Is our sense of ourselves as Ameri-cans patent only when challenged? "Does it," Huntington asks, "take an Osama bin Laden . . . to make us realize that we are Americans? If we do not experience recurring de-structive attacks, will we return to the fragmentation and eroded Americanism before September 11?"

One hopes that the answer is No. I am writing around the tenth anniversary of 9/11. The behavior of those school-children at Fort McHenry—behavior that was, I am happy to report, quietly encouraged by their teachers—suggests that the answer cannot simply be No. But I fear that for every schoolchild standing at attention for the National Anthem, there is a teacher or lawyer or judge or politician or ACLU employee militating against the hegemony of the dominant culture, the insupportable intrusion of white, Christian, "Eurocentric" values into the curriculum, the school pageant, the town green, etc., etc. The demonstration of national character and resolve following September 11 was extraordinary. It did not, however, purchase immunity from the virus of cultural dissolution. The usually percep-tive commentator Max Boot, writing about the issue of gay marriage, remarked in passing that "no one who saw the response to 9/11 can think we are soft or decadent" or that "America is in cultural decline." Alas, the display of nation-al heroism and resolve following 9/11 has had little if any effect on the forces behind the fragmentation and "eroded Americanism" to which Huntington refers.

Those forces are not isolated phenomena; they are not even confined to America. They are part of a global crisis in national identity, coefficients of the sudden collapse of self-confidence in the West—a collapse that shows itself in everything from swiftly falling birthrates in "old Europe" to the attack on the whole idea of the sovereign nation state. It is hard to avoid thinking that a people that has lost the will to reproduce or govern itself is a people on the road to destruction.

ONLY A FEW YEARS AGO we were invited to contemplate the pleasant spectacle of the "end of history" and the establish-ment of Western-style liberal democracy the world over.

Things look rather different now as a variety of centrifugal forces threatens to undermine the sources of national identity and, with it, the sources of national strength and the security which that strength underwrites.

The threat shows itself in many ways, from culpable complacency to the corrosive imperatives of "multiculturalism" and political correctness. (I use scare quotes because what generally travels under the name of "multiculturalism" is really a form of mono-cultural animus directed against the dominant culture.) In essence, as Huntington notes, multiculturalism is "anti-European civilization. . . . It is basically an anti-Western ideology." The multiculturalists claim to be fostering a progressive cultural cosmopolitanism distinguished by superior sensitivity to the downtrodden and dispossessed. In fact, they encourage an orgy of self-flagellating liberal guilt as impotent as it is insatiable. The "sensitivity" of the multiculturalist is an index not of moral refinement but of moral vacuousness. As the French essayist Pascal Bruckner observed, "An overblown conscience is an empty conscience."

> Compassion ceases if there is nothing but compassion, and revulsion turns to insensitivity. Our "soft pity," as Stefan Zweig calls it, is stimulated, because guilt is a convenient substitute for action where action is impossible. Without the power to do anything, sensitivity becomes our main aim, the aim is not so much to do anything, as to be judged. Salvation lies in the verdict that declares us to be wrong.

Multiculturalism is a moral intoxicant; its thrill centers around the emotion of superior virtue; its hangover subsists on a diet of nescience and blighted "good intentions."

Wherever the imperatives of multiculturalism have touched the curriculum, they have left broad swaths of anti-Western attitudinizing competing for attention with quite astonishing historical blindness. Courses on minorities, women's issues, and the Third World proliferate; the teaching of mainstream history slides into oblivion.

"The mood," Arthur Schlesinger wrote in *The Disuniting of America* (1992), his excellent book on the depredations of multiculturalism, "is one of divesting Americans of the sinful European inheritance and seeking redemptive infusions from non-Western cultures."

A profound ignorance of the milestones of American culture is the predictable result of this mood. The statistics have become proverbial. Huntington quotes one poll from the 1990s showing that while 90 percent of Ivy League students could identify Rosa Parks, only 25 percent could identify the author of the words "government of the people, by the people, for the people." (Yes, it's the Gettysburg Address.) In a 1999 survey, 40 percent of seniors at fifty-five top colleges could not say within half a century when the Civil War was fought. Another study found that more high school students knew who Harriet Tubman was than knew that Washington commanded the American army in the Revolution or that Abraham Lincoln wrote the Emancipation Proclamation. Doubtless you have your own favorite horror story.

But multiculturalism is not only an academic phenomenon. The attitudes it fosters have profound social as well as intellectual consequences. One consequence has been a sharp rise in the phenomenon of immigration without—or with only partial—assimilation: a dangerous demographic trend that threatens American identity in the most basic way.

These various agents of dissolution are also elements in a wider culture war: the contest to define how we live and what counts as the good in the good life. Anti-Americanism occupies such a prominent place on the agenda of the culture wars precisely because the traditional values of American identity—articulated by the Founders and grounded in a commitment to individual liberty and public virtue—are deeply at odds with the radical, de-civilizing tenets of the "multiculturalist" enterprise.

To get a sense of what has happened to the institution of American identity, compare Robert Frost's performance at John F. Kennedy's inauguration in 1961 with Maya Angelou's performance thirty-two years later. As Huntington reminds us, Frost spoke of the "heroic deeds" of America's founding, an event, he said, that with God's "approval" ushered in "a new order of the ages." By contrast, Maya Angelou never mentioned the words "America" or "American." Instead, she identified twenty-seven ethnic or religious groups that had suffered repression because of America's "armed struggles for profit," "cynicism," and "brutishness."

Repellent though Maya Angelou's performance was, it did seem the appropriate rhetorical embroidery to welcome Bill Clinton, a president infatuated with the blandishments of multiculturalism and who sought a third "great revolution" to emancipate America from the legacy of European civilization and its Anglo-Protestant values. It has to be acknowledged that considerable progress toward that goal was made during his administration. And further progress has been made by Barack Obama, who pointedly downgraded claims to American exceptionalism—if America is exceptional, he said, it is merely in the same way that Greece or Britain, say, is exceptional—even as he presided over the downgrading of the country's credit rating.

A favorite weapon in the armory of multiculturalism is the lowly hyphen. When we speak of an African-American or Mexican-American or Asian-American these days, the aim is not descriptive but deconstructive. There is a polemical edge to it, a provocation. The hyphen does not mean "American, but hailing at some point in the past from someplace else." It means "only provisionally American: my allegiance is divided at best." (I believe something similar can be said about the feminist fad for hyphenating the bride's maiden name with her husband's surname. It is a gesture of independence that is also a declaration of divided loyalty.) It is curious to what extent the passion for hyphenation is fostered more by the liberal elite than the populations it is supposedly meant to serve. How does it serve them? Presumably by enhancing their sense of "self-esteem." Frederick Douglass saw through this charade some one hundred and fifty years ago. "No one idea," he wrote, "has given rise to more oppression and persecution toward colored people of this country than that which makes Africa, not America, their home."

The indispensable Ward Connerly would agree. Connerly has campaigned vigorously against affirmative action across the country. This of course has made him a pariah among the politically correct elite. It has also resulted in some humorous exchanges, such as this telephone interview with a reporter from *The New York Times* in 1997.

> REPORTER: What are you?
> CONNERLY: I am an American.
> REPORTER: No, no, no! What are you?
> CONNERLY: Yes, yes, yes! I am an American.
> REPORTER: That is not what I mean. I was told that you are African American. Are you ashamed to be African American?
> CONNERLY: No, I am just proud to be an American.

Connerly went on to explain that his ancestry included Africans, French, Irish, and American Indians. It was too much for the poor reporter from our Paper of Record: "What does that make you?" he asked in uncomprehending exasperation. I suspect he was not edified by Connerly's cheerful response: "That makes me all-American."

The multicultural passion for hyphenation is not simply a fondness for syntactical novelty. It also bespeaks a commitment to the centrifugal force of anti-American tribalism. The division marked by the hyphen in African-American (say) denotes a political stand. It goes hand-in-hand with other items on the index of liberal desiderata—the redistributive impulse behind efforts at "affirmative action," for example. Affirmative action was undertaken in the name of equality. But, as always seems to happen, it soon fell prey to the Orwellian logic from which the principle that "All animals are equal" gives birth to the transformative codicil: "but some animals are more equal than others."

Affirmative action is Orwellian in a linguistic sense, too, since what announces itself as an initiative to promote equality winds up enforcing discrimination precisely on the grounds that it was meant to overcome. Thus we are treated to the delicious, if alarming, contradiction of college applications that declare their commitment to evaluate candidates "without regard to race, gender, religion, ethnicity, or national origin" on page 1 and then helpfully inform you on page 2 that it is to your advantage to mention if you belong to any of the following designated victim groups. Among other things, a commitment to multiculturalism seems to dull one's sense of contradiction.

The whole history of affirmative action is instinct with that irony. The original effort to redress legitimate grievances—grievances embodied, for instance, in the discriminatory practices of Jim Crow—have mutated into new forms of discrimination. In 1940, Franklin Roosevelt established the Fair Employment Practices Committee because blacks were openly barred from war factory jobs.

But what began as a Presidential Executive Order in 1961 directing government contractors to take "affirmative action" to assure that people be hired "without regard" for sex, race, creed, color, etc., has resulted in the creation of vast bureaucracies dedicated to discovering, hiring, and advancing people chiefly on the basis of those qualities. White is black, freedom is slavery, "without regard" comes to mean "with regard for nothing else."

Had he lived to see the evolution of affirmative action, Tocqueville would have put such developments down as examples of how in democratic societies the passion for equality tends to trump the passion for liberty. The fact that the effort to enforce equality often results in egregious inequalities he would have understood to be part of the "tutelary despotism" that "extends its arms over society as a whole; it covers its surface with a network of small, complicated, painstaking, uniform rules through which the most original minds and the most vigorous souls cannot clear a way to surpass the crowd."

MULTICULTURALISM and "affirmative action" are allies in the assault on the institution of American identity. As such, they oppose the traditional understanding of what it means to be an American—an understanding hinted at in 1782 by the French-born American farmer J. Hector St. John de Crèvecœur in his famous image of America as a country in which "individuals of all nations are melted into a new race of men." This crucible of American identity, this "melting pot," has two aspects. The negative aspect involves disassociating oneself from the cultural imperatives of one's country of origin. One sheds a previous identity before assuming a new one. One might preserve certain local habits and tastes, but they are essentially window-dressing. In essence one has left the past behind in order to become an American citizen.

The positive aspect of advancing the melting pot involves embracing the substance of American culture. The 1795 code for citizenship lays out some of the formal requirements.

I do solemnly swear (1) to support the Constitution of the United States; (2) to renounce and abjure absolutely and entirely all allegiance and fidelity to any foreign prince, potentate, state, or sovereignty of whom or which the applicant was before a subject or citizen; (3) to support and defend the Constitution and the laws of the United States against all enemies, foreign and domestic; (4) to bear true faith and allegiance to the same; and (5) (A) to bear arms on behalf of the United States when required by law, or (B) to perform noncombatant service in the Armed Forces of the United States when required by law . . .

For over two hundred years, this oath had been required of those wishing to become citizens. In 2003, Huntington tells us, federal bureaucrats launched a campaign to rewrite and weaken it.

I shall say more about what constitutes the substance of American identity in a moment. For now, I want to underscore the fact that this project of Americanization has been an abiding concern since the time of the Founders. "We must see our people more Americanized," John Jay declared in the 1780s. Jefferson concurred. Teddy Roosevelt repeatedly championed the idea that American culture, the "crucible in which all the new types are melted into one," was "shaped from 1776 to 1789, and our nationality was definitely fixed in all its essentials by the men of Washington's day."

It is often said that America is a nation of immigrants. In fact, as Huntington points out, America was initially a country of *settlers*. Settlers precede immigrants and make their immigration possible. The culture of those mostly English-speaking, predominantly Anglo-Protestant settlers defined American culture. Their efforts came to fruition with the generation of Franklin, Washington, Jefferson, Hamilton, and Madison. The Founders are so denominated because they founded, they inaugurated a state. Immigrants were those who came later, who came from elsewhere, and who became American by embracing the Anglophone culture of the original settlers. The English language, the rule of law, respect for individual rights, the industriousness and piety that flowed from the Protestant work ethic—these were central elements in the culture disseminated by the Founders. And these were among the qualities embraced by immigrants when they became Americans. "Throughout American history," Huntington notes, "people who were not white Anglo-Saxon Protestants have become Americans by adopting America's Anglo-Protestant culture and political values. This benefitted them and the country."

Justice Louis Brandeis outlined the pattern in 1919. Americanization, he said, means that the immigrant "adopts the clothes, the manners, and the customs generally prevailing here . . . substitutes for his mother tongue the English language" and comes "into complete harmony with our ideals and aspirations and cooperate[s] with us for their attainment." Until the 1960s, the Brandeis model mostly prevailed. Protestant, Catholic, and Jewish groups, understanding that assimilation was the best ticket to stability and social and economic success, eagerly aided in the task of integrating their charges into American society.

The story is very different today. In America, there is a dangerous new tide of immigration from Asia, a variety of Muslim countries, and Latin America, especially from Mexico. The tide is new not only chronologically but also in substance. First, there is the sheer matter of numbers. More than 2,200,000 legal immigrants came to the U.S. from Mexico in the 1990s alone.

The number of illegal Mexican immigrants is staggering. So is their birth rate. Altogether there are more than 8 million Mexicans in the U.S. Some parts of the Southwest are well on their way to becoming what Victor Davis Hanson calls "Mexifornia," "the strange society that is emerging as the result of a demographic and cultural revolution like no other in our times." A professor at the University of New Mexico predicts that by 2080 parts of the Southwest United States and Northern Mexico will join to form a new country, "La Republica del Norte."

The problem is not only one of numbers, though. Earlier immigrants made—and were helped and goaded by the ambient culture to make—concerted efforts to assimilate. Important pockets of these new immigrants are not assimilating, not learning English, not becoming or thinking of themselves primarily as Americans. The effect of these developments on American identity is disastrous and potentially irreversible.

Such developments are abetted by the liberal political and educational elites of this country, whose dominant theme is the perfidy of traditional American values. Hence the passion for multiculturalism and the ideal of ethnic hyphenation that goes with it. This has done immense damage in schools and colleges as well as in the population at large. By removing the obligation to master English, multiculturalism condemns whole sub-populations to the status of permanent second-class citizens. By removing the obligation to adopt American values, it fosters what the German novelist Hermann Broch calls a "value vacuum," a sense of existential emptiness that breeds anomie and the pathologies of nihilism.

As if in revenge for this injustice, however, multiculturalism also weakens the social bonds of the community at large. The price of imperfect assimilation is imperfect loyalty. Take the movement for bilingualism. Whatever it intended in theory, in practice it means not mastering English. It has notoriously left its supposed beneficiaries essentially monolingual, often semi-lingual. The only "bi" involved is a passion for bifurcation, which is fed by the accumulated resentments instilled by the anti-American multicultural orthodoxy. Every time you call directory assistance or some large corporation and are told "Press One for English" and "Para español oprime el numero dos" it is another small setback for American identity.

Meanwhile, many prominent academics and even businessmen come bearing the gospel of what John Fonte has dubbed "transnational progressivism"—an anti-patriotic stew of politically correct ideas and attitudes distinguished partly by its penchant for vague but virtuous-sounding abstractions, partly by its moral smugness. In *Sovereignty or Submission: Will Americans Rule Themselves or be Ruled by Others?* (2011), Fonte describes it as "the suicide of liberal democracy." It is a familiar litany. The philosopher Martha Nussbaum warns that "patriotic pride" is "morally dangerous" while Princeton's Amy Gutmann reveals that she finds it "repugnant" for American students to learn that they are "above all, citizens of the United States" instead of partisans of her preferred abstraction, "democratic humanism." New York University's Richard Sennett denounces "the evil of a shared national identity" and concludes that the erosion of national sovereignty is "basically a positive thing." Cecilia O'Leary of American University identifies American patriotism as a right-wing, militaristic, male, white, Anglo, and repressive force while Peter Spiro of Hofstra University says it "is increasingly difficult to use the word 'we' in the context of international affairs."

Of course, whenever the word "patriotism" comes up in left-wing circles, there is sure to be some allusion to Samuel Johnson's observation that "patriotism is the last refuge of scoundrels." Right on cue, George Lipsitz of the University of California sniffs that "in recent years refuge in patriotism has been the first resort of scoundrels of all sorts." Naturally, Dr. Johnson's explanation to Boswell that he did not mean to disparage "a real and generous love of our country" but only that "pretended patriotism" that is a "cloak for self-interest" is left out of account.

The bottom line is that the traditional ideal of a distinctive American identity, forged out of many elements but unified around a core of beliefs, attitudes, and commitments is now up for grabs. One academic epitomized the established attitude among our liberal elites when she expressed the hope that the United States would "never again be culturally 'united,' if united means 'unified' in beliefs and practices."

Nor is this merely an academic crotchet. Many politicians—and many courts—have colluded in spreading the multicultural gospel. The nation's motto—E pluribus unum—was chosen by Franklin, Jefferson, and Adams to express the ideal of faction- and heritage-transcending unity. America forged one people out of many peoples. Former Vice President Al Gore interpreted the tag to mean "Out of one, many." This might have been inadvertence. It might have been simple ignorance. It might have been deliberate ideological provocation. Which is worst?

The combined effect of the multicultural enterprise has been to undermine the foundation of American national identity. Huntington speaks dramatically but not inaptly of "Deconstructing America." What he has in mind are not the linguistic tergiversations of a Jacques Derrida or Michel Foucault but the efforts—politically if not always intellectually allied efforts—to disestablish the dominant culture by fostering a variety of subversive attitudes, pieces of legislation, and judicial interventions. "The deconstructionists," Huntington writes,

> promoted programs to enhance that status and influence of subnational racial, ethnic, and cultural groups. They encouraged immigrants to maintain their birth-country cultures,

granted them legal privileges denied to native-born Americans, and denounced the idea of Americanization as un-American. They pushed the rewriting of history syllabi and textbooks so as to refer to the "peoples" of the United States in place of the single people of the Constitution. They urged supplementing or substituting for national history the history of subnational groups. They downgraded the centrality of English in American life and pushed bilingual education and linguistic diversity. They advocated legal recognition of group rights and racial preferences over the individual rights central to the American Creed. They justified their actions by theories of multiculturalism and the idea that diversity rather than unity or community should be America's overriding value. The combined effect of these efforts was to promote the deconstruction of the American identity that had been gradually created over three centuries.

Taken together, Huntington concludes, "these efforts by a nation's leaders to deconstruct the nation they governed were, quite possibly, without precedent in human history."

The various movements to deconstruct American identity and replace it with a multicultural "rainbow" or supranational bureaucracy have made astonishing inroads in the last few decades and especially in the last several years. And, as Huntington reminds us, the attack on American identity has counterparts elsewhere in the West wherever the doctrine of multiculturalism has trumped the cause of national identity. The European Union—whose leaders are as dedicated to multicultural shibboleths as they are to rule by top-down, anti-democratic bureaucracy—is a case in point. But the United States, the most powerful national state, is also the most attractive target for deconstruction.

It is a curious development that Huntington traces. In many respects, it corroborates James Burnham's observation, in *Suicide of the West* (1964), that "liberalism permits Western civilization to be reconciled to dissolution." (I have more to say about Burnham below in "The Power of James Burnham.") For what we have witnessed with the triumph of multiculturalism is a kind of hypertrophy or perversion of liberalism, as its core doctrines are pursued to the point of caricature. "Freedom," "diversity," "equality," "tolerance," even "democracy"—how many definitive liberal virtues have been redacted into their opposites by the imperatives of political correctness? If "diversity" mandates bilingual education, then we must institute bilingual education, even if it results in the cultural disenfranchisement of those it was meant to benefit. The passion for equality demands "affirmative action," even though the process of affirmative action depends upon treating people unequally. The French philosopher Jean-François Revel put it well when he observed, in 1970, that "Democratic civilization is the first in history to blame itself because another power is trying to destroy it."

IF THERE IS a bright spot in the portrait that Huntington paints, it revolves around the fact that centrifugal forces of multiculturalism are espoused chiefly by the intellectual and bureaucratic elite. For many ordinary people, the developments that Huntington outlines represent a catastrophe, not progress. What prospects do ordinary people have against the combined forces of the courts, the educational establishment, the "mainstream" media, and much popular culture? It is hard to say—at least, it is hard to say anything cheerful. But Huntington does provide several rays of hope. There are many movements to "take back America," to resuscitate the core values that, traditionally, have defined us as Americans. Indeed, Huntington's book may be regarded as a manifesto on behalf of that battle. The home-schooling movement is one example. Only a few years ago, it was a fringe phenomenon, allied almost exclusively to certain conservative evangelical sects. Today, home schoolers come from every religious and social background. In 1990–1991, 76,000 children were home-schooled. The estimate for 2011 is more than 2 million. That explosion is not only evidence of disenchantment with the intellectual failure of public schools: much more it betokens disenchantment with the moral tenor of public education.

WE STAND at a crossroads. The future of America hangs in the balance. Huntington outlines several possible courses that the country might take, from the loss of our core culture to an attempt to revive the "discarded and discredited racial and ethnic concepts" that, in part, defined pre-mid-twentieth century America.

Huntington argues for a third alternative. If we are to preserve our identity as a nation we need to preserve the core values that defined that identity. This is a point that the political philosopher Patrick, Lord Devlin (whose work we will meet again below in Chapter 6) made in his book *The Enforcement of Morals* (1965):

> [S]ociety means a community of ideas; without shared ideas on politics, morals, and ethics no society can exist. Each one of us has ideas about what is good and what is evil; they cannot be kept private from the society in which we live. If men and women try to create a society in which there is no fundamental agreement about good and evil they will fail; if having based it upon a common set of core values, they surrender those values, it will disintegrate. For society is not something that can be kept together physically; it is held by the invisible but fragile bonds of common beliefs and values. . . . A common morality is part of the bondage of a

good society, and that bondage is part of the price of society which mankind must pay.

What are those beliefs and values? They embrace several things, including religion. You wouldn't know it from watching CNN or reading *The New York Times*, but there is a huge religious revival taking place now, affecting just about every part of the globe except Western Europe, which slouches towards godlessness almost as fast as it slouches towards bankruptcy and demographic catastrophe (neither Spain nor Italy are producing enough children to replace their existing populations, while the Muslim birthrate in France continues to soar).

Things look different in America. For if America is a vigorously secular country—which it certainly is—it is also a deeply religious one. It always has been. Tocqueville was simply minuting the reality he saw around him when he noted that "On my arrival in the United States the religious aspect of the country was the first thing that struck my attention." As G. K. Chesterton put it a century after Tocqueville, America is "a nation with the soul of a church." Even today, America is a country where an astonishing 92 percent of the population says it believes in God and 80 to 85 percent of the population identifies itself as Christian. Hence Huntington's call for a return to America's core values is also a call to embrace the religious principles upon which the country was founded, "a recommitment to America as a deeply religious and primarily Christian country, encompassing several religious minorities adhering to Anglo-Protestant values, speaking English, maintaining its cultural heritage, and committed to the principles" of political liberty as articulated by the Founders.

Naturally, Huntington was sharply criticized for prescribing a return to "Anglo-Protestant values" as an antidote for faltering American identity. For example, Michiko Kakutani, reviewing *Who Are We?* for *The New York Times*, dismissed it as a "portentous," "crotchety," "highly polemical book" that merely "recycl[ed] arguments from earlier thinkers" while imparting to them a "bellicose new spin." Oh dear. Kakutani was particularly exercised by Huntington's criticism of multiculturalism and his advocacy of Anglo- Protestant values. But she missed something important. For Huntington was careful to stress that what he offers is an "argument for the importance of Anglo-Protestant culture, not for the importance of Anglo-Protestant people"— that is, a culture and set of values that "for three and a half centuries have been embraced by Americans of all races, ethnicities, and religions and that have been the source of their liberty, unity, power, prosperity, and moral leadership."

American identity was originally founded on four things: ethnicity, race, ideology, and culture. By the mid-twentieth century, ethnicity and race had sharply receded in importance. Indeed, one of America's greatest achievements is having eliminated the racial and ethnic components that historically were central to its identity. Ideology—the package of Enlightened liberal values championed by the Founders—are crucial but too thin for the task of forging or preserving national identity by themselves. ("A nation defined only by political ideology," Huntington notes, "is a fragile nation.") Which is why Huntington, like virtually all of the Founders, explicitly grounded American identity in religion.

Opponents of religion in the public square never tire of reminding us that there is no mention of God in the Constitution. This is true. Neither is the word "virtue" mentioned. But both are presupposed. As the historian Gertrude Himmelfarb points out, virtue, grounded in religion, was presumed "to be rooted in the very nature of man and as such . . . reflected in the moeurs of the people and in the traditions and informal institutions of society." It is also worth pointing out that if the Constitution is silent on religion, the Declaration of Independence is voluble, speaking of "nature's God," the "Creator," "the supreme judge of the world," and "divine Providence."

We are often told that the Founders were, almost to a man, Deists listing toward atheism. In *Washington's God: Religion, Liberty and the Father of Our Country* (2006), Michael and Jana Novak did a great deal to disabuse us of that idea. And in *The Roads to Modernity: The British, French, and American Enlightenments* (2004), Himmelfarb showed how a distinctively American form of Enlightenment, deeply informed by the British Enlightenment and differing sharply from the anti-clerical rationalism of the French variety, nourished the Founders' understanding of politics and what constitutes the good life for man. It was a form of Enlightenment that, Himmelfarb observes, regarded religion as an indispensable ally of reason, not an enemy. In America, Tocqueville observed, unlike in France, the "spirit of religion" and "the spirit of freedom" support rather than oppose each other. "Religion," he wrote

> sees in civil freedom a noble exercise of the faculties of man; in the political world, a field left by the Creator to the efforts of intelligence. . . . Freedom sees in religion the companion of its struggles and its triumphs, . . . the divine source of its rights. It considers religion as the safeguard of mores; and mores as the guarantee of laws.

Today, we are encouraged to interpret "freedom of religion" to mean "freedom from religion"—unless, of course, your religion is suitably exotic. (One recalls Chesterton's observation that "Religious liberty might be supposed to mean that everybody is free to discuss religion. In practice it means that hardly anybody is allowed to mention it.") The

ACLU is tortured by the thought of school children uttering the phrase "under God"; in June 2002, the Ninth Circuit Court of Appeals in California ruled that the phrase violated the principle of the separation of church and state. Yet until recently, Florida (among other states) allowed Muslim women to pose for a driver's license photograph with their faces veiled. The Founders would have been astounded—not to say alarmed—at this selective exclusion of religion from public life. They would have been even more astounded that it has been carried forward under the aegis of the First Amendment, perhaps the most wilfully misinterpreted text in America legal history.

Notwithstanding the ACLU and their allies, Himmelfarb is surely right that "The separation of church and state, however interpreted, did not signify the separation of church and society." Benjamin Rush, one of the signers of the Declaration of Independence, summed up the common attitude of the Founders toward religion when he insisted that "The only foundation for a useful education in a republic is to be laid in religion. Without it there can be no virtue, and without virtue there can be no liberty, and liberty is the object of all republican governments." George Washington concurred: "Reason and experience both forbid us to expect that national morality can prevail in exclusion of religious principles."

Even Benjamin Franklin, one of the least religious of the Founders, wanted some mention of God in the Constitution and, according to Himmelfarb, proposed that the proceedings of the Constitutional Convention begin with a daily prayer. Militant secularists will quote Jefferson's brusque dismissal of religion in *Notes on the State of Virginia*: "It does me no injury for my neighbor to say there are twenty gods or no god. It neither picks my pocket nor breaks my leg." But they somehow never get around to quoting the passage that occurs a few pages later: "Can the liberties of a nation be thought secure when we have removed their only firm basis, a conviction in the minds of people that these liberties are the gift of God?" As President, Himmelfarb notes, Jefferson was even more respectful of religion, and specifically Christianity, as the foundation of liberty and public virtue. On his way to church one Sunday, Jefferson was met by a friend.

> "You going to church Mr. J. You do not believe a word in it."
> "Sir [Jefferson replied], no nation has ever yet existed or been governed without religion. Nor can be. The Christian religion is the best religion that has been given to man and I as chief Magistrate of this nation am bound to give it the sanction of my example. Good morning Sir."

It is sometimes objected that, whatever lip-service the Founders gave to Christianity, their conception of religion was (the word "merely" implicitly supplied) pragmatic or utilitarian. Well, there was no doubt that the Founders thought religion was pragmatic, that is, socially useful, i.e., not merely a private affair with God. But why the implicit "merely"? As Himmelfarb argues, "this view of religion is not unworthy."

> To look upon religion as the ultimate source of morality, and hence of a good society and a sound policy, is not demeaning to religion. On the contrary, it pays religion—and God—the great tribute of being essential to the welfare of mankind. And it does credit to man as well, who is deemed capable of subordinating his lower nature to his higher, of venerating and giving obeisance to something above himself.

NO NATION lasts forever. An external enemy may eventually overrun and subdue it; internal forces of dissolution and decadence may someday undermine it, leaving it prey to more vigorous competitors. Sooner or later it succumbs. The United States is still the most powerful and productive nation the world has ever seen. Its astonishing military might, economic vitality, and political vigor are unprecedented. But someday, as Huntington reminds us, it too will fade or perish as Athens, Rome, and other great civilizations have faded or perished. Is the end, or the beginning of the end, at hand? No one's crystal ball is sufficiently clairvoyant to allow us to say. For decades—no, longer—we have been getting bulletins about the decline of the West, the rise and (especially) the fall of great powers, etc., etc.

So far, the West—or at least the United States—has disappointed its self-appointed undertakers. How do we stand now, near the beginning of the twenty-first century? It is worth remembering that besieged nations do not always succumb to the forces, external or internal, that threaten them. Sometimes, they muster the resolve to fight back successfully, to renew themselves. Today, America faces a host of new challenges. A rapidly arming and economically puissant China introduces new complexities to America's strategic calculations. Militant Islam and global terrorism continue their battle to spread Sharia law to the West. Those minatory forces will fail in proportion to our resolve to defeat them. The question is, Do we still possess that resolve? Inseparable from resolve is self-confidence, faith in the essential nobility of one's regime and one's way of life. To what extent do we still possess, still practice that faith?

America also faces numerous internal threats, from the rise of immigration without assimilation to the dissolute forces of cultural decadence and radical multiculturalism, to the destabilizing assaults of a protracted financial crisis. A stupefying mountain of debt threats the economic future of America while the forces of multiculturalism preach the dogma of bureaucratic cosmopolitanism. They encourage us to shed what is distinctively American in order to accommodate the quivering sensitivities of "humanity"—that imperious abstraction whose exigent mandates are updated regularly by such bodies as the United Nations, the World Court, and their allies in the professoriate and the liberal media. Huntington is right that "America cannot become the world and still be America." We face a choice between a multicultural future and an American future. Which will it be?

In *Washington's Crossing* (2004), his marvelous book on Washington's leadership in the Revolutionary War, David Hackett Fischer argues that America won the war against a much larger, better trained, and better equipped army partly because of the "moral strength of a just cause" and partly because of "religion": "Americans," he notes, "were a deeply spiritual people, with an abiding faith that sustained them in adversity." Americans are still a deeply spiritual people, though many of our intellectual, cultural, and political leaders would have us forget that fact. In 1973, the late Irving Kristol observed that

> for well over a hundred and fifty years now, social critics have been warning us that bourgeois society was living off the accumulated moral capital of traditional religion and traditional moral philosophy, and that once this capital was depleted, bourgeois society would find its legitimacy ever more questionable. These critics were never, in their lifetime, either popular or persuasive. The educated classes of liberal-bourgeois society simply could not bring themselves to believe that religion was that important to a polity. They could live with religion or morality as a purely private affair, and they could not see why everyone else—after a proper secular education, of course—could not do likewise.

Today, Kristol wrote two decades later, "the delicate task" we face is not to reform "the secular rationalist orthodoxy."

> Rather, it is to breathe new life into the older, now largely comatose, religious orthodoxies—while resisting the counterculture as best we can, adapting to it and reshaping it where we cannot simply resist.

Now, in the second decade of the twenty-first century, we have a glorious opportunity—perhaps it is the last such opportunity—to start repaying some of the moral capital we have been so profligate with in recent decades. Some sages assure us that our fate is sealed, that inevitable forces have scripted the (unhappy) denouement of American civilization. I do not believe them. Those children I saw at Fort McHenry are—potentially—insurance against that gloomy prognostication. They, and thousands like them, are potent weapons against the dissolutions that threaten us. Will we have the wit to use those weapons effectively? Samuel Huntington urges us to foster "those qualities that have defined America since its founding," above all the Anglo-Protestant values that wed liberty to order. Many in the liberal, multicultural establishment have rejected Huntington's vision of American unity as nativist or worse. I believe that his critics are wrong. Benjamin Franklin got to the nub of the matter when, more than two hundred years ago, he observed that "We must all hang together or assuredly we shall all hang separately."

Pericles and the Foreseeable Future:
9/11 a Decade Later

History is strewn with the wrecks of nations which have gained a little progressiveness at the cost of a great deal of hard manliness.
—Walter Bagehot, 1872

MIDWAY THROUGH the long article on Afghanistan in the great eleventh edition of *The Encyclopædia Britannica*, one comes across this description of the inhabitants of that ancient mountain country:

> The Afghans, inured to bloodshed from childhood, are familiar with death, and audacious in attack, but easily discouraged by failure; excessively turbulent and unsubmissive to law or discipline; apparently frank and affable in manner, especially when they hope to gain some object, but capable of the grossest brutality when that hope ceases. They are unscrupulous in perjury, treacherous, vain and insatiable, passionate in vindictiveness, which they will satisfy at the cost of their own lives and in the most cruel manner. Nowhere is crime committed on such trifling grounds, or with such general impunity, though when it is punished the punishment is atrocious. Among themselves the Afghans are quarrelsome, intriguing and distrustful; estrangements and affrays are of

constant occurrence; . . . The Afghan is by breed and nature a bird of prey. If from habit and tradition he respects a stranger within his threshold, he yet considers it legitimate to warn a neighbour of the prey that is afoot, or even overtake and plunder his guest after he has quitted his roof.

That refreshingly frank passage, by Colonel Sir Thomas Hungerford Holdich, was published in 1910. I hope that the American and British troops who still, in the autumn of 2011, are enjoying the hospitality of the Afghans are acquainted with this travel advisory. It is as pertinent today, a decade after 9/11, as it was 100 years ago.

I was put in mind of Sir Thomas's insightful commentary when *The New York Times* took its quote of the day from one Faqir Muhammad, an officer in one of the many squabbling anti-Taliban armies: "This is what Afghanistan is," he said. "We kill each other."

Indeed. And not only each other, of course. Item from *The New York Post* September 2011: "Fearing attack by Afghan 'allies,' Brit troops to sleep with pistols." The scare quotes around the word "allies" is a nice touch.

Sir Thomas's remarks are valuable not only because of their contemporaneity but also because they help us set today's issues in historical context. "The farther backward you can look," Winston Churchill once observed, "the farther forward you are likely to see." Early in the Peloponnesian War, a plague swept through Athens, killing thousands and demoralizing the survivors. In a rallying speech, Pericles (himself soon to die) noted that "When things happen suddenly, unexpectedly, and against all calculation, it takes the heart out of a man." Against the temptations of apathy and acquiescence, Pericles urged his listeners to recall the greatness of Athens, to face calamity with an "unclouded mind and react quickly against it."

It has been several weary years since the shock of September 11 gave way to the reality of America at war. In attempting to assess the significance of 9/11 a decade on, it is useful to take a page from Churchill and cast a backward glance. The pressure of contemporary events crowds us into the impatient confines of the present, rendering us insensible to the lessons of history—not least the lesson that tomorrow's dramas are typically unforeseen by the scripts we abide by today. Language itself conspires to keep us in the dark. I will return in a moment to Pericles. But I want first to dwell briefly on our tendency to use language to emasculate surprise.

Consider only that marvelous phrase "the foreseeable future." With what cheery abandon we employ it! Yet what a nugget of unfounded optimism those three words encompass. How much of the future, really, do we foresee? A week? A day? A minute? "In a minute," as T. S. Eliot said in "The Love Song of J. Alfred Prufrock," "there is time/For decisions and revisions which a minute will reverse." So much of life is a juggling with probabilities, a conjuring with uncertainties, that we often forget upon what stupendous acts of faith even the prudent conduct of life depends.

Had I been asked, on September 10, 2001, whether New York's Twin Towers would continue standing for "the foreseeable future," I should have answered "Yes." And so, in one sense, they did. Only my foresight was not penetrating enough, not far-seeing enough, to accommodate that most pedestrian of eventualities: an event.

An event is as common as dirt. It is also as novel as tomorrow's dawn. "There is nothing," the French writer Charles Péguy noted in the early years of the twentieth century, "so unforeseen as an event." The particular event Péguy had in mind was the Dreyfus Affair. Who could have predicted that the fate of an obscure Jewish Army captain falsely accused of spying would have such momentous consequences? And yet this unforeseen event, as Proust observed in *À la recherche du temps perdu*, suddenly, catastrophically, "divided France from top to bottom." Its repercussions were felt for decades. We plan, stockpile, second-guess, buy insurance, make allowances, assess risks, play the odds, envision contingencies, calculate interest, tabulate returns, save for a rainy day . . . and still we are constantly surprised.

IN A THOUGHTFUL ESSAY called "What Is Freedom?," the philosopher Hannah Arendt noted the extent to which habit—what she disparages somewhat with the name "automatism"—rules life. We are creatures of habit, schedules, and conventions. And thank God for that. For without habit we could never build character. And yet we are also creatures who continually depart from the script. Human beings do not simply behave in response to stimuli. We act—which means that our lives, though orchestrated largely by routine, are at the same time everywhere edged with the prospect of novelty. "Every act," Arendt wrote,

> seen from the perspective not of the agent but of the process in whose framework it occurs and whose automatism it interrupts, is a "miracle"—that is, something which could not be expected. . . . It is in the very nature of every new beginning that it breaks into the world as an "infinite improbability," and yet it is precisely this infinitely improbable which actually constitutes the very texture of everything we call real.

Every moment of every day presents us with the potential for what Arendt calls the "miracle" of human action, so familiar and yet ultimately unfathomable. That is why we find proleptic phrases like "the foreseeable future" indispensable. They declare the flag of our confidence, the reach of our competence. They domesticate the intractable mystery of everyday novelty. But they also serve to remind us that our confidence is deeply complicit with luck—that most fickle of talismans—our competence instantly revocable without notice. Which is to say that our foresight is always an adventure, practiced at the pleasure of the unpredictable.

This is something that P. G. Wodehouse, a philosopher of a somewhat merrier stamp than Hannah Arendt, put with his customary grace when his character Psmith observed that "in this life . . . we must always distinguish between the Unlikely and the Impossible." On September 10 it was unlikely that a small band of murderous fanatics should destroy the Twin Towers and fundamentally alter the political landscape of the world. It was not, alas, impossible.

The eruption of the unlikely is an affront to our complacency, an insult to our pride. We tend to react by subsequently endowing the unlikely with a pedigree of explanation. This reassures us by neutralizing novelty, extracting the element of the unexpected from what actually happened. I think again of Churchill. Summarizing the qualities that a budding politician should possess, he adduced both "The ability to foretell what is going to happen tomorrow, next week, next month, next year"—and the compensating ability "afterwards to explain why it didn't happen."

Today, the events of September 11 can seem almost inevitable. Reasons have been furnished for every detail. Pundits have rehearsed knowing genealogies for all the actors. Plausible itineraries have been repeated until they seem like predictions. All of those reasons and explanations were available on September 10. A look at the literature shows that some had been propounded for years. But they lacked the traction that events give to hindsight. Where were they when they were needed, at 8:00 A.M. on September 11?

They were not part of the foreseeable future until that future, unforeseen, overtook us.

I mention these homely incapacities to provide a kind of signpost or reminder. Even the extraordinary circumstance of wartime begets its anesthetizing versions of the ordinary. Our complacency exposed us to surprise on September 11. New complacencies now compete for our allegiance. In part, this results from the pressure of familiarity. Sooner or later, a state of permanent emergency comes to seem like a normal state of affairs. Ceaseless vigilance by nature ceases to be vigilant. But there are other ingredients involved in the return of complacency. Already one senses impatience on the part of the media. From the very beginning of this conflict, President Bush warned that the struggle against terrorism was going to be long, that it would be measured in years, not weeks or months. But a protracted battle does not accord well with a 24-hour news cycle, with the demand for screaming headlines, new developments, clear victories.

There is no single antidote to these liabilities. Nevertheless, Churchill was right about history providing the best corrective to our myopia. We need to look backwards if we are to extricate ourselves from the constrictions of the present. The "relevance" sought for the present time is best acquired from guideposts that have outlived the hectoring gabble of contemporary fashion. We are often asked if our "values" have kept pace, have "evolved," with the dramatic changes our political and social reality has seen in the past several decades. But values, I think, do not so much "evolve" as change keys. That is to say, our underlying humanity—with its essential moral needs and aspirations—remains constant. And this is why, for example, the emotional and psychological taxonomy that Aristotle provides in his *Ethics* and *Rhetoric* is as fresh and relevant to humanity today as it was two and a half millennia ago.

Which brings me back to Pericles. What lessons does the great Greek statesman have for us today? Does his example as a leader of the Athenians at the beginning of the Peloponnesian War have a special pertinence for us as we think back on the West's long struggle with Islamic terrorism? Does Pericles, in short, point the way for us?

To answer these questions, one first wants to know: what is it that Pericles stood for? To what sort of society was he pointing? What way of life, what vision of the human good did he propound?

IN HIS HISTORY of the Peloponnesian War, Thucydides recounts the public funeral oration that Pericles, as commander of the army and first citizen of Athens, delivered to commemorate those fallen after the first year—the first of twenty-seven years, be it noted—of war with Sparta. The short speech is deservedly one of the most famous in history.

The funeral oration outlines the advantages of Athenian democracy, a bold new system of government that was not simply a political arrangement but a way of life. There were two keynotes to that way of life: freedom and tolerance, on the one hand, responsible behavior and attention to duty on the other.

The two go together. We Athenians, Pericles said, are "free and tolerant in our private lives; but in public affairs we keep to the law"—including, he added in an important proviso, "those unwritten laws"—the lawlike commands of taste, manners, and morals—"which it is an acknowledged shame to break." Freedom and tolerance, Pericles suggested, were blossoms supported by roots that reached deep into the soil of duty.

Athens had become the envy of the world, partly because of its wealth, partly because of its splendor, partly because of the freedom enjoyed by its citizens. Athens' navy was unrivaled, its empire unparalleled, its civic and cultural in-stitutions unequalled. The city was "open to the world," a cosmopolitan center, political life was "free and open," as was private life: "We do not get into a state with our next-door neighbor," Pericles said, "if he enjoys himself in his own way."

Of course, from the perspective of twenty-first century America, democracy in Athens may seem limited and im-perfect. Women were entirely excluded from citizenship in Athens and there was a large slave class that underwrote the material freedom of Athens' citizens. These things must be acknowledged. But must they be apologized for? Whenever 5th-century Athens is mentioned these days, it seems that what is stressed is not the achievement of Athenian democ-racy but its limitations.

To my mind, concentrating on the limitations of Athe-nian democracy would be like complaining that the Wright brothers neglected to provide transatlantic service with their airplanes. The extraordinary achievement of Athens was to formulate the ideal of equality before the law. To be sure: that ideal was not perfectly instantiated in Athens. Perhaps it never will be perfectly instantiated, it being in the nature of ideals to inspire emulation but also to exceed it.

The point to bear in mind is that both the ideal of equal-ity before the law and the cultivation of an open, tolerant society were new. They made Athens the model of democ-racy for all the republics that sought to follow the path of freedom—just as America is the model of freedom today. Pericles was right to boast that "Future ages will wonder at us, as the present age wonders at us now." To continue the theme of aviation, we might say that in Athens, after innu-merable trials elsewhere, democracy finally managed to get off the ground and stay aloft. In Periclean Athens what mat-tered in assuming public responsibility, as Pericles said, was "not membership in a particular class, but the actual ability which the man possesses." To an extraordinary extent, within the limits of its franchise, Athens lived up to that ideal.

It is also worth noting that life in Athens was not only free but also full. When the day's work was done, Pericles boasted, Athenians turned not simply to private pleasure but also to ennobling recreation "of all kinds for our spirits." For the Age of Pericles was also the age of the great dramatists, the age of Socrates, the great artist Phidias, and others. Freedom, skill, and ambition conspired to make Athens a cultural as well a political paragon.

A RECURRENT THEME of the funeral oration is the importance of sound judgment, what Aristotle codified as the virtue of prudence. The blessing of freedom requires the ballast of duty, and informed judgment is the indispensable handmaiden of duty. A free society is one that nurtures the existential slack that tolerance and openness generate. Chaos and anarchy are forestalled by the intervention of politics in the highest sense of the term: deliberation and decision about securing the good life. When it comes to cultural activities, Pericles said, Athenians had learned to love beauty with moderation—the Greek word is *euteleias*, "without extravagance"—and to pursue philosophy and the life of the mind "without effeminacy," *aneu malakias*. Culture and the life of the mind were to be ennoblements of life, not an escape from its burdens, not a decadent pastime.

The exercise of sound judgment was required in other spheres as well. In their conduct of policy, Athenians strove to be bold, but prudent, i.e., effective. "We are," Pericles wrote, "capable at the same time of taking risks and of estimating them beforehand." The exercise of sound judgment was not simply an intellectual accomplishment; it was the tithe of citizenship. "We do not say that a man who takes no interest in politics is a man who minds his own business," Pericles observed, "we say that he has no business here at all."

He did not mean that every citizen had to be a politician. What he meant was that all citizens had a common stake in the commonwealth of the city. And that common stake brought with it common responsibilities as well as common privileges. At a time when everyone is clamoring for his or her "rights"—when new "rights" pop up like mushrooms throughout society—it is worth remembering that every right carries with it a corresponding duty. We enjoy certain rights because we discharge corresponding responsibilities. Some rights may be inalienable; none is without price.

SOMETHING SIMILAR can be said about democracy. Today, the word "democracy" and its cognates are often used as fancy synonyms for mediocrity. When we read about plans to "democratize" education or the arts or athletics, we know that is shorthand for plans to eviscerate those activities, for lowering standards and pursuing them as instruments of racial or sexual redress or some other form of social engineering. Alexis de Tocqueville was right to warn about the dangers of generalizing the principle of equality that underlies democracy. Universalized, the principle of equality leads to egalitarianism, the ideology of equality.

The problem today is that the egalitarian imperative threatens to overwhelm that other great social impulse, the impulse to achieve, to excel, to surpass: "always to be best and to rise above others," as Homer put it in one classic expression of the agonistic spirit. Radical egalitarianism—egalitarianism uncorrected by the aspirations of excellence—would have us pretend that there are no important distinctions among people; where the pretense is impossible, it would have us enact compensatory programs to minimize, or at least to paper over, the differences. The results are a vast increase in self-deception, cultural degradation, and bureaucratic meddlesomeness.

It is refreshing to turn to Pericles and remind ourselves that a passion for democracy need not entail the pursuit of mediocrity. Democracy is a high maintenance form of government. Freedom requires the disciplines restraint and circumspection if it is to flourish. Athenian democracy was animated by freedom, above all the freedom to excel, and it inspired in citizens both a healthy competitive spirit and "shame," as Pericles said, at the prospect of "falling below a certain standard."

In all this, Pericles noted, Athens was "an education to Greece," a model for its neighbors. At the moment he spoke, at the beginning of a long and ultimately disastrous war, his words must have had special resonance. In celebrating what the Athenians had achieved, he was also reminding them of all they stood to lose. His funeral oration was therefore not only an elegy but also a plea for resoluteness and a call to arms. It is a call that resonates with special significance now that the United States and indeed all of what used to be called Christendom is under attack by a worldwide network of terrorists. Pericles was right: The open society depends upon the interdiction of forces calculated to destroy. "We who remain behind," he said, "may hope to be spared the fate [of the fallen], but must resolve to keep the same daring spirit against the foe."

The view of society and the individual's responsibility that Pericles put forward was rooted in tradition but oriented toward the future. He did not think much of the custom of public funeral orations, he said, but he felt bound to observe it: "this institution was set up and approved by our forefathers, and it is my duty to follow the tradition." At the same time Pericles reminds us of the claims of the future by stressing the future's main emissaries: the children of Athens. "It is impossible," he suggests, for a man to put forward fair and honest views about our affairs if he has not . . . children whose lives are at stake."

The vision of society that Pericles articulated in the funeral oration has exercised a permanent fascination on the political imagination of the West. Although occasionally lost sight of, it has always returned to inspire apostles of freedom and tolerance. But it is imperative that we understand that the view of society that Pericles described is not inevitable. It represents a choice—a choice, moreover, that must constantly be renewed. It is one version of the good life for man. There are other, competing versions that we would find distinctly less attractive. In the West, Pericles' vision, modified by time and circumstance, has proven to be a peculiarly powerful one. It was absorbed by Christendom in the eighteenth century and helped to inform the democratic principles that undergird British and American democracy.

But we would be untrue to Pericles' counsel of vigilance were we to think that some of the alternatives to this vision were incapable of inspiring strong allegiance. This was true when Pericles spoke. His entire speech presupposes the contrast between the Athenian way of life and another that was inimical to it. It continues to be true. The spectacle of radical Islamists dancing joyfully in the street when news broke of the September 11 attacks on New York and Washington should remind us of that fact.

Indeed, the status of Pericles' vision of society as one alternative among others was dramatically sharpened by the events of September 11. For that attack was not simply an attack on symbols of American capitalism or American military might. Nor was it simply a terrorist attack on American citizens. It was all those things but more. It was an attack on the idea of America as a liberal democratic society, which means that it was an attack on an idea of society that had one of its primary sources in the ideals enunciated by Pericles. Above in "The Fortunes of Permance," I quoted Binyamin Netanyahu's astringent observation that 9/11 was a furious salvo in "a war to reverse the triumph of the West." Netanyahu's words should be constantly borne in mind lest the emollient tide of rationalization blunt the angry reality of those attacks.

MANY ILLUSIONS were challenged on September 11. One illusion, as I noted above in "Institutionalizing Our Demise," concerns the fantasies of academic multiculturalists, so-called. I say "so-called" because what goes under the name of multiculturalism in our colleges and universities today is really a polysyllabic form of mono-culturalism fueled by ideological hatred. Genuine multiculturalism involves a great deal of work, beginning with the arduous task of learning other languages, something most of those who call themselves multiculturalists are conspicuously loath to do.

Think of the fatuous attack on "dead white European males" that stands at the center of the academic multiculturalist enterprise. As a specimen of that maligned species, one could hardly do better than Pericles. Not only is he a dead white European male, but he is one who embodied in his life and aspirations an ideal of humanity completely at odds with academic multiculturalism. He was patriarchal, militarist, elitist, and Eurocentric, indeed, Hellenocentric, which is even worse.

The good news is that Pericles survived September 11. The spurious brand of multiculturalism that encourages us to repudiate "dead white European males" and insists that all cultures are of equal worth may finally be entering a terminal stage. Figures like Edward Said and Susan Sontag, Harold Pinter and Noam Chomsky continued to bay about the iniquity of America, the depredations of capitalism, and so on, but their voices fell on increasingly deaf ears. The liberal media began by wringing its hands and wondering whether the coalition would hold, whether we were fair to "moderate" members of the Taliban, whether the Afghans were too wily for Americans, whether the United States was acting in too "unilateral" a fashion. On Christmas Eve 2001, in a masterpiece of understatement, *The Wall Street Journal* ran a story under the headline "In War's Early Phase, News Media Showed a Tendency to Misfire." "This war is in trouble," quoth Daniel Schorr on NPR. Not to be outdone, R. W. Apple warned readers of *The New York Times* that "signs of progress are sparse." *Et cetera*. Every piece of possible bad news was touted as evidence that we had entered a "quagmire," that we were "overextended," "arrogant," "unresponsive" to the needs and desires of indigenes. Even now, a decade later, it is too soon to say which way the rhetorical chips will ultimately fall. The elimination of Osama bin Laden by a team of Navy SEALs in 2011 marked the end of a chapter but it was quickly absorbed into a larger metabolism of doubt.

The hollowness of the left-liberal wisdom about the war brings me to another illusion that was challenged by the events of 9/11. I mean the illusion that the world is basically a benevolent, freedom-loving place, and that if only other people had enough education, safe sex, and access to National Public Radio they would become pacific celebrants of democracy and tolerance. This is the temptation of utopia—Greek for "nowhere"—and it must be acknowledged that America's fortunate geographical position in the world has long encouraged certain versions of this temptation. The extraordinary growth of America's wealth and military power in the twentieth-century—like Athens' great wealth and power in the fifth-century B.C. have kept the wolf from the door and the marauder from our throats. They have also abetted the illusion of invulnerability. But increased international mobility and the widespread dissemination of technological know-how have conspired to neutralize or at least attenuate those advantages. And let's not forget the world-wide economic crisis that, since 2008, has introduced a new current of anxious uncertainty into our deliberations about the future. September 11, which brought the destruction of war to American soil for the first time since the war of 1812, made it abundantly clear that we have implacable enemies, enemies we can not hide from, effectively appease, or negotiate with, enemies that will struggle to the death to destroy us. "Allah Akbar!" shout a group of Taliban prisoners, and then they set about detonating hand grenades, killing themselves and their guards. The supreme Taliban leader Mullah Mohammed Omar put it with all possible clarity when he said that for him and his followers "The real matter is the extinction of America, and God willing, it will fall to the ground."

A third illusion that was challenged on September 11 concerns the morality of power. It has been fashionable among trendy academics, CNN commentators, and other armchair utopians to pretend that the use of power by the powerful is by definition evil. Violence on the part of anyone claiming to be a victim was excused as the product of "frustration" or "rage"—emotions that for mysterious reasons are held to be exonerating for the dispossessed but incriminating when exhibited by legitimate authority. Hence the ponderous scramble to uncover "root causes": that is, the search for sociological alibis that might absolve the perpetrators of evil from the inconveniences of guilt. Another quotation from Charles Péguy: "Surrender is essentially an operation by means of which we set about explaining instead of acting."

This favorite liberal pastime has not been abandoned, but it looks increasingly rancid. As the commentator Jonathan Rauch wittily put it shortly after the terrorist attacks, the cause of terrorism is terrorists. September 11 reminded us that with power comes responsibility. Power without resolution is perceived as weakness, and weakness is always dangerously provocative. In the aftermath of September 11, we in the West have often been cautioned against exciting Islamic rage. My own feeling is that it is salutary for our allies and our enemies alike to understand that American rage, too, is an unpleasant thing. Pericles commended the Athenians on their "adventurous" spirit that had "forced an entry into every sea and into every land." Everywhere, he noted, Athens "left behind . . . everlasting memorials of good done to our friends or suffering inflicted on our enemies."

Since the 1970s, we have tended to flinch from such frank talk; we shy away from talk of forcing anyone to do anything; we seem ashamed of acknowledging that we have enemies let alone acknowledging that we wish them ill; we are embarrassed alike by the perquisites and the obligations of power. Such squeamishness is precisely part of the "effeminacy" against which Pericles warned. We desperately wish to be liked. We forget that true affection depends upon respect.

At least since the end of the Vietnam conflict, the United States has vacillated in discharging its responsibilities to power. Whatever the wisdom of our involvement in Vietnam, our way of extricating ourselves was ignominious and an incitement to further violence. The image of that U.S. helicopter evacuating people from our embassy in Saigon is a badge of failure, not so much of military strategy but of nerve.

Even worse was our response to the hostage crisis in Iran in 1979 and 1980. Our hesitation to act decisively was duly noted and found contemptible by our enemies. And the fiasco of President Carter's botched rescue attempt, when a transport vehicle and one of our helicopters collided on

the sands of the Iranian desert, was a national humiliation. President Reagan did effectively face down the Soviet
Union, but his halfhearted response to the terrorist bombing
of a U.S. Marine barracks in Lebanon in 1983 contributed
to the tattered reputation of America as (in Mao's phrase)
"a paper tiger."

The Clinton administration sharply exacerbated the
problem. From 1993 through 2000, United States again and
again demonstrated its lack of resolve even as it let the U.S.
military infrastructure decay. In Somalia at the end of 1992,
two U.S. helicopters were shot down, several Americans
were killed, the body of one was dragged naked through the
streets of Mogadishu. We did nothing—an action, or lack
of action, that prompted Osama bin Laden way back then
to reflect that his followers were "surprised at the low morale of the American soldiers and realized more than before
that the American soldier was a paper tiger and after a few
blows ran in defeat."

It was the same in 1993, when terrorists bombed the
World Trade Center, killing six people and wounding scores.
Bin Laden applauded the action but denied responsibility.
No one really believed him; nevertheless nothing was done.
(One of the wretches jailed for that atrocity commented:
"Next time we'll do it right.")

It was the same in June 1996, when a truck bomb explod-
ed outside a U.S. military barracks in Saudi Arabia, killing
nineteen Americans. There were some anguished words but
we did—nothing. It was the same in 1998 when our embas-
sies were bombed in Kenya and Tanzania, killing hundreds.
The response was to rearrange some rocks in the Afghanistan desert with a few cruise missiles in a half-hearted attempt to target bin Laden.

It was the same in October 2000, when suicide terrorists
blew a gigantic hole in USS Cole, killing seventeen sailors

and almost sinking one of the U.S. Navy's most advanced ships. Like Hamlet, we responded with "words, words, words," and only token military gestures.

In the wake of September 11, this policy of bellicose vacillation changed. Still, there were plenty of voices urging not caution but abdication. The left-liberal establishment cannot long bear to see a strong America regnant. It was chastened by disaster but incited by the prospect of losing hold of its illusions. Missteps in Iraq gave its opposition to the war new strength. A decade on, despite some high profile assassinations of terrorist leaders, there are fewer signs that America remains prepared to follow through on its promise to eradicate terrorism and hold responsible those states that sponsor, finance, or abet it. There are even fewer signs that America, or the West generally, is prepared to stand up for its own cultural and political legacy in the face of the existential threat of Islamism and its encroaching effort to establish Sharia law the world over.

If so, we are abandoning a central part of Pericles' vision. "Make up your minds," Pericles said toward the end of his great oration, "that happiness depends on being free, and freedom depends on being courageous. Let there be no relaxation in the face of the perils of the war."

LET ME END with a different historical parallel. Among the neglected masterpieces of Victorian political thought is Walter Bagehot's book *Physics and Politics*. Published in 1872, it outlines the requirements for the survival and advance of civilization. Bagehot's ideal is the civilization that he inhabited himself: the liberal democratic polity of nineteenth-century Britain where most disputes were settled in law courts and politics was pursued through discussion, not arms. But Bagehot was canny enough—one might say he was grown-up enough—to understand that such a polity had been made possible in the first instance by force and that it could be maintained in the long run only through the distillates of force that economic might and military prowess represent. "History," Bagehot wrote, "is strewn with the wrecks of nations which have gained a little progressiveness at the cost of a great deal of hard manliness, and have thus prepared themselves for destruction as soon as the movements of the world gave a chance for it." In the context of our discussion here, Bagehot's observation looks like a summary of Pericles' funeral oration, or at least a central part of it. Does Pericles point the way? The alternative is cultural suicide.

Part Two

Rereading John Buchan

*Life is barren enough surely with all her trappings; let us
be therefore cautious of how we strip her.*
—Dr. Johnson, quoted by John Buchan

*The life of reason is our heritage and exists only through
tradition. Now the misfortune of revolutionists is that
they are disinherited, and their folly is that they wish to be
disinherited even more than they are.*
—George Santayana, quoted by John Buchan

*"You think that a wall as solid as the earth separates
civilization from barbarism. I tell you the division is a
thread, a sheet of glass. A touch here, a push there, and
you bring back the reign of Satan."*
—Andrew Lumley, in Buchan's *The Power-House*

"REALLY?" I believe that was my cautious response when
a friend urged me to read John Buchan's memoir *Pilgrim's Way*. It was, he said, "a remarkable spiritual testament,"
or words to that effect. Hmm. The source of the recommendation was unimpeachable: one of the most intelligent and
least frivolous people I know. Yet I had read Buchan—probably the same books you have: *The Thirty-Nine Steps* (1915),

for example, the short, bracing spy thriller (or "shocker," as Buchan called it) in which the dashing Richard Hannay battles a perfidious German spy ring and—after a series of wild, pulse-rattling cliffhangers—emerges triumphant in the nick of time. I had also read *Greenmantle* (1916), the somewhat longer, but still bracing, spy thriller in which the dashing Richard Hannay battles a perfidious German spy ring and—after a series of wild, pulse-rattling cliffhangers—emerges triumphant in the nick of time. I had even read *Mr. Standfast* (1919), the moderately long spy thriller in which a dashing Richard . . . German . . . wild . . . emerges . . . nick of t.

I HASTEN TO ADD that the preceding sentences are not fair to my experience of reading those books. I gobbled them up gratefully if heedlessly. And that, I suspect, is precisely how Buchan intended them to be read. His biographers make a point of telling us that he disliked talking about his "shockers." He was pleased that people liked them—pleased that they sold well—but at bottom they were a bit of a lark, a recreation rather than a vocation.

Buchan once said that if there were six literary categories from "highbrow to solid ivory" he belonged in the middle, to the "high-lowbrow." He understood perfectly that his popular fiction was a species of "romance where the incidents defy the probabilities, and march just inside the borders of the possible." That indeed was part of its attraction. As the critic John Gross observed in his review of Janet Adam Smith's biography of Buchan (1965), "one of the main reasons for enjoying Buchan is because he is so preposterous." But do note that the emphasis here is as much on "enjoying" as on "preposterous."

In any event, there is nothing that prevents the preposterous from possessing contemporary relevance. I reread *Greenmantle* in 2001, just after al Qaeda destroyed the World Trade Towers. It really is an extravagant period piece. But I am surprised that the book has not made a conspicuous comeback. The story turns on a German effort to enlist and enflame a radical Islamist sect in Turkey, where things are touch-and-go for the Allies. Sir Walter Bullivant of the Foreign Office summons Hannay and puts him in the picture. "The ordinary man" believes that Islam is succumbing to "Krupp guns," to modernity. "Yet—I don't know," Sir Walter confesses. "I do not quite believe in Islam becoming a back number." Hannay agrees (natch): "It looks as if Islam had a bigger hand in the thing than we thought. . . . Islam is a fighting creed, and the mullah still stands in the pulpit with the Koran in one hand and a drawn sword in the other." Indeed.

Later in the book, another character observes,

"There's a great stirring in Islam, something moving on the face of the waters. . . . Those religious revivals come in cycles, and one was due about now. And they are quite clear about the details. A seer has arisen of the blood of the Prophet, who will restore the Khalifate to its old glories and Islam to its old purity."

How do you spell "Muslim Brotherhood"?

Greenmantle was published in 1916. Perhaps we've finally caught up with it.

Buchan often deliberately poached on contemporary historical events and places in his shockers. He was aiming less at verisimilitude than at the piquancy that the appearance of verisimilitude provided. He did it all with a wink. In the dedication to *The Thirty-Nine Steps*, Buchan explains that, convalescing from an illness, he had exhausted his supply of thrillers—"those aids to cheerfulness"—and so decided to write one of his own. He tossed it off in a matter of weeks in the autumn of 1914 and was duly startled by its immense success. (An earlier shocker, *The Power-House*, had been serialized in 1913 but wasn't published in book form until 1916.) A million copies of *The Thirty-Nine Steps* sold, I read somewhere, and that is an old figure. Timing played a part in the huge sale. The book was published in October 1915, early in the First World War. Tales about brave chaps hunting down dastardly German spies had an audience primed and waiting.

But the success of *The Thirty-Nine Steps* was not due to timing alone. It is a remarkable book. Like Mr. Hannay himself, the book hits the ground running and barely stops for breath in the course of its 110 pages. *On your mark* (first sentence): Hannay, back from South Africa having made his pile, is "pretty well disgusted with life"; he contemplates Albania, "a place that might keep a man from yawning."

> I made a vow. I would give the Old Country another day to fit me into something; if nothing happened, I would take the next boat for the Cape.

Get set (a few pages later): Hannay comes home to find the man with a dark secret he'd met a few days earlier murdered in his apartment. *Go*: Hannay, pursued by both the police (who suspect him of the murder) and the bad guys (who done it), races from London to Scotland, clambers over endless Scottish moors, is caught by the baddies, escapes, and zigzags back by the cliffs of Dover to reveal the secret of the Black Stone. Whew: "All Europe" had been "trembling on the edge of an earthquake." Not to worry: Hannay nabs the spy; England is safe. (In his famous 1935 film version of the book, Alfred Hitchcock took many liberties with the text, but he did manage to preserve Buchan's uncanny union of velocity and menace.)

The *Thirty-Nine Steps* recounts all this with an urgent but evocative economy. It owes as much to Sir Walter Scott and Robert Louis Stevenson (fellow Scots and two of Buchan's models) as E. Phillips Oppenheim (a less august though no less favored model: "my master in fiction . . . the greatest Jewish writer since Isaiah").

BUCHAN DID NOT INVENT a genre with *The Thirty-Nine Steps*. Conan Doyle, Wilkie Collins, and others beat him to it. And let's not forget Erskine Childers's classic *The Riddle of the Sands* (1903). But Buchan did supply some novel furnishings, a distinctive tone and atmosphere instantly recognizable as the Buchanesque. The scholar Robin Winks called Buchan "the father of the modern spy thriller," a genre whose beneficiaries include Graham Greene, Ian Fleming, and John le Carré. The chase scenes, the villain who belongs to the upper reaches of respectable society, the breeding and derring-do of the hero: they're reasonably fresh in Buchan, overripe in Fleming, often a bit rancid in later authors.

But the Buchanesque involved other elements. It has something to do with his breathless plots and flat but somehow compelling characters—not only Hannay (modelled, it is said, on the young Edmund Ironside, later Field Marshall Lord Ironside of Archangel), but also figures like Peter Pienaar, the wiry Dutch hunter; Dickson McCunn, the retired Glasgow grocer; Sir Edward Leithen, the high-powered lawyer. None is three-dimensional; none seems "real"; all are curiously memorable in the context of their actions. I suspect that Buchan would have agreed with—let's see, Aristotle, wasn't it?—that plot is "the first principle and, as it were, the soul of the 'shocker'; character holds second place."

The Buchanesque also has something to do with the way place and landscape are woven into the bones of his stories (*vide* Stevenson here). *John Macnab* (1925) is in the form of a Buchan shocker. But it does not present a tale of high-stakes espionage. Instead, it tells the story of three middle-aged Buchan characters, Sir Edward Leithen, Palliser Yeates, and Lord Lamancha, who, at the pinnacles of their careers, find themselves bored and (like Hannay in *The Thirty-Nine Steps*) "disgusted with life." They need a challenge, the stimulus of danger, what William James called "the moral equivalent of war." So they betake themselves in secret to Scotland, where, under the name of John Macnab, they announce to some local grandees their intention of poaching two stags and a salmon over the course of a few days. The penalty if caught is public humiliation. As the historian Gertrude Himmelfarb observes in her classic essay on Buchan, there is a sense in which "the hunting and fishing scenes, . . . described in great and exciting detail, are not appendages to the plot; they are the plot." The relation between man and landscape, his behavior toward the land and its bounty, are part of the moral compact of society. One is not surprised to discover that Buchan was an avid, almost a compulsive walker. Ten, twenty, thirty miles a day—like Richard Hannay or Peter Pienaar, he also clambered over hill and dale, scouring the horizon, registering the lay of the land. Richard Usborne notes in his book *Clubland Heroes* (first published in 1953) that Buchan's characters "are attracted to exhaustion as a drinker to the bottle." It was an attraction that Buchan himself seemed to share.

John Macnab is a *tour de force*—some regard it as Buchan's best novel—an adventure story in which the McGuffin (to use Hitchcock's term) is deliberately reduced to a minimum: fish and fauna instead of foul play. Yet the result is more than a sprightly, slightly absurd adventure tale. Its theme, as Himmelfarb notes, "is not only the natural and rightful authority exercised by some men by virtue of their breeding, experience, and character, but also the natural and

rightful impulse to rebel against authority." That dialectic—
the implication of authority and independence, of conformity and innovation—are at the heart of Buchan's world view.

It is one version of the Tory creed. Democracy, Buchan
believes, is all well and good. In fact, he is a passionate democrat. But it is essential to remember that (as he puts it in
Pilgrim's Way) "Democracy . . . is a negative thing. It provides a fair field for the Good Life, but it is not itself the
Good Life." Buchan's view of democracy owes more to
Athens than to Jefferson. It is a political arrangement that
encourages striving and excellence—the agon of superior
achievement—but not the levelling imperative of equality.
This sobering truth is at the heart of *John Macnab*: "It is a
melancholy fact," a character muses, "which exponents of
democracy must face that, while all men may be on a level
in the eyes of the State, they will continue in fact to be pre-
posterously unequal."

All of which is to say that if Buchan is constitutionally
a Tory, he practices a slightly seditious—some might just
say "Scottish"—redaction of Toryism: its benediction is not
upon the pastness of the past but its compact with the energies of the present. Hence Buchan's (qualified) admiration
for such robust but un-Toryesque figures as Cromwell, to
whom he devoted a biography in 1934:

> His bequest to the world was not institutions, for his could
> not last, or a political faith, for his was more instinct and
> divination than coherent thought. It was the man himself,
> his frailty and his strength, typical in almost every quality of
> his own English people, but with these qualities so magnified
> as to become epic and universal.

As this passage suggests, another element of the Buchanesque involves highminded moral earnestness. Usborne

notes that there is throughout Buchan's fiction "a slight but persistent propaganda for the decencies as preached by the enthusiastic housemaster—for cold baths, for hard work, for healthy exhaustion in the playing-field, for shaking hands with the beaten opponent, for the attainment of Success in after-life." In *Mr. Standfast* (remember *The Pilgrim's Progress?*), Hannay has a clear shot at the evil Moxon Ivery, who is planning to infect the British army with anthrax. He doesn't fire because Ivery is sitting down and facing away from him: a sportsman does not shoot a man in the back. In *Greenmantle*, when it's clear that the bloody battle of Erzerum is going the right way, Hannay's sidekick Sandy Arbuthnot exclaims, "Oh, well done our side!" It wasn't only Waterloo that was won on the playing fields of Eton.

USBORNE RATHER deprecates the public-school "success ethic" in Buchan. It is I suppose easy to mock, though perhaps less easy to replace (apart from the cold baths, I mean). Buchan's characters are the best-est, most-est at whatever they do. The financier Julius Victor is "the richest man in the world." Sandy Arbuthnot was "one of the two or three most intelligent people in the world." Everyone has made, or is about to make, a "big name" for himself. Of a character at a dinner party of luminaries, "it was rumored that in the same week he had been offered the Secretaryship of State, the Presidency of an ancient University, and the control of a great industrial corporation." That is business as usual in Buchanland. Likewise Buchan's villains. In *Mr. Standfast*, the good guys are not just hunting bad chaps, they are "hunting the most dangerous man in all the world." Hilda von Einem (*Greenmantle*), Dominick Medina (*The Three Hostages*, 1924), Moxon Ivery (a repeat character): When they are bad, they are very bad indeed (though few are without a redeeming dollop of courage). Buchan was writing a species of romance, not tragedy, but perhaps here, too, he followed Aristotle and aimed at presenting men "better than in actual life." At first blush, anyway, it is easy to see why Buchan was an author approved by parents, teachers, pastors. As Usborne put it, he "backed up their directives and doctrines. Buchan wrote good English. Buchan taught you things. Buchan was good for you."

In fact, I believe that Buchan probably is good for you, especially considering the alternatives on offer. The question is whether the Buchan doctrine can still resonate meaningfully. In her essay on Buchan, Himmelfarb described him as "the last Victorian." What she had in mind was that extraordinary British amalgam of seriousness and eccentricity, energy and lassitude, adventurousness and propriety, world-conquering boldness and coddling domesticity; industry, yes; duty, yes; honor, yes; even a certain priggishness—all that but so much more: the whole complex package of moral passion at once goaded and stymied by spiritual cataclysm that made up (in Walter Houghton's phrase) "the Victorian frame of mind." Buchan, son of the manse, occupied a late-model version of that frame as magnificently as anyone.

One tends to think—I certainly thought—of Buchan primarily as a writer of thrillers. But that is like saying Winston Churchill was a painter. He did a few other things as well. In fact, Buchan comes closer than almost anyone to fulfilling Sydney Smith's definition of an "extraordinary man": "The meaning of an extraordinary man is that he is eight men in one man." Born in 1875 in Perth, Scotland, Buchan was the eldest of five children. Buchan père, a minister in the Free Church of Scotland, was, his son later recalled, "a man of wide culture, to whom, in the words of the Psalms, all things were full of the goodness of the Lord"—solemn, perhaps, but with "none of the harshness against which so many have revolted."

It was a close family, with the tensions but also the emotional bounty that closeness brings. In *Pilgrim's Way*, Buchan described his father as "the best man I have ever known" and noted that "not many sons and mothers can have understood each other better than she and I"—"indeed," he continues with a smile, "in my adolescence we sometimes arrived at that point of complete comprehension known as a misunderstanding."

The Buchan family, of decidedly modest means, moved south in 1876 to Pathhead, near the Firth of Forth. Buchan's childhood was instinct partly with the magic of bonny braes and burns, tarns, haughs, and other burry ornaments of the Scottish countryside, partly with the magic of a gentle though unwavering Calvinism. The Bible and *The Pilgrim's Progress* loomed large, rich literary and rhetorical as well as spiritual reservoirs.

Buchan conjectured that his "boyhood must have been one of the idlest on record," yet he managed to get through one or two books.

> Early in my teens I had read Scott, Dickens, Thackeray, and a host of other story tellers; all Shakespeare; a good deal of history, and many works of travel; essayists like Bacon and Addison, Hazlitt and Lamb, and a vast assortment of poetry including Milton, Pope, Dante (in a translation), Wordsworth, Shelley, Keats, and Tennyson. Matthew Arnold I knew almost by heart; Browning I still found too difficult except in patches.

If Buchan was idle, what are we?

In 1888, the Buchans moved to Glasgow. John was educated at Hutchesons' Grammar School and then (from 1892–1895) at Glasgow University, where he studied and became friends with the classicist Gilbert Murray. In 1895, he won a place at Brasenose College, Oxford, an institution of barely a hundred students and known chiefly for rowdiness and prowess at games. Buchan distinguished himself in other areas. He just missed a first in Mods but managed a first in Greats the following year. He won (after a few tries) both the Stanhope and Newdigate Prizes. He was elected President of the Union and, by 1899 when he was graduated, already had six or seven books to his credit, including a novel, a collection of essays, and an edition of Bacon's essays. He was, Janet Adam Smith speculated, possibly the only person in the 1898 edition of *Who's Who* whose occupation was listed as "undergraduate."

Brasenose both extended and mollified Buchan's temperament. Growing up, he recalled in *Pilgrim's Way* (called *Memory Hold-the-Door* in England), he instinctively subscribed to Lord Falkland's famous dictum: "When it is not necessary to change, it is necessary not to change." But his exposure to philosophy led him to become "skeptical of dogmas," which he more and more looked upon "as questions rather than answers."

> The limited outlook of my early youth had broadened. Formerly I had regarded life as a pilgrimage along a strait and steep path on which the pilgrim must keep his eyes fixed. I prided myself on a certain moral austerity, but now I came to realise that there was a good deal of self-interest in that outlook, like the Puritan who saw in his creed not only the road to heaven but the way to worldly success. I began to be attracted by the environs as well as by the road, and I became more charitable in my judgment of things and men.

Buchan considered staying on at Oxford and becoming a don or professor. He concluded that he was not sufficiently devoted to any subject to give up his life to it. "I wanted a stiffer job, one with greater hazards in it, and I was not averse to one which offered bigger material rewards." So after four years he traded Oxford for London and philosophy for the law.

In 1900, Buchan was in London working for *The Spectator*, reading for the Bar, and, as always, writing, writing, writing. (One sees different figures for his total output: one plausible sum is 130 books.) In 1901, he was called to the Bar, practiced briefly, but then accepted an offer from Lord Alfred Milner to join him in South Africa. Buchan became a distinguished member of Milner's "Kindergarten," the brilliant young men who helped the British High Commissioner for South Africa establish order in the aftermath of the Boer War and raise the standard of civilization among the natives.

The youth and inexperience of Milner's staff raised eyebrows, but he knew what he was doing. "There will be a regular rumpus and a lot of talk about boys and Oxford and jobs and all that," Milner wrote to a friend.

> Well, I value brains and character more than experience. First-class men of experience are not to be got. Nothing one could offer would tempt them to give up what they have. . . . No! I shall not be here for very long, but when I go I mean to leave behind me young men with plenty of work in them.

Buchan was one such, and South Africa was a revelation to him. For one thing, invested with enormous administrative responsibility during his two years in South Africa, this bookish youth discovered that "there was a fine practical wisdom which owed nothing to books and academies." He met Cecil Rhodes when the great imperialist was at the end of his life. Rhodes was a fount of pragmatic wisdom. "You can make your book with roguery," he told the young Buchan, "but vanity is incalculable."

Buchan was the perfect acolyte for Milner's reformist zeal and benefits-of-Empire campaign. And if Milner discerned great potential in his youthful recruits, at least some of his Kinder returned the admiration. Milner, Buchan noted, was an administrative genius. "The drawback to a completely rational mind is that it is apt to assume that what is flawless in logic is therefore practicable. Milner never made that mistake." He possessed an unerring "instinct for what is possible. . . . He could do what the lumberman does in a log-jam, and pick out the key log which, once moved, sets the rest going."

Buchan's stint in South Africa—reading Euripides on the veldt, absorbing that surprising new landscape—plumbed a current of almost mystical feeling that, in fact, is an aspect of Buchan's character often overlooked on account of his worldly competence and the practical can-do bustle of many of his heroes. In South Africa, Buchan reported in *Pilgrim's Way*, he enjoyed "moments, even hours, of intense exhilaration."

> There are no more comfortable words in the language than Peace and Joy. . . . Peace is that state in which fear of any kind is unknown. But Joy is a positive thing; in Joy one does not only feel secure, but something goes out from oneself to the universe, a warm, possessive effluence of love. There may be Peace without Joy, and Joy without Peace, but the two combined make Happiness. It was Happiness that I knew in those rare moments. The world was a place of inexhaustible beauty, but still more it was the husk of something infinite, ineffable, and immortal, in very truth the garment of God.

I cannot recall Richard Hannay expressing such feelings, but they are on view in other books by Buchan—*The Dancing Floor* (1926), for example, or his last, posthumously published novel, *Sick Heart River* (1940, published in America as *Mountain Meadow*).

In 1903, Buchan returned to London, resumed work for *The Spectator* and the Middle Temple, and wrote, among other books, *The Law Relating to the Taxation of Foreign Income* (1905), a work I have no intention of reading. In 1906, he became a partner in the publishing firm of his old Oxford friend Tommy Nelson. The following year, Buchan married Susan Grosvenor, a granddaughter of Lord Ebury, and great-great-grandniece of the Duke of Wellington. It was a splendid match, which brought four children and much happiness. "I have," Buchan wrote toward the end of his life, "been happy in many things, but all my other good fortune has been as dust in the balance compared with the blessing of an incomparable wife." Susan was not rich, but she was well-connected and her marriage came as an agreeable surprise to some. One friend wrote, "So you aren't going to be a fat Duchess after all. I had always looked forward to being given one finger to shake at one omnium-gatherum garden-party by your Grace, and now you're going to marry something like a genius instead."

From his perch in the publishing world, Buchan naturally came into contact with many writers and public figures. "With G. K. Chesterton and Hilaire Belloc and Maurice Baring," Buchan reports with Chestertonian slyness, "I never differed—except in opinion." He knew Kipling and Asquith, Stanley Baldwin and Lord Balfour. Balfour, Buchan wrote, was "the only public figure for whom I felt a disciple's loyalty." The Scottish-born earl is remembered today, I suspect, chiefly for the Balfour Declaration (1917), the instrument through which the state of Israel was created. But he was, in addition to his gifts as a statesman, the only Prime Minister who was also an accomplished academic philosopher. Among his works are *Defense of Philosophic Doubt* (1879) and *Questionings on Criticism and Beauty*, the Romanes lectures for 1909.

Pilgrim's Way is a sort of memoir, but an impersonal one; it is less an autobiography than a portrait of an age. With typical decorum, Buchan leaves out of his account contemporaries who were still living. Much of the book is devoted to sketches of Buchan's Oxford friends who died in the Great War: Tommy Nelson, Raymond Asquith, and Aubrey Thomas Herbert, who was a model for Sandy Arbuthnot.

Buchan's recollections are invariably affectionate but seldom uncritical. Of the famous lawyer Richard Haldane, Buchan noted that "to differ from him seemed to be denying the existence of God." Haldane was steeped in the philosophy of Hegel, and his arguments, though brilliant, gave to the uninitiated "No light, but darkness visible," as Milton might put it. Buchan recalls one episode when the bench mistook Haldane's use of the word "antinomy" to mean the metal "antimony." It is clear that Buchan admired Haldane. It is also clear that he regarded him as a sort of object lesson in the dangers of Teutonic intellectualization. "A man who has been nourished on German metaphysics," Buchan observed, "should make a point of expressing his thoughts in plain workaday English, for the technical terms of German philosophy have a kind of hypnotic power; they create a world remote from common reality where reconciliations and synthesis flow as smoothly and with as little meaning as in an opiate dream." This is an observation that aspiring graduate students in the humanities ought to memorize and repeat three times daily before breakfast.

Although a man of immense intellectual cultivation, Buchan had his feet planted firmly on the ground. He understood the dangers of political as well as intellectual infatuation. He understood that responsiveness to the unexpected—which means responsiveness to reality—was a key political asset. Of Prime Minister Asquith, Buchan concluded that he possessed "every traditional virtue—dignity, honor, courage, and a fine selflessness. . . . He was extremely intelligent, but he was impercipient."

> New facts made little impression on his capacious but insensitive mind. Whatever ran counter to his bland libertarianism seemed an impiety. I remember, when the audacities of Lytton Strachey's Victorian Studies were delighting the world, suggesting to Mr. Asquith that the time was ripe for a return match. It was easy, I said, to make fun of the household of faith, but I thought just as much fun could be made out of the other side, even with the most respectful and accurate presentation. I suggested a book to be called "Three Saints of Rationalism" on the lines of *Eminent Victorians*, and proposed for the chapters John Stuart Mill, Herbert Spencer, and John Morley. He was really shocked, as shocked as a High Churchman would be who was invited to consider the comic side of the Oxford Movement.

That "Three Saints of Rationalism" is a volume still waiting to be written.

"Experimentalism" in art (or life) had little appeal for Buchan. In the late Teens and early Twenties, he made an effort to read his contemporaries. "Alas! I had put it off too long. My ear simply could not attune itself to their rhythms, or lack of rhythms." T. S. Eliot's poetry he regarded as "a pastiche of Donne" that reproduced "only his tortured conceits . . . not his sudden flute notes and moments of shattering profundity." Still, Buchan's intelligence admitted the merits of the great modernists, though his heart did not respond. On Proust, for example: "I disliked his hothouse world, but it was idle to deny his supreme skill in disentangling subtle threads of thought and emotion." Buchan befriended T. E. Lawrence ("a mixture of contradictories which never were—perhaps could never have been—harmonised") and Henry James. Although he did not care for James's late novels ("tortuous arabesques"), he "loved the man" and "revelled in the idioms of his wonderful talk."

Once Buchan acted as host at a relative's country house where James was a guest. He knew that James, like most sophisticated New Englanders of his day, would appreciate a good Madeira. The house had a wonderful cellar. Buchan promised James something special.

> He sipped his glass, and his large benign face remained impassive while he gave his verdict. I wish I could remember his epithets; they were a masterpiece of the intricate, evasive, and non-committal, and yet of an exquisite politeness. Then I tasted the wine and found it swipes. It was the old story of a dishonest butler who was selling famous vintages and replacing them by cheap stuff from a neighboring public house.

On another occasion, an aunt of Buchan's wife, the widow of Byron's grandson, asked Buchan and James to examine the archives in order to write an opinion on the quarrel between Byron and his wife. Over the course of a summer weekend, Buchan and James "waded through masses of ancient indecency, and duly wrote an opinion. The thing nearly made me sick, but my colleague never turned a hair. His only words for some special vileness were 'singular'—'most curious'—'nauseating, perhaps, but how quite inexpressibly significant.'"

WHEN BUCHAN was five years old, he fell out of a carriage and fractured his skull when the back wheel rolled over his head. He spent the better part of a year in bed recovering, but Buchan himself attributes a long run of good health to the episode. Before, he had been "a miserable headachy little boy"; afterwards he was in a nearly continuous bloom of health until 1911. From then until his early death in 1940, Buchan was beset by painful stomach problems. The onset of World War I found him in bed for three months recovering from an operation for a duodenal ulcer.

Buchan was too old for the infantry, but he served the war effort well, first as a correspondent in France for *The Times*, then working for Lord Beaverbrook as Director of the Department of Information and, briefly, as Director of Intelligence. In order to keep the presses of Thomas Nelson and Sons running, he also undertook Nelson's *History of the War*, which was published in twenty-four volumes from 1915–1919. I have read in several places that Buchan's quota was 50,000 words a fortnight. That depressing number works out to 5,000 words a day, Monday through Friday. Try it sometime, especially when you are Director of your country's intelligence service, raising a family, and writing a clutch of novels and a volume of verse.

Buchan's *History* is no piece of makework, either. For sheer narrative verve, it may outdo even Churchill's multivolume history of the Great War. Buchan had a genius for making military operations clear to the layman. Writing as events were unfolding, in the confusing smoke-and-mirrors chaos of war, he nevertheless managed to see beyond sorties, troop movements, and individual campaigns. His deep reading in history allowed him to keep the larger picture in view. The larger picture concerned civilization: its requirements and enemies. Summing up toward the end of his final volume, Buchan optimistically suggests that one benefit of the war was to have shaken the world "out of its complacency." The ensuing years showed how resilient a trait is human complacency. We are never done with it—a fact that Buchan implicitly acknowledged when he observed that "The world is at no time safe for freedom, which needs vigilant and unremitting guardianship."

Andrew Lownie said in his biography of Buchan, *The Presbyterian Cavalier* (1995), that the War left Buchan "physically and emotionally shattered." That seems to me to overstate things. He suffered the loss of many close friends (including Tommy Nelson, who fell at the Somme). His stomach problems had become chronic. But shattered men do not continue turning out the books; they do not become Director of Reuters, as Buchan did in 1919, or buy and restore a manor house, as Buchan did with Elsfield near Oxford that same year. In 1927, when he was first elected Conservative MP for Scottish Universities, Buchan was working on five books. In 1929, he finally resigned from Nelson's. A few years later, he was created High Commissioner to the General Assembly of the Church of Scotland, the representative of the Crown to the Church. (In 1929, Buchan had co-authored *The Kirk in Scotland*, so he was prepared by industry as well as background for the pomp-filled post.) The apex of Buchan's public career came in 1935 when he was created Baron Tweedsmuir of Elsfield and was appointed Governor General of Canada, a post he held until his death in Ottawa in February 1940.

BUCHAN WAS SCHOOLED to an intelligent toughness—to an independence bred in reverence—that would twist and bristle in the self-self-self moral atmosphere of today. There was a strong streak of lyricism in his make up, yet candor and forthrightness were among the primary virtues he cultivated. Heckling, he noted with some pride, was an art "pursued for the pure love of the game" in the Border Country. Candidates were sometimes heckled to a standstill by their own supporters. Buchan recalled an incident shortly after Lloyd George's Insurance Act had been introduced. A speaker was defending the welfare policy on the grounds that it was a practical application of the Sermon on the Mount. A shepherd rose to chivvy the speaker:

> "Ye believe in the Bible, sir?"
> "With all my heart."
> "And ye consider that this Insurance Act is in keepin' with the Bible?"
> "I do."
> "Is it true that under the Act there's a maternity benefit, and that a woman gets the benefit whether she's married or no?"
> "That is right."
> "D'ye approve of that?"
> "With all my heart."
> "Well, sir, how d'ye explain this? The Bible says the wages of sin is death and the Act says thirty shillin's."

Of the Border folk he represented in Parliament, Buchan said he particularly admired their "realism coloured by poetry, a stalwart independence sweetened by courtesy, a shrewd kindly wisdom." These were qualities that by most accounts Buchan himself embodied.

ONE CANNOT READ far into the commentary on Buchan, however, before encountering some stiff criticism of some of his attitudes and language. The criticism resolves into three main charges. 1. Buchan was a colonialist, a champion of the British Empire. 2. Buchan was a racist: he said and believed unpleasant things about Negroes. 3. Buchan was an anti-Semite: he said and believed unpleasant things about Jews.

On the first matter, Buchan must stand guilty as charged, though "guilty" is assuredly not the right word. Buchan was a partisan of the British colonialist enterprise; he did believe in the civilizing mandate of the British Empire. The only question is whether that is something of which Buchan ought to have been ashamed. In fact, what was already crystal clear in the early 1900s when Buchan was with Milner in South Africa has become sadly, grimly reinforced in recent decades: everywhere Britain went benefitted immensely from its wise and beneficent intervention. Were there mistakes? Yes. Were there unnecessary cruelties, stupidities, miscalculations? You bet. But the British colonial adventure was an incalculable gain for the colonized. The British brought better hygiene, the rule of law, better schools, roads, industry, and manners. Santayana was right about the colonial rule of the Englishman: "Never since the heroic days of Greece," the philosopher wrote in *Soliloquies in England*, "has the world had such a sweet, just, boyish master. It will be a black day for the human race when scientific blackguards, conspirators, churls, and fanatics manage to supplant him." What's happened in Africa in the period of de-colonization—better call it "rebarbarization," a much more accurate name—is stark evidence that Santayana was right.

But what about the other charges against Buchan? In *Mr. Standfast*, when Richard Hannay is asked to pose as a pacifist, he objects: "there are some things that no one has a right to ask of any white man." You'll find similar locutions salted throughout Buchan's novels. You'll also find, as you will in the novels of Mark Twain or Joseph Conrad (for example), the use of the word "nigger." Is that objectionable? Today it would be. Indeed, a few decades ago a publisher refused to re-issue Buchan's adventure novel *Prester John* (1910) because of the "N" word.

You will find similar language about Jews. At the beginning of *The Thirty-Nine Steps*, Franklin Scudder is ranting about the international Jewish conspiracy and conjures up the evil figure of the mastermind behind the scenes, a "little white-faced Jew in a bath chair with an eye like a rattlesnake." Of course, Scudder is potty and winds up a few pages later with a knife in his back. But Buchan's portrayal of Jews, at least in his early novels, is not glamorous. With some exceptions, they are rag dealers or pawnbrokers or else nefarious anarchists or shady financiers. There are exceptions—Julius Victor, for example, "the richest man in the world," who is a thoroughly noble chap. But then he is described by the dyspeptic American John S. Blenkiron as "the whitest Jew since the apostle Paul." It was meant as praise, but still . . .

Buchan's biographer Lownie said that "It is difficult to find any evidence of anti-Semitism in Buchan's own personal views." Well, maybe. It's much more likely that—up to the 1930s, anyway—Buchan was anti-Semitic (and anti-foreigner) in the way nearly everyone in his society was. At the time, Gertrude Himmelfarb notes, "Men were normally anti-Semitic, unless by some quirk of temperament or ideology they happened to be philo-Semitic. So long as the world itself was normal, this was of no great consequence. . . . It was Hitler . . . who put an end to the casual, innocent anti-Semitism of the clubman." And by the time the Nazis came along, Buchan had abandoned any casual aspersions against Jews in his novels. Moreover, he publicly denounced Hitler's anti-Semitism in 1934. (Which was one reason, no doubt, that he was on the Nazi's post-invasion list of people to be imprisoned for "Pro-Jewish activity.") Like Milner, Buchan was ardently pro-Zionist, and his name was later ceremoniously inscribed in the Golden Book of the Jewish National Fund.

Buchan wrote at a time less constrained than ours by the imperatives of political correctness. He didn't try to second-guess his audience. He had confidence not only in his knowledge, but also, as Himmelfarb observed, in his opinions, attitudes, intuitions, and prejudices. What he wrote for the public was what he felt in private; he did not labor for a subtlety or profundity that did not come spontaneously, or censor his spontaneous thoughts before committing them to paper. He had none of the scruples that are so inhibiting today. He was candid about race, nation, religion, and class, because it did not occur to him that anything he was capable of feeling or thinking could be reprehensible. . . . What some have condemned as insensitivity or condescension may also be taken as a forthright expression of opinion—or not so much opinion, because that is to dignify it as a conscious judgment, but rather impression or experience.

In *The Three Hostages*, Sandy Arbuthnot gives voice to feelings of exasperation that, I suspect, come close to Buchan's own feelings:

> "The old English way was to regard all foreigners as slightly childish and rather idiotic and ourselves as the only grownups in a kindergarten world. That meant that we had a cool detached view and did even-handed unsympathetic justice. But now we have to go into the nursery ourselves and are bear-fighting on the floor. We take violent sides, and make pets, and of course if you are -phil something or other you have got to be -phobe something else."

It was precisely that unreasoning attachment to ideology—to the grim nursery of human passions—that Buchan resisted.

HIMMELFARB DESCRIBED Buchan as "the last Victorian" because the world that could nurture such a character has long since vanished. But one may hope that Buchan will have successors, for the creator of Richard Hannay, Sandy

Arbuthnot, and the others was a great and potent friend of civilization. Robin Winks remarked that "What Buchan feared most was unreasoning passion"—that, and the complacency which renders passion toxic. In his biography of Augustus (1937), Buchan wrote that the Emperor's "true achievement . . . is that he saved the world from disintegration." At the end of his life Buchan saw the world once again threatened by a storm of irrational violence and hatred. Yet again it was revealed that (as his character Dickson McCunn put it) "civilisation anywhere is a very thin crust." Nevertheless, what Buchan feared above all was not "barbarism, which is civilisation submerged or not yet born, but de-civilisation, which is civilisation gone rotten." In his posthumously published memoir, he describes a "nightmare" world in which science had transformed the world into "a huge, dapper, smooth-running mechanism."

> Everyone would be comfortable, but since there could be no great demand for intellectual exertion everyone would be also slightly idiotic. Their shallow minds would be easily bored, and therefore unstable. Their life would be largely a quest for amusement. . . . Men would go everywhere and live nowhere; know everything and understand nothing. . . . In the tumult of a jazz existence what hope would there be for the still small voices of the prophets and philosophers and poets? A world which claimed to be a triumph of the human personality would in truth have killed that personality. In such a bagman's paradise, where life would be rationalised and padded with every material comfort, there would be little satisfaction for the immortal part of man. It would be a new Vanity Fair. . . . The essence of civilisation lies in man's defiance of an impersonal universe. It makes no difference that a mechanised universe may be his own creation if he allows his handiwork to enslave him. Not for the first

time in history have the idols that humanity has shaped for its own ends become its master.

Buchan thought the dictators of the 1930s and 1940s had paradoxically "done us a marvellous service in reminding us of the true values of life," awakening men to the dangers of complacency.

Yet Buchan knew that, whatever questions the war answered, the compact of routinization and unruly passion—the marriage of hyper-rationalization and irrationality—was a problem that transcended the savagery of war. It was a problem built into the nature of modernity. How that problem would be solved—or, rather, how that unthinking version of life was to be avoided, for it was not a problem susceptible of any one solution—was something Buchan regarded with a mixture of foreboding and faith. He regarded the extinction of eccentricity, the homogenization of the world with a distaste bordering on horror. What he feared was failure bred in success: "a deepening and narrowing of ruts" that technological and economic success regularly brought in their wake. "The world," he wrote towards the end of *Pilgrim's Way*, "must remain an oyster for youth to open. If not, youth will cease to be young, and that will be the end of everything." Buchan speculated that "the challenge with which we are now faced may restore us to that manly humility which alone gives power."

The campaign against genuine individuality is much further advanced today than it was in 1940 when Buchan wrote. We seem further than ever from the "manly humility" he prescribed. Which is one reason that rereading John Buchan is such a tonic exercise. His adventures are riches that help remind us of our poverty. If, as Montaigne wrote, admonition is the highest office of friendship, that counsel is a precious bounty.

A Dangerous Book for Boys

JOHN BUCHAN, I think, would have enjoyed *The Dangerous Book for Boys*, a surprise hit by the brothers Iggulden, Conn and Hal. They share Buchan's concern that the world remain "an oyster for youth to open. If not, youth will cease to be young, and that will be the end of everything." That feeling must be pretty widely disseminated for, as I say, *The Dangerous Book for Boys* was a wild publishing success. Nevertheless, it is something of a miracle that it hasn't been banned by zealous school groups, social workers, and other moral busybodies. Or perhaps I am precipitate: perhaps it has been banned.

I first encountered this admirable work when it was published in London in 2006. I liked its retro look—the lettering and typography of the cover recall an earlier, more swashbuckling era—and I thought at first it must be a reprint. Imagine my surprise when I discovered that a book containing instructions on how to make catapults, how to hunt and cook a rabbit, how to play poker, how to make a waterbomb, was published today, the high noon of nannydom.

The first chapter, "Essential Gear" ("Essential Kit" in the English edition), lists a Swiss Army knife, for God's sake, not to mention matches and a magnifying glass, "For general interest. Can also be used to start fires." Probably, the book would have to be checked with the rest of your luggage at the airport: If you can't bring a bottle of water on the airplane, how do you suppose a book advocating knives and incendiary devices is going to go over? Why, even the title is a provocation. The tort lawyers must be salivating over the word "dangerous," and I can only assume that the horrible grinding noise you hear is from Title IX fanatics (see "Institutionalizing Our Demise" above) congregating to protest the appearance of a book designed for the exclusive enjoyment of boys.

And speaking of "boys," have you noticed how unprogressive the word sounds in today's English? It is almost as retrograde as "girls," a word that I knew was on the way out when an academic couple I know proudly announced that they had just presented the world with a "baby woman."

No, I did not make that up, and even after due allowances are made for the fact that the couple were, after all, academics and therefore peculiarly susceptible to such p.c. deformations, it's clear that something fundamental is happening in our society. Some speak about the "feminization" of America and Europe. Scholars like Christina Hoff Sommers have reported on the "war against boys." A public school near where I live gets high marks for "academic excellence," but I note that they allow only 15 minutes of recess a day for kindergarteners and first graders. Result: By 2 PM the boys are ready to explode. That turns out to be a solvable problem, though, because a little Ritalin with the (whole grain) Cheerios does wonders to keep Johnny from acting up.

In a recent interview, Conn Iggulden, speaking about his collaboration with his brother in writing *The Dangerous Book for Boys*, dilated on this campaign against the boylike side of boyhood. "They need to fall off things occasionally," Iggulden said, "or . . . they'll take worse risks on their own. If we do away with challenging playgrounds and cancel school trips for fear of being sued, we don't end up with

safer boys—we end up with them walking on train tracks."
Quite right. *The Dangerous Book for Boys* is alive with
such salubrious challenges. Its epigraph, a 1903 letter from
an army surgeon to the young Prince of Wales, advises, "The
best motto for a long march is 'Don't grumble. Plug on.'"
How antique that stiff-upper-lippery sounds to our ears!

The book includes instructions on making "The Greatest Paper Plane in the World." Did you know that many
schools have outlawed paper airplanes? Might strike a
child in the eye, don't you know. And of course, that's only
the beginning of what many schools outlaw. The game of
tag is verboten almost everywhere, a fact I learned when
our then-eight-year-old son fell and broke his elbow while
playing the game. The final indignity came when, being
down, he was tagged by the chap who was "it." Even that
had its compensations, though, since James was looking
forward to suspending his allegiance to the principles of
the Sermon on the Mount and getting the fellow back when
he fully recovers. Besides, although it hurts to break your
arm, it is quite nifty to have your arm in a cast, especially
if one of your heroes is Lord Nelson, to whom (or so one's
parents assure you) you bear a strong resemblance when
sporting a sling. Of course, I am sorry that James broke his
arm, but I prefer his school's (unofficial) motto—"Better a
broken bone than a broken spirit"—to the pusillanimous
alternative.

Into the swamp-like miasma of contemporary life *The
Dangerous Book for Boys* blows like a healing zephyr.
Mark Twain once included a note about "the weather in
this book," explaining that there wasn't any. There is a lot of
weather in *The Dangerous Book for Boys*, and I do not just
mean the sections devoted to cloud formations and such
questions as Why is the Sky blue? What causes the wind?
and Why is it hotter at the Equator? True, this book in-

cludes lots of indoor activities. You'll find out how to make a simple battery out of a bunch of quarters, aluminum foil, vinegar, and salt, for example, as well as how to make secret inks, fireproof cloth, and marbled paper. There's a section on timers and tripwires—"very simple to make—and deeply satisfying," the authors explain. Let's say you want a light bulb to turn on in 20 minutes "to win a bet perhaps, or frighten your little sister with the thought that a mad axe murderer is upstairs." Look no further: It's all here.

There's a section of useful quotations from Shakespeare, "Latin Phrases Every Boy Should Know," and "Books Every Boy Should Read" (*The Dangerous Book for Boys* is one of them, though it's not on the list). There are several engaging sections on words and grammar. There are also two sections devoted to famous battles, from Thermopylae and Cannae up through Waterloo, Gettysburg, and the Somme. If you want a quick timeline of U.S. history, it's here. So is information about "the golden age of piracy," spies, codes, and ciphers, as well as coin tricks, dog tricks, and first aid. There's also—uh-oh: P.C. alert!—a chapter on the history of artillery.

STILL, this is essentially an outdoor book. Not that it deals chiefly with outdoor subjects, though it has splendid advice about building treehouses, fishing, and growing sunflowers (and I suppose artillery is, usually, a subject best pursued outside). Rather, it understands that boys and the outdoors go together like a hammer and nails. It is sympathetic to dirt and looks kindly upon rocks, bugs, snakes, and woodpiles. It is a book, in other words, that approves of derring-do and the testosterone that fires it. This is clear in the informative chapter devoted to the mysterious subject of Girls who, many feminists will be surprised to discover, are "quite different" from boys. By this, the authors explain:

We do not mean the physical differences, more the fact that [girls] remain unimpressed by your mastery of a game involving wizards, or your understanding of Morse Code. Some will be impressed, of course, but as a general rule, girls do not get quite as excited by the use of urine as a secret ink as boys do.

That's been my experience. In fact, the chapter on girls is full of good advice. Here are two bits: 1. "Play a sport of some kind," they advise. "It doesn't matter what it is, as long as it replaces the corpse-like pallor of the computer programmer with a ruddy glow." 2. "If you see a girl in need of help—unable to lift something, for example—do not taunt her. Approach the object and greet her with a cheerful smile, whilst surreptitiously testing the weight of the object. If you find you can lift it, go ahead. If you can't, try sitting on it and engaging her in conversation." Ovid couldn't have put it any better. (His advice about girls is to be found in a book for older boys called *Ars Amatoria*.)

The Dangerous Book for Boys is a book that implicitly endorses Aristotle's observation that courage is the most important virtue because, without courage, it is impossible to practice the other virtues. "In this age of video games and mobile phones," the authors write, "there must still be a place for knots, treehouses and stories of incredible courage." Indeed, physical courage looms large in *The Dangerous Book for Boys*. That's another reason John Buchan would have approved of it. One of its best features is a series of "extraordinary stories." Remember the bracing story of Robert Scott, the intrepid English explorer who suffered untold hardships in his race to be the first to reach the South Pole? In the event, the Norwegian explorer Roald Amundsen beat him, just barely. Scott and his team arrived there on January 17, 1912, only to find Amundsen's empty tent and a note announcing their presence on December 14, 1911. Scott made it back to within 11 miles of his last camp before he and the rest of his team froze to death. In his last hours, he managed to write a few letters, including one to his wife which mentioned their only son:

> I had looked forward to helping you to bring him up, but it is a satisfaction to know that he will be safe with you. . . . Make the boy interested in natural history if you can. It is better than games. They encourage it in some schools. I know you will keep him in the open air. Try to make him believe in a God, it is comforting. . . . and guard him against indolence. Make him a strenuous man. I had to force myself into being strenuous as you know—had always an inclination to be idle.

The Igguldens also include the story of Douglas Bader, an RAF pilot who crashed in 1931 when showing off doing rolls too close to the ground. He lost his right leg above the knee, his left below the knee. His flying log for the day reads: "X-country Reading. Crashed slow rolling near ground. Bad show." Fitted with metal legs, Bader was told he would never walk without sticks. "On the contrary," he replied, "I will never bloody walk with them." When World War II broke out, Bader was allowed to reenlist and even to fly, metal legs and all. He had 22-and-a-half air-to-air victories (he and a fellow RAF pilot both shot up one German plane, so they agreed to split the victory). In 1941, Bader collided with a German ME 109 over France.

> The tail of Bader's plane was torn off and he began plummeting towards the ground. He got the canopy off and climbed out into the wind to parachute clear. His right leg caught and he found himself nailed to the fuselage by the slipstream. . . .

At last, the belt holding the leg to him snapped and the leg
went off through his trousers, allowing him to break free of
the plane and parachute to safety.

Well, relative safety. He was scooped up by the Germans
and put in prison. He asked his captors if a message might
be sent to England to retrieve his spare right leg. Mirabile
dictu, the Germans agreed. The British dropped it off during a normal bombing run. Bader put on the leg and casu-
ally walked out of the hospital in an effort to escape. He
was promptly rounded up again, but tried to escape early
and often. Exasperated, the Germans took away his metal
legs, but the outcry from other prisoners was so great they
shamefacedly returned them.

These are stories, the Igguldens note, "that must be told
and retold, or the memories slowly die." The fact that *The
Dangerous Book for Boys* was a runaway bestseller in both
England and the U.S. gives one hope. And speaking of England, my chief recommendation is not just that you buy the
book, but that you buy it twice. Connoisseurs will want the
English as well as the American edition. There are numerous
differences. There are little things like prices being expressed
in dollars, not pounds, and a chapter on baseball instead of
one on cricket. American history has been substituted for
the story of the British Empire. I note that instead of a chapter called "Astronomy," the American edition offers us "Astronomy—the Study of the Heavens," which I suppose tells
us something about how the publisher views its American
readership.

All of that is minor—though I miss the list of kings and
queens of England, especially the mnemonic to keep the fate
of Henry VIII's wives straight: "Divorced, beheaded, died;
divorced, beheaded, survived." But having mentioned Admiral Nelson already, I have to say I was sorry to see that

the Wright brothers appear in his place in the American edition. I hasten to add that there are no flies on Wilbur and Orville—theirs is an exhilarating tale, eminently worthy of inclusion in this book—but the story of Horatio Nelson is essential, Master James Kimball requires me to state, absolutely essential.

I was also sorry to see that the chapter on catapults was dropped from the American edition. Ditto the chapter on conkers. Not that American boys play much with horse chestnuts attached to a bit of string, but the book's advice about how to make the hole in the chestnut is worth savoring. You can use a nail or spike, but "better to get your dad to use a drill on them." Don't try it yourself, by the way, because "the conkers spin round at high speed or crack when you put them in a vise. Much better to ask an adult to do it, but give them your worst conkers to start with until they have learned the knack."

Why not make do with the English edition, then? Well, for one thing, the American edition includes the Navajo Code Talkers' Dictionary. The U.S. Marines would have been lost without it in World War II. 'Nuff said.

Rudyard Kipling Unburdened

It is no use pretending that Kipling's view of life, as a whole, can be accepted or even forgiven by any civilized person.
—George Orwell, 1942

MY CHILDHOOD HOME did not boast many literary accoutrements. Apart from an imposing set of "World's Classics," bound in blue cloth with silver lettering, what I chiefly remember is a framed copy of (Joseph) Rudyard Kipling's poem "If—." It was printed with impressive gilt filigree on a sheet of foolscap and, together with a portrait of my Guardian Angel, it presided in quiet admonition on my bedroom wall.

I never memorized the poem, though I internalized its cadence while nervously savoring the impossible combination of virtues it pleaded:

> If you can keep your head when all about you
> Are losing theirs and blaming it on you;
> If you can trust yourself when all men doubt you,
> But make allowance for their doubting too;
> If you can wait and not be tired by waiting,
> Or, being lied about, don't deal in lies,

Or, being hated, don't give way to hating,
And yet don't look too good, nor talk too wise; . . .

Etc. Tough for an impatient eight- or ten- (or fifty-) year-old. There were thirteen such conditionals to be fulfilled before arriving at the consummating apodosis: "Yours is the Earth and everything that's in it,/And—which is more—you'll be a Man, my son!"

"All well and good," I remember musing, "but what 'if not'?"

"If—" is probably Kipling's most famous poem. As recently as 1995, a BBC poll named it Britain's favorite. Written in 1895, when Kipling was thirty and crossing the threshold to international celebrity, it was published as part of *Rewards and Fairies*, a set of historical stories, in 1910, when his reputation was already on the wane. In a celebrated essay on Kipling from 1942, George Orwell dismissed the poem as the sort of thing (about the only sort of thing) Colonel Blimp would like.

Today, I suspect, Kipling is regarded chiefly as that most anodyne of literary practitioners: a children's author, creator of the boy Mowgli, Kaa the python, and Shere Khan the Tiger, the genial-looking, pipe-puffing genius who wrote *Kim* and populated the imaginations of boys and girls with the sultry weather of the Raj, explained how the elephant got its trunk, and decorated it all with fastidious (little) poems that rhymed and scanned. Kipling was picturesque. He was born in romantic-sounding Bombay, and he got his precocious literary start in India after a decade of schooling in England. (His parents chose "Rudyard," by the way, after a lake in Staffordshire where they courted.) If his stories are exotic, even scary at times, they are nonetheless wholesome or at least susceptible to Disneyfication.

How different it once was. Around the turn of the last century, at the apogee of Kipling's fame, Mark Twain wrote that he was "the only living person not head of a nation, whose voice is heard around the world the moment it drops a remark, the only such voice in existence that does not go by slow ship and rail but always travels first-class by cable." In Kipling, the Zeitgeist briefly found its impresario. For a time, his authority was as much political as literary.

Kipling gave speeches advocating British supremacy in India and South Africa. He opposed the suffragettes and home rule for Ireland. He could be downright strident. It was Kipling, one of his biographers speculates, who popularized the metonymy "Huns" (actually, he insisted on "huns" with a small "h") for "Germans," a subject on which he grew increasingly ferocious. By 1915, Kipling was insisting that there were "only two divisions in the world . . . human beings and Germans." Kipling consistently refused state honors (a knighthood, the Order of Merit, the post of poet laureate) but by the late 1890s he was the undisputed if unofficial laureate—but also, which is sometimes forgotten, the Jeremiah—of Imperial Britain.

True, Kipling's celebrity was never universally applauded. Most literary folk instinctively disliked him. Henry James gave away the bride at Kipling's wedding, but he could be magisterially tart about Kipling the writer: "great talent," he wrote in a letter of 1897, but "almost nothing civilized save steam and patriotism." Oscar Wilde described Kipling as "our first authority on the second-rate," "a genius who drops his aspirates." And for Wilde's disciple Max Beerbohm, Kipling always exercised "the fascination of abomination": he was the man in whom "the schoolboy, the bounder, and the brute" found "brilliant expression."

This was, I've always felt, a bit stingy of Max, who ought to have harbored some gratitude to Kipling for provid-

ing him such valuable fodder for his own caricatures and
parodies. Particularly choice is P.C., X, 36, in which a Kiplingesque constable collars Santa Claus emerging from a
chimney on Christmas Eve:

> "Wot wos yer doin' hup there?" asked Judlip, tightening the
> grip.
> "I'm Santa Claus, Sir, p-please, Sir, let me g-go."
> "Hold him," I shouted, "He's a German."

Kipling's first book of poems, written when he was but
twenty, was called *Departmental Ditties*. Max slyly pref-
aced his parody with a "Police Station Ditty": "'Ustle 'im,
shake 'im till 'e's sick!/ . . . /An' it's trunch, trunch, trun-
cheon does the trick."

For his part, Kipling cordially returned the animus, writing about the "brittle intellectuals,/Who crack beneath the
strain" ("The Holy War") and "the flanneled fools at the
wicket"("The Islanders"). In 1889, shortly after returning
to London from his apprenticeship in India, Kipling published "In Partibus" in (note the venue) the *Civil and Military Gazette*:

> But I consort with long-haired-things,
> In velvet collar-rolls,
> Who talk about the Aims of Art,
> And "theories" and "goals,"
> And moo and coo with women-folk
>   About their blessed souls.

Kipling was pals with H. Rider Haggard (*King Solomon's
Mines, Allan Quartermain, She*). Arthur Conan Doyle came
to visit and give Kipling a golf lesson when he was ensconced
with his American wife in Brattleboro, Vermont, in the early

1890s. But by and large, Kipling consorted with politicians, generals, and magnates. George V was a close friend, so were Cecil Rhodes and Viscount Milner. When he won the Nobel Prize in 1907—the first English-language laureate, and still the youngest—the citation mentioned not only his "power of observation" and "originality of imagination" but also his "virility of ideas." By then, in the aftermath of the Boer War, the "virility" of Kipling's ideas was already a stumbling block; by the time the First World War was over—a war that Kipling had foretold with uncanny accuracy and in which he lost his only son, John—the nation was in wholesale retreat from Kiplingesque virility. (Today, of course, it is unimaginable that a Nobel citation—or most any other, for that matter—would commend someone for his "virility of ideas.") When Kipling died, in January 1936, age 70, his pallbearers included the Prime Minister, an Admiral, a General, various other friends, but no literary figures.

It would be instructive to trace the process that de-clawed and domesticated Rudyard Kipling, that gradually diminished that brusque and imposing giant to an entertaining homunculus. When the Zeitgeist shifted, Kipling's politics suddenly became a popular as well as an elite embarrassment. ("Poetry," T. S. Eliot, noted, "is condemned as 'political' when we disagree with the politics.") Typical was Orwell's savage outburst: "Kipling is a jingo imperialist, he is morally insensitive and aesthetically disgusting." It got to the point where people who had absorbed Kipling unwittingly suppressed his authorship. Orwell notes that Middleton Murry, quoting Kipling's famous lines "There are nine and sixty ways/Of constructing tribal lays," mistakenly attributed them to Thackeray. Kipling might have written good poetry, but it wasn't good for poetry to have been written by Kipling. Sanitizing Kipling, segregating his political and social opinions from his literary accomplishment, has had the unfortunate effect of diminishing the appreciation or even the knowledge of that accomplishment. A slim but representative selection of his poems, selected by Peter Washington for the attractive Everyman series (2008), offers a welcome occasion to return to that unfairly diminished master.

In 1941, T. S. Eliot edited and wrote an introduction for a plump collection of Kipling's poems. It was partly, but only partly, an effort at rehabilitation. Eliot noted Kipling's uncanny "second sight," his seeming ability to lift and peer beneath the curtain of history, also his habit of writing "transparently, so that our attention is directed to the object and not the medium." He spoke warmly of Kipling's "consummate gift of word, phrase, and rhythm" and praised his technical mastery: "no writer has ever cared for the craft of words more than Kipling." Kipling's prosody was generally so regular that it is easy to miss the subtlety of his music and rhythmical variation. Eliot singles out "Danny Deever," a typical Kipling "soldier's poem" from *Barrack-Room Ballads* (1892), that tells the story of the hanging of the eponymous Danny who "shot a comrade sleepin'." The poem begins in matutinal confusion—the bugles are blowing, but why? Eliot points out how Kipling insinuates a dread sense of acceleration and tautening step-step-step focus:

> "What's that so black agin' the sun?" said Files-on-Parade.
> "It's Danny fightin' 'ard for life," the Colour-Sergeant said.
> "What's that that whimpers over 'ead?" said Files-on-Parade.
> "It's Danny's soul that's passin' now," the Colour-Sergeant said.
> For they're done with Danny Deever, you can 'ear the quick-
> step play,
> The Regiment's in column, an' they're marchin' us away . . .

Eliot is all admiration for the seemingly effortless prosodic mastery Kipling displays. But (and it is a large "but") his essay turns on a distinction between "verse"—at which Kipling is said to excel—and "poetry," which, says Eliot, he approaches but rarely and then only by accident. In other words, Kipling, though good at what he does, isn't really playing in the big leagues. Eliot doesn't put it like that, not quite. He even notes that Kipling "is so different from other poets that the lazy critic is tempted merely to assert that he is not a poet at all and leave it at that."

Eliot forbears to make that assertion. He nonetheless manages to leave it echoing in the reader's mind. His essay is sensitive, intelligent, and a subtle masterpiece of deflation. The deflation operates primarily by apophasis. Eliot notes that one is usually called upon to defend modern poetry from the charge of excessive obscurity: with Kipling the culprit is "excessive lucidity." Similarly, where one hears of complaints about the metrical chaos of modern poetry, Kipling is so regular he can be accused of writing "jingles." Much modern poetry seems caught up in a sort of cosmic privateness: Kipling, who starts with "the motive of the ballad-maker," seems all too involved with the events of the day. In short, Eliot wants to preserve a place for Kipling, but he also wants to put him in his place—not, we are meant to understand, the same (and higher) place occupied by Eliot himself.

A good deal of intelligent commentary on Kipling operates like this. Irving Howe, for example, in his introduction to the *Viking Portable Kipling*, begins with the obligatory condemnation of Kipling the "tub-thumper" for imperialism, etc., but then proceeds to find numerous things to praise. His denouement is the conclusion that Kipling was "a brilliant if unacknowledged fellow traveller of literary modernism."

This strikes me as completely wrong. Kipling was in a different game altogether. Yes, he was sui generis, but only in the way—or rather, to the extent—that Eliot himself or other "strong voice" poets (Wallace Stevens, for example) are sui generis. You can't imagine Kipling beginning a long poem with the observation that "April is the cruellest month" (to say nothing of "Complacencies of the peignoir"). But then you can't imagine Eliot or Stevens writing "Now this is the Law of the Jungle—as old and as true as the sky;/And the Wolf that shall keep it may prosper, but the Wolf that shall break it must die." Which is better, more important, more serious?

I AM NOT SURE those are answerable questions. But if Auden is correct in defining poetry as "memorable speech," what Kipling wrote is surely poetry. Orwell lists several phrases that have entered the language:

> "East is East, West is West, [and never the twain shall meet.]"
> "The white man's burden."
> "Paying the Dane-geld."
> "The female of the species is more deadly than the male."
> "He travels the fastest who travels alone."

To which we might add (to show that Kipling had a sense of humor) "A woman is only a woman, but a good cigar is a smoke."

Writing about Auden, Edward Mendelson distinguished between the "vatic" and "civil" traditions in poetry. The former aspires to the splendid isolation of aesthetic autonomy, the latter to a more public vocation: "poets," says Mendelson, "who write as citizens, whose purpose is to entertain and instruct, and who choose subjects that would interest an audience even if a poet were not there to transform them into art."

That, I believe, brings us to the neighborhood where Kipling flourished. Although possessed of prodigious gifts of verbal and rhythmic invention, Kipling sought not the lyric moment but a more didactic end.

"Didactic"? I know that "didactic" is not what Stephen Potter (*Gamesmanship, One-Upmanship*) would call an "O.K. word" these days. We resist the presumption that art should aspire to teach almost as much as we resist the idea that we might be in need of tutelage. It is worth noting, then, that Kipling's didactic designs were capacious. As has often been pointed out, in much of his work, Kipling sought to give memorable voice to segments of society (even of animal society) hitherto lost in inarticulacy: the Indian beggar, the rude, uneducated solider, the hard-bitten colonial administrator. Kipling was especially good at capturing the sweaty rage of pride affronted, as here, in his great poem "Tommy":

> Yes, makin' mock o' uniforms that guard you while you sleep
> Is cheaper than them uniforms, an' they're starvation cheap;
> An' hustlin' drunken soldiers when they're goin' large a bit
> Is five times better business than paradin' in full kit.
> Then it's Tommy this, an' Tommy that, an' "Tommy,
>   'ow's yer soul?"
> But it's "Thin red line of 'eroes" when the drums begin
>   to roll . . .

I have always greatly admired "Tommy," not least for its psychological acuity. The good citizens of Berkeley, California, would profit from taking its message to heart. They might also get outside "The Gods of the Copybook Headings," a poem that is full of sage but perpetually forgotten advice:

> They swore, if we gave them our weapons, that the wars of
>   the tribes would cease.
> But when we disarmed They sold us and delivered us bound
>   to our foe,

And the Gods of the Copybook Headings said: "Stick to the
>> Devil you know."

And let's not forget "Dane-Geld":

It is always a temptation to a rich and lazy nation,
To puff and look important and to say:
"Though we know we should defeat you, we have not the
>> time to meet you.
We will therefore pay you cash to go away."
And that is called paying the Dane-geld;
But we've proved it again and again,
That if once you have paid him the Dane-geld
You never get rid of the Dane.

"[N]ever pay any-one Dane-geld," Kipling advised, "No
matter how trifling the cost,/For the end of that game is
oppression and shame,/And the nation that plays it is lost!"

SAGE, if not particularly "poetic," advice. But Kipling was
not all barracks-room bluster or overt moralizing. Far
from it. As Robert Conquest notes in his excellent "Note
on Kipling's Verse," if Kipling's was a "poetry of clarifica-
tion rather than of subtlety and suggestion," you could also
easily make a selection of his poems that would show him
to be "a poet of sensitivity and sorrow." Poems like "The
Craftsman," about the burgeoning Shakespeare, or "The
Way Through the Woods," a haunting, Hardyesque lyric,
reveals another, less declamatory side of Kipling:

They shut the road through the woods
Seventy years ago.
Weather and rain have undone it again,
And now you would never know

There was once a road through the woods
Before they planted the trees.

And anyone who thinks of Kipling as a poet celebrating war hasn't read enough Kipling: "If any question why we died,/Tell them, because our fathers lied." ("Common Form").

In fact, Kipling was a poet of considerable emotional range and conspicuous majesty. "Recessional," the poem that catapulted Kipling from mere fame to nationwide celebrity, was written in 1897 for Victoria's Diamond Jubilee. It is an ever-pertinent masterpiece about hubris and the evanescence of power. Instinct with Biblical echoes, it issues a lofty call to humility and awe; it also contains one of the two most politically incorrect lines in all of Kipling:

If, drunk with sight of power, we loose
Wild tongues that have not Thee in awe,
Such boasting as the Gentiles use
Or lesser breeds without the Law—
Lord God of Hosts, be with us yet,
Lest we forget—lest we forget!

As Orwell noted, the line about "lesser breeds" is "always good for a snigger in pansy-left circles."

But the line does not refer, as Orwell also noted, to "coolies" being kicked about "by pukka sahib in a pith helmet" but rather to the awe-less multitudes "without the Law," Germans, first of all, but also anyone who glorified power without restraint or obeisance.

The other gem of political incorrectitude, for the record, is "the white man's burden," title and recurrent phrase of another famous poem: "Take up the White Man's burden—/And reap his old reward:/The blame of those ye better,/The hate of those ye guard—." How we squirm at that today! But as David Gilmour points out in *The Long Recessional: The Imperial Life of Rudyard Kipling*, the word "white" "plainly refers to civilization and character more than to the colour of men's skins. The 'white men' are those who conduct themselves within the Law for the good of others: Gunga Din may have a 'dirty' hide, but he is 'white, clear white, inside.'"

The key word is "civilization." Kipling was above all the laureate not of Empire, but of civilization, especially civilization under siege. Henry James once sniffed that there was only one strain absent in Kipling: that of "the civilized man."

It's a frequent refrain. But in a deeper sense, Kipling was about almost nothing else—not the civilization of elegant drawing rooms, but something more primeval and without which those drawing rooms would soon be smashed and occupied by weeds. Kipling, Evelyn Waugh wrote toward the end of his life, "believed civilization to be something laboriously achieved which was only precariously defended. He wanted to see the defenses fully manned and he hated the liberals because he thought them gullible and feeble, believing in the easy perfectibility of man and ready to abandon the work of centuries for sentimental qualms." Kipling endeavored to man those defenses partly through his political oratory, but more importantly through a literary corpus that taught the explicit lessons and the implicit rhythms of emotional continence and restraint.

G. K. Chesterton: Master of Rejuvenation

And God saw every thing that he had made, and, behold, it was very good.
—Genesis

The ordinary modern progressive position is that this is a bad universe, but will certainly get better. I say it is certainly a good universe, even if it gets worse.
—G. K. Chesterton, As I Was Saying

Despair does not lie in being weary of suffering, but in being weary of joy.
—G. K. Chesterton, *The Everlasting Man*

IN LIFE, there was always something unwieldy about Gilbert Keith Chesterton. Mentally as well as physically, he was a man who tended to . . . *overflow*. Like Flambeau, the criminal mastermind of his Father Brown mysteries, Chesterton was fully six-foot-four. Vertically, he left off growing in adolescence. Horizontally, he kept going. Slender in youth, he was solid as a young man and positively rotund in his thirties. His body was the perfect correlative for the drama he enacted. Chesterton always seems to have favored pince-nez, but it was his wife, Frances, who advocated the familiar equipage that defined his public image. With billowing cape and wide-brimmed hat, brandishing a sword stick and often sporting a pistol from his pocket as he strode up and down his beloved Fleet Street, Chesterton cut a figure as imposing as one of his famous epigrams.

The impression of superabundance continued on the page. His prose bristles with encompassing vitality. No matter the ostensible subject, Chesterton was always present amongst the syllables with his view of the universe. T. S. Eliot said that his 1906 study of Dickens was "the best essay on that author that has ever been written." Maybe so. But as his friend Ronald Knox noted, even that book is "really the Chestertonian philosophy illustrated by the life of Dickens." Chesterton wrote:

> To every man alive, one must hope, it has in some manner happened that he has talked with his more fascinating friends round a table on some night when all the numerous personalities unfolded themselves like great tropical flows. All fell into their parts as in some delightful impromptu play. Every man was a beautiful caricature of himself. The man who has known such nights will understand the exaggerations of *Pickwick*. The man who has not known such nights will not enjoy *Pickwick* nor (I imagine) heaven. . . . [Dickens] is there, like the common people of all ages, to make deities; he is there . . . to exaggerate life in the direction of life. The spirit he at bottom celebrates is that of two friends drinking wine together and talking through the night. But for him they are two deathless friends talking through an endless night and pouring wine from an inexhaustible bottle.

"To exaggerate life in the direction of life": that might describe the author of *The Pickwick Papers*; it was the perpetual credo of the author of *Dickens*.

Chesterton was a literary cornucopia. The tally includes some 100 books. His first two volumes, published in 1900 when he was in his mid-twenties, were collections of poems (of *Greybeards at Play*, the first, W. H. Auden said, that it contained "some of the best pure nonsense verse in English"). There followed many collections of columns and essays (he wrote some 4,000), biographical studies (of Browning, the Victorian painter G. F. Watts, Aquinas, and St. Francis Assisi, among others), hundreds of short stories (including the Father Brown series), more collections of poems, several plays, a clutch of famous phantasmagorical novels (*The Napoleon of Notting Hill, The Man Who Was Thursday*), and several classic—if also idiosyncratic—works of Christian apologetics. No less an authority than Etienne Gilson called *Orthodoxy* (1908) "the best piece of apologetic the century produced." "I did try to found a heresy of my own," Chesterton cheerfully acknowledges; "and when I had put the last touches to it, I discovered that it was orthodoxy." If you can read only one of Chesterton's nonfictional works, make it *Orthodoxy*: it is as eloquent as it is insightful. (Although posterity regards Chesterton as Catholic through and through, he was raised Anglican and wasn't received into the Church until 1922: *Orthodoxy* is a Catholic work by a practicing Protestant.)

All in all it was a bravura performance. By 1900, Chesterton had made a name for himself in literary London, and by 1904, when he published *The Napoleon of Notting Hill*, he was well on his way to international celebrity. His influence was enormous. Invitations to write and speak poured in. C. S. Lewis said his reading of *The Everlasting Man* helped spark his conversion. Dorothy L. Sayers similarly credited Chesterton with her return to the Church.

Chesterton's success would have been hard to predict. He was the opposite of precocious. He didn't learn to read until his ninth year (but after that he was unstoppable). His performance at lower school was lackluster. One schoolmaster exclaimed in exasperation that "if we could open your head we should not find any brain but only a lump of white fat." Chesterton began to blossom at St. Paul's (whose notable alumni include Milton, Pepys, and Judge Jeffries), where he met and befriended E. C. Bentley, the creator of the Clerihew, a form Chesterton would have been proud to invent. After St. Paul's, Chesterton first contemplated a career in art. For a couple of years, he dabbled in classes at the Slade while also attending lectures in English, French, and Latin at University College, London. He took no degree. And art turned out to be an entrée, an avocation, not an end. He went on to entertain friends with his drawings. But his main revelation concerned criticism. Years later, Chesterton recalled that, "having failed to learn how to draw or paint, I tossed off easily enough some criticisms of the weaker points of Rubens or the misdirected talents of Tintoretto. I had discovered the easiest of all professions; which I have pursued ever since."

"JOURNALIST," the music critic Ernest Newman once said, "is a term of contempt applied by writers who are not much read to writers who are." Chesterton would have liked that mot. He saw himself as a journalist—a "Jolly Journalist," in his wife's partially affectionate term—and he gloried in the semi-bohemian life of a Fleet Street pro. A column wasn't properly executed unless the printer's boy was kept waiting at the door for copy. (After 1909, when Chesterton moved to Buckinghamshire, the mad dash was to get copy to the London-bound train.) His earliest professional outlets were liberal-radical venues like *The Speaker* and the *Daily News*, but soon he was appearing in dozens of papers. Deadlines were like gauntlets. Chesterton regarded them as

Winston Churchill regarded public forms of transportation: they should be given a sporting chance of getting away. In later life, after he had acquired a secretary, he would sometimes dictate one article while simultaneously writing another in his own hand. Especially in the incandescent decade of 1900–1910, he wrote everywhere and anywhere—and about anything: "The Advantages of Having One Leg," "A Piece of Chalk," "What I Found in My Pocket," "On Gargoyles," "Cheese." These 1,000-word bijoux he would scribble in cabs, public houses, upon shirt cuffs, the backs of play bills.

It was never merely chalk or cheese, though. In Chesterton's hands, even the most pedestrian subject grew wings. "There is," Chesterton assured readers at the beginning of an essay on Kipling, "no such thing on earth as an uninteresting subject." In "The Unthinkable Theory of Professor Green," an astronomer delivers a lecture on his exciting discovery of a new planet. Only gradually do we realize that this marvelous new world with all its wonders is what we've already seen but somehow never known: Earth. What Chesterton called the "mere excitement of existence" countermanded boredom. "It is dull as ditch-water," you say. But think about it: "Is ditch-water dull? Naturalists with microscopes have told me that it teems with quiet fun." Again: "It is one thing," Chesterton reminded his readers, "to describe an interview with a gorgon or a griffin, a creature who does not exist. It is another to discover that the rhinoceros does exist and then take pleasure in the fact that he looks as if he didn't."

The uncommonness of the commonplace, and the proximity of what we lightly call nonsense to faith, was a prominent theme in *The Defendant* (1901), Chesterton's first collection of prose. "The simple sense of wonder at the shapes of things, and at their exuberant independence of our intellectual standards and our trivial definitions, is the basis of spirituality as it is the basis of nonsense," Chesterton wrote.

> Nonsense and faith (strange as the conjunction may seem) are the two supreme symbolic assertions of the truth that to draw out the soul of things with a syllogism is as impossible as to draw out Leviathan with a hook. The well-meaning person who, by merely studying the logical side of things, has decided that "faith is nonsense," does not know how truly he speaks; later it may come back to him in the form that nonsense is faith.

The poverty of looking at things solely from the "logical side of things" was a central plank of the Chestertonian gospel. "The madman," he observed in *Orthodoxy*, "is not the man who has lost his reason. The madman is the man who has lost everything except his reason." *Le coeur a ses raisons que la raison ne connaît point*: that Pascalian dictum might be engraved on the Chesterton escutcheon.

But engraved with a light touch. Humor was a familiar weapon in Chesterton's armory, and he was adept at deploying it to make serious points. The professors of "critical thinking" would be aghast, but at the beginning of his *Autobiography* (finished but weeks before his death, at sixty-two, in June 1936) Chesterton makes a startling confession: "Bowing down in blind credulity, as is my custom, before mere authority and the tradition of the elders, superstitiously swallowing a story I could not test at the time by experiment or private judgment, I am firmly of the opinion that I was born on the 29th of May, 1874." Born, he adds, to "respectable but honest parents" (savor that "but"), of that "old-fashioned" middle class for which "a business man was still permitted to mind his own business." That's all said with a smile, but it makes a deep point about the place of tradition in the economy of belief.

Chesterton gloried in eccentricity. When he married Frances Blogg in June 1901, they betook themselves to the Norfolk Broads for their honeymoon. Along the way, Chesterton stopped with his bride to have a glass of milk at a dairy he used to frequent with his mother. "It seemed to me," Chesterton wrote in his *Autobiography*, "a fitting ceremonial to unite the two great relations of a man's life." He then paused in another shop to procure a revolver and cartridges.

> Some have seen these as singular wedding presents for a bridegroom to give to himself; and if the bride had known less of him, I suppose she might have fancied that he was a suicide or a murderer, or, worst of all, a teetotaller. They seemed to me the most natural things in the world. I did not buy the pistol to murder myself or my wife; I never was really modern. I bought it because it was the great adventure of my youth, with the general notion of protecting my wife from the pirates doubtless infesting the Norfolk Broads . . . where, after all, there are still a suspiciously large number of families with Danish names.

This light-hearted reflection (Vikings!) has not satisfied the amateur psychoanalysts bent on inspecting the Chestertons' marital relations. Ada Chesterton, his sister-in-law, added the typical embellishments in her waspish 1941 book on the couple. "He was fathoms deep in love . . . and then the whole world went crash. The woman he worshipped shrank from his touch and screamed when he embraced her. . . . Frances couldn't resign herself to the physical realities of marriage. . . . Gilbert in a vital hour condemned to a pseudo-monastic life in which he lived with a woman but never enjoyed one." All very dramatic but, though eagerly repeated by some of Chesterton's biographers, not very credible. That first night may have been awkward for the shy and virginal couple—Frances was sickly, especially in later years—but she and Gilbert passionately wanted children. She even underwent an operation to cure her sterility—a pointless exercise absent the sexual prerequisites.

ADA CHESTERTON envied and disliked her sister-in-law, but the real significance of the episode en route to the Norfolk Broads is to underscore Chesterton's singularity. He was a gift to caricaturists. The calculated persona. The bonhomous advocacy of beer and beef. The avoirdupois. The boisterous polemic and studied absent-mindedness. "Am at Market Harborough," Chesterton once telegraphed his wife. "Where ought I to be?" Came the answer: "Home." It was a splendid confection. His friend Max Beerbohm "did" Chesterton several times, singly and with friends. One image from 1909 depicts the bean-thin, ascetic George Bernard Shaw, head back, hands behind him, standing ramrod straight in front of the disheveled beach-ball, hands stuffed in his pockets, that was Chesterton. ("To look at you," Chesterton once said to his favorite debating foil, "anyone would think a famine had struck England." "To look at you," Shaw shot back, "anyone would think you had caused it.") "Leaders of Thought," Max called the caricature, the humor inhering partly in the incongruity of the image, partly in the truth of the title.

Chesterton was eighteen years Shaw's junior. But he early on impressed the dramatist and vegetarian campaigner for eugenics, teetotalism, and the New Man. Chesterton first came to Shaw's attention with an article on *Ivanhoe* in the *Daily News*. Probably, they first encountered each other in the flesh at a Fabian meeting. "From the start," observed Dudley Barker in his 1973 biography of Chesterton, "they were jovially opposed to each other in debate, and warmly attached in friendship. Each attacked the other in public and valued him in private. They influenced each other's opinions not at all; unless it be influence to strengthen by opposition." When Shaw declared that Shakespeare was a hack who turned out pot-boilers to please the multitude and make money, Chesterton replied with "The Great Shawkspear Mystery," "Sorry, I'm Shaw," and other satirical ripostes. His *George Bernard Shaw* (1909) was, Shaw said, "the best work of literary art I have yet provoked." The rhetorical salvos traveled in both directions. Particularly memorable was Shaw's creation of that improbable beast, the Chesterbelloc, who was Chesterton's friend and intermittent mentor Hilaire Belloc stridently leading in front, a flailing Chesterton struggling to keep in step behind.

Debate was a crucial tonic for Chesterton. He started young, arguing endlessly with Cecil, his younger, politically dyspeptic brother. According to family lore, the longest uninterrupted argument, when Gilbert was nineteen and Cecil fourteen, took place during a seaside holiday. It commenced after breakfast at 8:15 A.M., traversed luncheon, tea, and dinner, and concluded, their father noted, sometime after 2:00 A.M., eighteen hours and thirteen minutes by the clock.

Although his adolescence was tinctured with loneliness and angst—it was then, he remarked, that he acquired certitude about "the objective solidity of Sin"—Chesterton enjoyed a conspicuously happy childhood. "I regret I have no gloomy and savage father to offer to the public gaze," Chesterton wrote in his posthumously published *Autobiography*, "no pale-faced and partially poisoned mother whose suicidal instincts have cursed me with the temptations of the artistic temperament . . . and that I cannot do my duty as a true modern by cursing everybody who made me what I am."

Among his fondest memories were the performances of fairy tales he and his father, a moderately prosperous estate agent, put on in a toy theater at their Kensington home. It was a habit he carried with him to adulthood. Indeed, the moral universe to which fairy tales introduced him became an abiding metaphysical staple. "My first and last philosophy," he wrote in *Orthodoxy*, "I learnt in the nursery. . . . The things I believed most then, the things I believe most now, are the things called fairy tales. . . . They seem to me to be the entirely reasonable things. They are not fantasies: compared with them other things are fantastic." As Dudley Barker observed, Chesterton "never lost the sense that his life as a child was his real life." The seat of "that ancient instinct of astonishment," childhood is not something one should endeavor to outgrow; it is something one should aspire to grow into. "I believe," Chesterton wrote, "in prolonging childhood. . . . I had in childhood, and have partly preserved out of childhood, a certain romance of receptiveness." "Romance" was a master word for Chesterton ("wonder" was another). His great achievement as a writer was to render those qualities palpably communicable.

CHESTERTON IS deliciously quotable. No one who wrote as much and as quickly as he escapes without longueurs and repetitions. His facility can at times seem merely facile, his penchant for paradox rote. (William James, though an admirer, spoke of his "mannerism of paradox.") After a mysterious, near-fatal illness in 1914–15 (Chesterton languished in a semi-coma for months), his energies contracted more than his appetite for work. Chesterton's brother Cecil died in an army hospital in 1918. Out of fraternal piety, Chesterton took over his paper, *New Witness* (started a few years before by Belloc), eventually renaming it *G.K.'s Weekly*. It was an invitation to literary dissipation. But at his not infrequent best Chesterton was wise as well as memorable. "When everything about a people," he wrote in *Heretics* (1905), "is for the time being growing weak and ineffective, it begins to talk about efficiency. So it is that when a man's body is a wreck he begins, for the first time, to talk about health. Vigorous organisms talk not about their processes, but about their aims." Worth pondering, that. And speaking of "aims," how's this, on the "new humility": "The old humility made a man doubtful about his efforts, which might make him work harder. But the new humility makes a man doubtful about his aims, which will make him stop working altogether." Prescient, no? One more: "Do not be proud of the fact that your grandmother was shocked at something which you are accustomed to seeing or hearing without being shocked. . . . It may be that your grandmother was an extremely lively and vital animal, and that you are a paralytic."

Although the Father Brown mysteries are widely read (still helped, I suspect, by Alec Guinness's portrayal in the 1954 film by Robert Hamer), for many readers today Chesterton exists primarily as a source of such aperçus:

> "An adventure is only an inconvenience rightly considered. An inconvenience is only an adventure wrongly considered."

> "If a man cannot make a fool of himself, we may be quite certain that the effort is superfluous."

> "Religious liberty might be supposed to mean that everybody is free to discuss religion. In practice it means that hardly anybody is allowed to mention it."

> "Pragmatism is a matter of human needs; and one of the first of human needs is to be something more than a pragmatist."

> "Some dogma, we are told, was credible in the twelfth century, but is not credible in the twentieth. You might as well

say that a certain philosophy can be believed on Mondays, but cannot be believed on Tuesdays."

"The true soldier fights not because he hates what is in front of him, but because he loves what is behind him."

"Tradition means giving votes to the most obscure of all classes, our ancestors. It is the democracy of the dead."

"The Christian ideal has not been tried and found wanting. It has been found difficult; and left untried."

One of my favorite Chesterton apothegms is the observation that "if a thing is worth doing, it is worth doing badly." I had thought he was referring to the practice of Christianity: he might have been, but in fact Chesterton is describing (in *What's Wrong with the World*) what he calls "the prime truth of woman, the universal mother." (Chesterton, I might remark in passing, would not have approved of Title IX "gender equity" legislation: "there is no boy's game, however brutal, which these mild lunatics have not promoted among girls.")

Some of Chesterton's maxims are mere elegant variations à la Oscar Wilde: "Literature and fiction are two entirely different things. Literature is a luxury; fiction is a necessity." But some encapsulate an important critical judgment or sociological observation. On Tennyson, for example: "He could not think up to the height of his own towering style." On America: "a nation with the soul of a church." On "the false theory of progress," according to which "we alter the test instead of trying to pass the test." (How Chesterton would have savored the phrase "affirmative action.") It is, I suppose, a measure of Chesterton's popular authority that he, like George Orwell, Mark Twain, and Winston

Churchill, is also a repository of clever sayings that he never said. "When a man stops believing in God he doesn't then believe in nothing, he believes anything." I always admired that Chestertonian formulation, only it turns out not to be by Chesterton (though it might have been).

Chesterton's exuberance didn't countenance scholarly apparatus or exactitude. He was a master of many genres, but I am not sure he ever indited a footnote. Not that he lacked precision. His command of the semicolon (look out for it) was subtle and masterly. But he didn't go in for the academic side of his calling. His research, though exhaustive, took place in the library of the heart, not the other kind. He misquoted and misattributed. His overall effect, as the critic John Gross observed, "is to animate rather than inform." Some of his recent admirers have endeavored to fill the gap. A serious "Collected Works" by Ignatius Press got going in 1986 and, as of this writing, is nearing its fortieth stout volume. *Chesterton and the Romance of Orthodoxy,* William Oddie's recent study of Chesterton's development, and *G. K. Chesterton,* the brick-like 750-page biography by Ian Ker, the authoritative biographer of Cardinal Newman, are models of academic diligence. These stately tomes are bulletins in what seems to be a renaissance of interest in (to adopt Oddie's shorthand) GKC. Both make large claims for their subject. Cardinal Newman was canonized last year; why not Chesterton next? Ker nominates Chesterton as "the successor of the great Victorian 'sages,' and particularly Newman," and suggests that we place him in the pantheon of English literary critics alongside Dr. Johnson, Matthew Arnold, and Ruskin.

I can envision Chesterton in a niche next to Dr. Johnson and Arnold; seeing him next to Newman is more difficult. Worldliness is not necessarily at odds with holiness; I wonder, though, about ruddiness. (Quoth Chesterton: "And

Noah he often said to his wife when he sat down to dine/'I don't care where the water goes if it doesn't get into the wine.'") Chesterton was assuredly devout. But he fought as many social and political battles as he did literary or religious ones. And in that arena he did not always distinguish himself. One tort that has shadowed him for decades is the charge of anti-Semitism. Auden, in the preface to his anthology of Chesterton's nonfictional prose, admits that, though he always enjoyed Chesterton's poetry and fiction, he had avoided his nonfictional prose because of his reputation as an anti-Semite. Ker, in his extensive index, has a longish entry devoted to "Chesterton, anti-Semitism of, alleged." The adjective is meant to be extenuating. Kerr's conclusion is that "he was anti-Jewish just as he was anti-Prussian, but only in the sense that he associated Jews with capitalism and international finance, just as he associated Prussians with barbarism and military aggression." Ker seems to regard this as an exoneration. I think Auden is right that Chesterton cannot be "completely exonerated." "I said," Chesterton wrote in one typical passage,

> that a particular kind of Jew tended to be a tyrant and another particular kind of Jew tended to be a traitor. . . . Patent facts of this kind are permitted in the criticism of any other nation on the planet. It is not counted illiberal to say that a certain kind of Frenchman tends to be sensual. . . . I cannot see why the tyrants should not be called tyrants and the traitors traitors merely because they happen to be members of a race persecuted for other reasons and on other occasions.

The problem, as Auden notes, is the "quiet shift from the term *nation* to the term *race*." Any nation, any religion or culture, is open to criticism. But a person's ethnic heritage is beyond his power to alter; it is therefore not subject to the scrutinies of moral judgment. Chesterton's anti-Semitism shouldn't be overstated. It existed, and was abetted by his brother and by Hilaire Belloc, who seemed to regard government corruption as a largely Jewish concession. But, as John Gross notes in his splendid pages on Chesterton in *The Rise and Fall of the Man of Letters*, anti-Semitism did not obscure Chesterton's "fundamental decency." "He hated oppression; he belonged to the world before totalitarianism." And it is also worth noting that he was one of the very first in England to attack Hitler and Hitlerism.

IN THE SCHEME of things, Chesterton's anti-Semitism seems to me less obtuse than the set of attitudes of which it was a part: I mean his "medievalism," his allergy to modernity. Chesterton had huge strengths as a writer and moralist. He also had significant blindspots. Chesterton may have been right that "The vice of the modern notion of mental progress is that it is always something concerned with the breaking of bonds, the effacing of boundaries, the casting away of dogmas." But what are we to make of his claim that "Mankind has not passed through the Middle Ages. Rather mankind has retreated from the Middle Ages in reaction and rout"? According to Chesterton, "Too much capitalism does not mean too many capitalists, but too few capitalists." An energizing thought. But what are we to make of his insistence that property should be redistributed "almost as sternly and sweepingly as did the French Revolution . . . so as to produce what is called Peasant Proprietorship"? That way lies not more capitalists but more poverty and institutionalized terror. Who was it who observed that the only real alternative to the cash nexus (which Marx abhorred) was the terror nexus (which Marx helped pave the way for)? Under Belloc's influence, Chesterton and his brother espoused "Distributism," supposedly a "middle way" between Socialism and Capitalism. But like most such middle ways, it puts one in mind of Hazlitt's observation about the lamentable critic who seeks truth "in the middle, between the extremes of right and wrong."

One of the delights of reading Chesterton is his seemingly inexhaustible fund of good humor. I don't just mean the laughs, but rather the abiding sense that "the aim of life is appreciation." It is startling, then, to wander among some of his social and political pronouncements. The rich of every nation, he said with unparalleled brutality, are "the scum of the earth." John Gross was right in observing that much of the "positive side" of Chesterton's politics—"Distributism, peasant small holdings, Merrie Englandism—led him into a hopeless cul-de-sac."

Chesterton did not like, I am not sure he really understood, wealth and the mechanisms responsible for its creation. He declared that "our industrial civilization" is "rooted in injustice," but compared to what other civilization? Medieval Europe? That is a fantasy. Chesterton was sincerely on the side of the "common man." But he was blind to the extent to which money, as Friedrich Hayek put it, is "one of the great instruments of freedom ever invented," opening "an astounding range of choice to the poor man—a range greater than that which not many generations ago was open to the wealthy."

The truth is that the Chestertonian optics worked best peering into the interstices of the quotidian. Their lenses were equipped for the grandeur of the humble, the small, the seemingly (but only seemingly) insignificant. They faltered when presented with the patently grand. It is edifying to read Chesterton on the desirability of supplying heraldry to the common man: "A grocer should have a coat-of-arms worthy of his strange merchandise gathered from distant and fantastic lands; a postman should have a coat-of-arms capable of expressing the strange honour and responsibility of the man who carries men's souls in a bag." Neatly put. But when presented with the British Empire upon which the sun never sets, Chesterton sniffs that he is not much interested in an empire without sunsets. Cleverly put, but how much magnificence is thereby discarded!

The other side of Chesterton's embrace of eccentricity was a horror of homogeneity. Rhetorically, it informed his knack of discovering neglected significances in everyday language, and the adumbration of a "promise" in "compromise," for example. "He focuses on a cliché or a battered simile," John Gross wrote, "until it begins to recover its original brightness. He brings out the wealth of implication in everyday speech, and also its inadequacy: we habitually say more than we realize, but less than we intend." Chesterton was a prominent defender of tradition, of the way things have been, not because he championed the status quo but because he saw tradition as a fertile resource for beneficent change: "All conservatism," he noted, "is based upon the idea that if you leave things alone you leave them as they are. But you do not. If you leave a thing alone you leave it to a torrent of change."

The science writer Martin Gardner, a prominent admirer of Chesterton's work, got to the existential heart of the matter. "No modern writer," Gardner noted, "lived with a more pervasive sense of ontological wonder, of surprise to find himself alive, than Gilbert Chesterton." Such wonder was the source of his uncanny powers of rejuvenation, of making fresh, young, new. Wonder, Chesterton said in the Autobiography, "was the chief idea of my life." Surprise, as Gardner noted, is a regular concomitant of wonder. Another is gratitude. It was a prime Chestertonian gift, the sense of grateful wonder before the fathomless mystery of life. "The comedy of man," as he put it in a 1935 radio broadcast, "survives the tragedy of man."

I have found no evidence that Chesterton read Søren Kierkegaard, who died in 1855 but was not translated into English until much later. Kierkegaard was a sort of connoisseur (and expert anatomist) of boredom. Boredom was, Kierkegaard said, "the demonic side of pantheism." Chesterton would have understood and savored that formulation. Boredom's pact with the devil yielded staleness and weariness where joy ought to have predominated. It was, he would have pointed out, one of the disadvantages of pantheism and the doctrinaire naturalism from which pantheism flows. One does not need to embrace Chesterton's religious views to understand that he who wonders at life cannot be bored, while he who is bored cannot experience wonder or the gratitude that blossoms alongside it. Chesterton's inestimable achievement is to have salvaged wonder for himself and, by so doing, for his readers. "A man does not grow old without being bothered," he wrote; "but I have grown old without being bored." Chesterton was not wrong to see modern, capitalist society as a solvent of the heterogeneity he championed. It's just that his imagination rebelled at the spectacle. For once, the inconvenience was an inconvenience, not an adventure.

Does Shame Have a Future?

No society can do without intolerance, indignation, and disgust.
—Patrick Devlin, *The Enforcement of Morals*

[A] liberal society has particular reasons to inhibit shame and protect its citizens from shaming.
—Martha C. Nussbaum, *Hiding from Humanity*

I heard thy voice in the garden, and I was afraid, because I was naked; and I hid myself.
—*Genesis*, 3:10

In Masaccio's great fresco depicting the expulsion of Adam and Eve from the Garden of Eden (ca. 1426), the Angel of the Lord hovers, sword in hand, above and behind the First Couple. Adam strides forward, naked, his face buried in his hands. Eve, however, a look of wailing misery on her upturned face, covers her breasts and privates as she walks. She is ashamed of her nakedness and strives to conceal it.

I thought of Masaccio when I stumbled upon Martha Nussbaum's essay "Danger to Human Dignity: The Revival of Disgust and Shame in the Law" in *The Chronicle of Higher Education* in August 2004. How Nussbaum would disapprove of Eve!, I thought. For Martha Nussbaum—a classicist who is currently the Ernst Freund Distinguished Service Professor of Law and Ethics in the Philosophy Department, Law School, and Divinity School at the University of Chicago—does not approve of shame. She is not too keen about disgust, either. Both emotions, she thinks, impede "the moral progress of society." And here we have Eve, ashamed of her body, modestly shielding her sex from view: how very unprogressive!

"Danger to Human Dignity" is an oddly vertiginous work, as is the book from which it is drawn, *Hiding from Humanity: Disgust, Shame, and the Law* (2004). (It is appropriate that the book should feature on its cover a fleshy, unpleasant nude by Otto Dix: how different it is—morally as well as aesthetically—from Masaccio's Eve!) Professor Nussbaum begins "Danger to Human Dignity" with the following show-stopper: "The law, most of us would agree, should be society's protection against prejudice." Really? I thought "most of us would agree" that the law ought to be society's protection against *crime*. After all, a crime is an action while a prejudice is merely an attitude.

But perhaps Professor Nussbaum thinks that prejudice is itself a crime—though surely not all prejudice. Edmund Burke said that prejudice "renders a man's virtue his habit." He meant that if we have a predisposition—i.e., a prejudice—toward the right things, they more easily become second nature. Surely Professor Nussbaum would not wish the law to protect us from that sort of prejudice? And it must be said that she herself is clearly prejudiced against anything she labels "conservative." I doubt that she believes that the law should be society's protection against prejudice directed at conservatives.

Well, let's leave prejudice to one side. The ostensible burden of both these works, the essay and the book, is to warn readers about the "remarkable revival" of shame and disgust in our society, especially as they impinge upon the law. Now when I read that, I thought "Nussbaum, on top of everything else, must be a student of Stephen Potter," a philosopher I mentioned above in discussing Rudyard Kipling (speaking of personages of whom Martha Nussbaum would disapprove). For anyone as intelligent as she could not really believe that shame and disgust are enjoying a renaissance in our culture. She must be employing a variation of a gambit Potter describes in his book *Lifemanship*, "Going One Better." It works like this. First you find out the quality for which an author is most famous, then you blame him for not having enough of it. An example from *Lifemanship*: "The one thing that was lacking, of course, from D. H. Lawrence's novels, was the consciousness of sexual relationship, the male and female element in life." (The "of course" is the classic Potter touch.) Look around at our society: flip on your television; browse the interent for a few minutes; saunter down to your local newsstand; visit a local theater or museum; inspect the nose rings, the tongue or eyebrow or nipple studs that are so popular with the young and not-so-young today. One thing indisputably missing in our society is anything like a traditional sense of shame or disgust. So how clever of Professor Nussbaum to devote an entire book to the malignant presence of something that has all but disappeared.

Professor Nussbaum is particularly exercised by the sentences, handed down by various courts, which involve some public declaration of the perpetrator's wrongdoing. A child molester, for example, might be required to post a sign on his property warning children to stay away. Another chap, convicted of larceny, is required to wear a shirt with the advice: "I am on felony probation for theft." A drunk driver is made to sport a bumper sticker advertising the fact of his infraction to other motorists.

Professor Nussbaum approvingly quotes a spokesman from the American Civil Liberties Union who angrily objects to such punishments: "Gratuitous humiliation of the individual serves no social purpose at all . . . [a]nd there's been no research to suggest it's been effective in reducing crime." To which one might reply that the humiliation was not "gratuitous" but, on the contrary, was meted out in response to a criminal violation. And as for the "research," it doesn't take much to tell you that, having been duly put on notice, the neighbors of that convicted child molester will keep a wary eye out for him, thus reducing the chance of a repeat performance. Likewise, the shopkeeper who espies the banner-wearing thief enter his store is sure to watch the till, once again reducing the chance that the crime will be repeated.

But Professor Nussbaum doesn't confine herself to mere pragmatic issues, such as whether a given policy in fact reduces crime. Her objection is more fundamental. "Shaming penalties," she notes, "encourage the stigmatization of offenders, asking us to view them as shameful." Er, yes: they would have that effect, wouldn't they? *Hiding from Humanity* is full of such near tautologies. You do something bad, something, in fact, that is shameful. The legal punishment calls attention to your bad, your shameful, action, partly in order to encourage you to reflect on your fault, partly to alert others to it. Is that a bad thing?

Professor Nussbaum brandishes the verb "stigmatize" early and often in this book. She doesn't approve of stigmatizing people. Originally, a stigma was a mark burned into the skin of a criminal or slave. It has acquired an additional meaning: "A mark or token of infamy, disgrace, or reproach," as my dictionary puts it. Professor Nussbaum several times raises the specter of unfairly stigmatizing innocent people or groups of people. She quotes A. Hitler on the Jews, for example. As you'd expect, he said some very unpleasant things that were definitely intended to stigmatize the Jewish people. But how about Joe, the convicted child molester, who moves in next door? A thoughtful judge has ordered him to post a sign on his front lawn advertising his crime. That sign is indeed "A mark or token of infamy, disgrace, or reproach," and you can bet that it's one for which the mothers in the neighborhood are grateful. Which brings us to something that gets lost in Professor Nussbaum's discussion: the distinction between unfairly stigmatizing an innocent person or group of people and stigmatizing someone or some group because they deserve a mark or token of infamy, disgrace, or reproach. Of course one wishes to avoid the former. Does that mean that we should in principle forswear the latter?

Professor Nussbaum doesn't say. But she has a deeper objection to penalties that shame a criminal. She thinks that calling attention to Joe's penchant for sexually molesting little girls or boys is incompatible with the ideals of "human dignity and the equal worth of persons." That's another phrase Professor Nussbaum deploys regularly. She tells us, toward the beginning of her book, that her guiding motivation is to "construct a public myth of equal humanity, to substitute for other pernicious myths that have long guided us." That sounds nice. Why not toss out all those "pernicious myths" that have guided humanity until fifteen minutes ago and sign on to the one that says "human dignity" and "equality"?

Professor Nussbaum speaks of the "equal worth of persons." What do you suppose she means? In America, all citizens are meant to enjoy equality before the law. The figure of justice is often portrayed blindfolded because the scales she carries are meant to operate dispassionately, without the ballast of interest or parti-pris. That is one sort of equality. Then there is what the philosopher Harvey Mansfield called "the self-evident half-truth that all men are created equal." It's only a half-truth because, except for the special case of our status as legal actors, nothing could be more obvious than the gross inequality of men. As the journalist William Henry put it in his book *In Defense of Elitism* (1994),

> the simple fact [is] that some people are better than others— smarter, harder working, more learned, more productive, harder to replace. Some ideas are better than others, some values more enduring, some works of art more universal. Some cultures, though we dare not say it, are more accomplished than others and therefore more worthy of study.

Something similar can be said about "human dignity." Professor Nussbaum finds a "deep tension" between the view that "law should shame malefactors and the view that law should protect citizens from insults to their dignity." Let's leave the question of whether the law really should concern itself with "insults" to a citizen's dignity. The critical point is that, by calling attention to a criminal violation of human dignity, the law reinforces the ideal of human dignity.

IN ANY EVENT, all these cases concern the outer scaffolding of Professor Nussbaum's argument. The inner core of her book is part of a revisionist morality, the emotional weather of which is summed up in a section that appears towards the end of her book: "The Case Against Disgust and Shame."

As Professor Nussbaum acknowledges, shame and its more visceral cousin, disgust, are semantically amphibious emotions. They are moral as well as physical creatures, depending as much upon an idea of the good as upon physical revulsion. Shame is deeply bound up with modesty, another moral sentiment that inscribes itself in immediate physical reaction. Similarly, disgust is the body's fire alarm for the

163

noxious, but not merely the physically noxious. As William Ian Miller puts it in his book *The Anatomy of Disgust* (1997), disgust, although inculcated in toddlerhood, is "above all . . . a moral and a social sentiment." Disgust highlights the good by violently excluding its opposite. Consequently, Miller argues, "contempt and disgust have their necessary role to play in a good, but not perfect, social order." Utopia, having excluded evil, would have no call for disgust. As Miller notes, these observations are hardly new: "The entire Latin Christian discourse of sin depended on the conceptualization of sin and hell as raising excremental stenches and loathsome prospects."

Professor Nussbaum wants us to get beyond all this. She acknowledges that "the person who is utterly shame-free is not a good friend, lover, or citizen," but she wants to privatize shame, as it were, to disenfranchise it from any role in public life. Similarly, Professor Nussbaum acknowledges that disgust may have played "a valuable role in our evolution"—making us recoil from various toxic elements in our environment; she even admits that it may continue to be a valuable guide in daily life. But because the "thought-content" of disgust is "typically unreasonable, embodying magical ideas of contamination, and impossible aspirations to purity, immortality, and nonanimality," disgust should "never be the primary basis for rendering an act criminal, and should not play either an aggravating or a mitigating role in the criminal law where it currently does."

Another way of putting this is to say that Professor Nussbaum wishes completely to emancipate law from the idea of sin. From a traditional point of view, of course, the law is seen as being rooted in a moral vision, which includes a recognition of sin. As the British jurist Patrick Devlin noted in *The Enforcement of Morals* (1965), "the complete separation of crime from sin . . . would not be good for the moral law and might be disastrous for the criminal." Why? Because without the idea of sin, moral life would be an empty calculus of pain and pleasure. "What makes a society of any sort," Lord Devlin noted, "is a community of ideas, not only political ideas but also ideas about the way its members should behave and govern their lives; these latter ideas are its morals."

IT WAS NOT SO long ago that sin—like disgust, like shame— was widely regarded as part of the permanent furniture of human reality. It was one of those abiding features of our moral existence that we felt even if we couldn't quite explain. But intellectuals like Martha Nussbaum are affronted by such phenomena. Sin—it is such an irrational idea, so hard to get hold of "theoretically." Professor Nussbaum finds disgust "perplexing in theory": "the theoretical literature," she says, reveals "considerable debate about whether shame and disgust ought to play the roles they currently play" in the moral and legal economy of life. ("That's all very well in practice," says the economist in the old joke, "but how does it work out in theory?") "To appeal to disgust," Professor Nussbaum concludes, "seems to be just to say 'I don't like that,' and stamp one's foot. No reasons are advanced that would make debate about such laws a real piece of public persuasion."

Professor Nussbaum is certainly right that feelings of disgust, like feelings of shame, are extra- if not irrational: we don't argue ourselves into disgust or shame: we feel it immediately. Professor Nussbaum is deeply suspicious of those feelings. She sharply criticizes the physician-philosopher Leon Kass for advocating the "wisdom of repugnance"—the wisdom of disgust and revulsion—because our disgust might be misplaced. She is even more severe about Lord Devlin, who argued that "for the difficult choice between a number of rational conclusions the ordinary man has to rely upon a 'feeling' for the right answer. Reasoning will get him nowhere."

A good conservative, Lord Devlin was a minimalist when it came to the law's province. "In any new matter of morals," he argued, "the law should be slow to act." Advocating "toleration of the maximum individual freedom that is consistent with the integrity of society," he noted that "the law is concerned with the minimum and not with the maximum": "the criminal law is not a statement of how people ought to behave; it is a statement of what will happen to them if they do not behave." At the same time, Lord Devlin recognized that "not everything is to be tolerated. No society can do without intolerance, indignation, and disgust."

> Every moral judgement, unless it claims a divine source, is simply a feeling that no right-minded man could behave in any other way without admitting he was wrong. It is the power of common sense and not the power of reason that is behind the judgements of society.

Professor Nussbaum is very impatient with the "power of common sense." Why? Because it is so often insufficiently enlightened, insufficiently progressive, insufficiently in agreement with the opinions of people like, well, like Martha Nussbaum. Lord Devlin appealed to the moral feeling of the ordinary man, "the man on the Clapham omnibus." Professor Nussbaum doubts "whether the disgust of the 'average' man would ever be a reliable test for what might be legally regulable."

So maybe many of the things that the inherited moral wisdom of millennia have taught us to find disgusting—and to which society has responded with various legal prohibitions—need to be reevaluated? What do you think? Take necrophilia. Professor Nussbaum finds this a thorny problem. Who, after all, is harmed in the transaction? Professor

Nussbaum wonders "whether necrophilia ought, in fact, to be illegal." She acknowledges that there is "something unpleasant" about a person who rapes a corpse, but it is "unclear" to her whether such conduct should be "criminal." Possibly, since a corpse is generally the property of its family, there should be "some criminal penalties" where "property violations" are involved, but otherwise not. Think about that for a moment . . .

Professor Nussbaum describes her intellectual-political pedigree as "less Millian than Whitmanesque." She may be right. I think, for example, of "Song of Myself," which has many Nussbaumian touches. Nussbaum: "[W]e wash our bodies, seek privacy for urination and defecation, cleanse ourselves of offending odors with toothbrush and mouthwash, sniff our armpits when nobody is looking, check in the mirror to make sure that no conspicuous snot is caught in our nose-hairs." Whitman: "The scent of these arm-pits is aroma finer than prayer,/This head is more than churches or bibles or creeds./ . . . I dote on myself . . . there is that lot of me, and all so luscious . . .").

But if there is a lot of Whitman blowing through Professor Nussbaum's book, there is also a good deal of Mill. I am thinking especially of the Mill of *On Liberty*, the Mill who advocated "new and original experiments in living" and argued that the "sole justification" society had for interfering with an individual "in the way of compulsion and control"—whether by "physical force in the form of legal penalties or the moral coercion of public opinion"—was "self-protection." If the individual is not harming others, then (says Mill) we have to leave him alone: "His own good, either physical or moral, is not a sufficient warrant" for interference. Mill's libertarian doctrine is our modern gospel. Professor Nussbaum is part of a large choir singing its praises.

But the popularity of Mill's doctrine says nothing about its cogency. As James Fitzjames Stephen pointed out in *Liberty, Equality, Fraternity* (1873), Mill's teaching would "condemn every existing system of morals."

> Strenuously preach and rigorously practise the doctrine that our neighbor's private character is nothing to us, and the number of unfavorable judgments formed, and therefore the number of inconveniences inflicted by them can be reduced as much as we please, and the province of liberty can be enlarged in corresponding ratio. Does any reasonable man wish for this? Could anyone desire gross licentiousness, monstrous extravagance, ridiculous vanity, or the like, to be unnoticed, or, being known, to inflict no inconveniences which can possibly be avoided?

As Stephen dryly observes, "the custom of looking upon certain courses of conduct with aversion is the essence of morality." But it is part of Professor Nussbaum's brief—as, in a way, it was of Mill's—to encourage us to dispense with moral aversion, of which shame and disgust are prominent allotropes.

One of the oddest features of *Hiding from Humanity* is Professor Nussbaum's recurring argument that the emotions of shame and disgust encourage us to ignore or discount our mortality, our incompleteness, our animality. No doubt Professor Nussbaum has managed to embrace her own animality without the benefit of shame or disgust. But for most of us, the emotions of shame and disgust are vivid reminders of our status as imperfect creatures, fragile, animal, and therefore mortal.

This is something embodied the world over in the idea of taboo, a concept with deep connections to the ideas of shame and disgust. These are insights we arrive at not by ratiocination but by feeling. As the philosopher Leszek Kolakowski writes, "We do not assent to our moral beliefs by admitting 'this is true,' but by feeling guilty if we fail to comply with them." What we are dealing with, he points out, is not an intellectual performance but "an act of questioning one's own status in the cosmic order, . . . an anxiety following a transgression not of a law but of a taboo." Professor Nussbaum wants us to "discard the grandiose demands for omnipotence and completeness that have been at the heart of so much human misery." Good idea! But shame and disgust are accomplices, not impediments, to that attack on hubris.

Hiding from Humanity is not only a polemic against the emotions of shame and disgust. It is also a political position paper. Professor Nussbaum is such a ferocious opponent of shame and disgust because she is such a passionate proponent of many things that shame and disgust recoil from. It is ironical that in a book which is partly an attack on "the grandiose" Professor Nussbaum should harbor such a grandiose agenda for social change. From public nudity to poverty, the global AIDS crisis, and homosexual marriage, Professor Nussbaum has embraced the entire menu of politically correct causes. Poverty, she says, is "one of the most stigmatized life-conditions, in all societies." Therefore it must be removed. And not just poverty: we must also supply items that are "part of the social definition of a decent living-standard," e.g., "a personal computer." Why not an iPad and high-speed internet service as well? AIDS is "a major cause of stigmatized lives." Something must be done!

Professor Nussbaum is one of those intellectuals whose intoxication with the thought of her own virtue is equalled only by her contempt for the opinions of the ordinary people whose lives she pretends to anguish over. Even without the inducement of the arguments she advances, her conviction of moral superiority would have led her to jettison shame as an impediment to "the moral progress of society." One saw this at work in the mid-1990s when she was called upon to give expert testimony in *Evans v. Romer*, which challenged a state constitutional amendment in Colorado that prohibited any official body from adopting a law or policy that grants homosexuals "minority status, quota preferences, protected status or claim of discrimination." As the philosopher John Finnis showed in an article for *Academic Questions*, Professor Nussbaum, by deliberately misrepresenting the meaning of certain Greek words and the work of other scholars, engaged in "wholesale abuse of her scholarly authority and attainments."

Among other things, Professor Nussbaum went back to a nineteenth-century edition of the standard Greek-English lexicon because it did not include a morally opprobrious definition of a contested Greek term. She took the trouble to white-out the name of a contributor to the later edition of the lexicon that the lawyers, unaware of her subterfuge, had supplied in the footnotes of a court document. Challenged about this, she claimed that she was simply correcting a clerical error because the earlier edition was "more reliable on authors of the classical period" than later editions. I asked a former Regius Professor of Greek about that and it took him about five minutes to stop laughing. It's clear that Professor Nussbaum doesn't believe it either, since it has been shown that her own work regularly relies on later editions.

It is a curious quirk of language that "shameless" entails "shameful"—that is, being without shame is something to be ashamed of. This is not, I suspect, something that much troubles the Ernst Freund Distinguished Service Professor of Law and Ethics in the Philosophy Department, Law School, and Divinity School at the University of Chicago. But the rest of us might regard a shameless life the real hiding from humanity.

The Consequences of Richard Weaver

*The past shows unvaryingly that when a people's freedom
disappears, it goes not with a bang, but in silence amid
the comfort of being cared for. That is the dire peril in
the present trend toward statism. If freedom is not found
accompanied by a willingness to resist, and to reject favors,
rather than to give up what is intangible but precarious, it
will not long be found at all.*
—Richard Weaver, 1962

*The simple process of preserving our present civilization
is supremely complex, and demands incalculably subtle
powers.*
—Ortega y Gasset, 1930

IN THE GREAT PANTHEON of half-forgotten conservative
sages, the southern writer Richard M. Weaver (1910–
1963) occupies an important, if curious, niche. I say "writer," but that is an imprecise designation. By trade, Weaver
was a professor of rhetoric. He is even the author of a textbook on the subject. One friend said that Weaver was "a
rhetor doing the work of a philosopher." It might be more
accurate to say that he was a critic doing the work of a
prophet. Prophets as a species tend to specialize in bad

news; they rarely return from the mountain reporting that management upstairs has concluded that everything down below is just fine.

Weaver was no exception to this rule. He made his reputation as a latter-day Isaiah, bearing admonitory tidings to an inattentive populace. Above all, perhaps, he was an acolyte of what he lovingly called "lost causes." The fact that a cause had lost, he argued, did not necessarily rob it of nobility; it did not mean that we could not learn something from the ideals that inspired it; it did not even mean that, ultimately, it was really lost. For what is lost might also be regained. It might serve not only as a reminder but also as a model, a new goal. In the "longer run," as Weaver put it, what seemed lost might eventually prove victorious.

Such, anyway, were among the explicit rationales that Weaver offered about the value of lost causes. An additional attraction, I suspect, lay in the romance of defeat. "Things reveal themselves passing away": Weaver liked to quote that Yeatsian line. I believe he cherished the passing away as much as the accompanying revelation.

EXHIBIT "A" in Weaver's dossier of lost causes—the cynosure to which he ritually returned, which he never really left—was the post-bellum American South. Its literature, manners, and aspirations, rooted in the life before the Civil War, were the subject of Weaver's dissertation, completed under Cleanth Brooks at Louisiana State University in 1943 but published, in revised form, only in 1968, five years after Weaver's death. *The Southern Tradition at Bay* is a brilliant, complex, cranky work, part literary criticism, part social commentary, part hortatory injunction. "From the bleakness of a socialist bureaucracy," Weaver wrote in his peroration, "men will sooner or later turn to something stirring: they will decide again to live strenuously, or romantically."

That was the ideal. The route to realizing it was to be found in the "Old South," which Weaver proposed as a co-conspirator in the pursuit of his strenuous, romantic oppositions.

As one of Weaver's biographers, Fred Douglas Young, notes, *The Southern Tradition at Bay* was less a dissertation than "an apologia." Most of Weaver's mature themes make their appearance in the book. Indeed, several critics have pointed out that Weaver's later work is essentially an elaboration and application of ideas he first formulated there. Weaver begins by laying out a constellation of four distinctively Southern, almost universally besieged, virtues: the feudal concept of society organized by an interlocking hierarchy of duties, filiations, and privileges; the code of chivalry; the ancient concept of the gentleman; and religion or at least "religiousness," which may have "little relation to creeds" but, prodded by "a sense of the inscrutable," "leaves man convinced of the existence of supernatural intelligence and power, and leads him to the acceptance of life as mystery."

But that scaffolding describes only one level of Weaver's argument. For every lost cause there is a victorious alternative. Weaver was interested in analyzing, elaborating, advocating what he took to be the virtues of the Old South; even more, he was interested in criticizing the forces that had undermined those virtues. The enemy, he thought, was not so much Grant's and Sherman's armies as the spirit that moved them. It was "science and technology." It was centralized government. It was the ethic of "total war." It was affluence, materialism, and the love of comfort. In a word, it was modernity. Hence the lessons of American's premier lost cause: "The mind of the South," Weaver wrote, is "conspicuous for its resistance to the spiritual disintegration of the modern world." Is such resistance futile? Never mind. Resistance itself is glorious: strenuous, romantic, precisely because—perhaps one should say "even if"—futile.

Later, Weaver came to acknowledge that the South's resistance in modern America had all but collapsed. But yesterday, in the 1940s, it still seemed like a magnificent ruin: "a hall hung with splendid tapestries in which no one would care to live." They may be inhospitable. They may be strange and even rebarbative. Nevertheless, Weaver concludes, they offer essential existential wisdom: "from them we can learn something of how to live." The Old South, he declared (and the italics are his) was *the last non-materialist civilization in the Western World.*

Students of the period will instantly recognize *The Southern Tradition at Bay* as an homage to, an extension of, the spirit of the Southern Agrarians whose famous manifesto *I'll Take My Stand* had been published in 1930. Many of the movement's founding members—John Crowe Ransom, Allen Tate, Donald Davidson—were among Weaver's mentors and friends. There is a lot of elegy in such writing, and not a little bitterness. Whatever the sins of the South, had not its punishment been excessive? The South had not so much been defeated as crushed by the Union armies: that was bad enough. Even worse were subsequent efforts to obliterate or efface Southern identity, to transform even its virtues into vices, its heroisms into crimes. "In short," Weaver put it tartly in a later essay, "the South either had no history, or its history was tainted with slavery and rebellion and must be abjured." Weaver, like the Agrarians, abjured the abjuration.

A rich mixture, this. What should we make of it? In a way, the work of Richard Weaver is not unlike the Old South he memorialized. It, too, is a splendidly appointed but, for most of us, an uninhabitable domicile. Still, it is one we cannot simply repudiate without diminishment. Weaver's work is a heady, sometimes an impossible stew. But it is one from which we can learn "something of how to live" or (what is almost the same thing) something of how not to.

Weaver the man was—or became—almost as eccentric as his work. Born in North Carolina, he was the first of four children. His father, an outgoing man who owned a livery stable, died when Richard was only six and his mother was expecting her last child. The family eventually resettled in Lexington, Kentucky, where his mother managed Embry and Company, a millinery business owned by her brother. Although Weaver became a formidable debater, he was a shy, bookish boy: his sister Polly remembers him sequestered in his bedroom for hours on end with the family typewriter. He blossomed socially in college, though his intellectual vocation seems to have settled upon him only gradually. In an autobiographical essay called "Up from Liberalism" (1958), Weaver recalls that in his undergraduate years at the University of Kentucky earnest professors had him "persuaded entirely that the future was with science, liberalism, and equalitarianism." By the time he graduated, in 1932, the Great Depression had swept the country and Weaver, like many others, had evolved into a full-fledged socialist. He served as secretary of the campus socialist party and, during Norman Thomas's presidential campaign, rose to be secretary of the statewide socialist party.

His metanoia began at Vanderbilt where he came under the mesmerising spell of John Crowe Ransom, the "subtle doctor" to whom he dedicated *The Southern Tradition at Bay*. What one might call the "localness" of Ransom's teaching—his agrarian emphasis on the importance of place, the genealogy of art and thought—began to wean Weaver from the centralizing imperatives of socialism. After taking a master's degree in 1937, he spent a restless few years teaching, first in Alabama, then Texas. It was while driving across the Texas prairies in 1939, he recalled later, that he had a revelation: "I did not have to go back to this job . . . I did not have to go on professing the clichés of liberalism, which were becoming meaningless to me. . . . At the end of that year I chucked the uncongenial job and went off to start my education over, being now arrived at the age of thirty." Weaver now switched into high intellectual gear. At LSU he studied not only with Cleanth Brooks but also with such commanding figures as Robert Penn Warren and the literary historian Arlin Turner. Summers found him at Harvard, the Sorbonne, or the University of Virginia pursuing his studies. He finished his dissertation in 1943 and, recommended by Brooks, landed a job at the University of Chicago.

Weaver's entire career unfolded at the University of Chicago. He taught there from 1944 until his early death, from heart failure, in 1963 at the age of fifty-three. Weaver was dutiful—he always insisted on keeping his hand in teaching introductory courses when most senior staff fobbed off that chore on junior colleagues—but he was never happy in Chicago. One biographer speaks of his "hermetically sealed existence" there. He had colleagues, but few if any close friends. He never married. He lived alone in a small apartment with his pipe, his books, and a nightly beer for company. In the summer, he would go south to stay with his mother in the house he had bought her. He traveled there by train—he boarded an airplane only once in his life, to lecture in California—and he always instructed his mother to have the garden plowed by horse or mule, not—abomination of desolation—by a tractor.

THERE WAS MORE than a little irony in Weaver's situation. The great Henry Regnery, who published Weaver's book *The Ethics of Rhetoric* in 1953, summed it up with his customary aptitude. How odd that a man who repudiated the modern world and all its works should spend virtually his entire career "at a university founded by John D. Rockefeller, where, not long before he arrived, the first chain reaction had taken place . . . and in the city where fifteen years before there had been a great exposition, 'A Century of Progress,' celebrating achievements of science and technology." As Regnery noted, being so out of place must have been a powerful goad to Weaver's ire, and hence to his work.

Weaver's star rose dramatically in 1948 when *Ideas Have Consequences* was published by the University of Chicago Press. He instantly went from being just another disgruntled prof to being a sort of academic celebrity. He had a knack for telling people what they didn't want to hear in such a way that they craved to hear it. "This is another book," he began mournfully, "about the dissolution of the West." It was Weaver's constant theme. *Ideas* is a brief book, fewer than 200 pages. But it crackles with passion and extensive, if sometimes imperfectly digested, erudition. Its success, or perhaps I should say its notoriety, astonished everyone, not least its author.

Paul Tillich—then at the height of his fame—spoke for one contingent when he declared the book "brilliantly written, daring, and radical. . . . It will shock, and philosophical shock is the beginning of wisdom." Others were less admiring. Writing in *The Antioch Review*, one critic denounced Weaver as a "pompous fraud" and his book as a retreat to "a fairyland of absolute essences." *Ideas* was not a measured, carefully modulated argument; it did not elicit a measured, carefully modulated response. I suspect that some part of the book's success lay in its title. It is not catchy, exactly, but it bluntly articulates an immovable intellectual truth: ideas do indeed have consequences. It is ironical, then, that Weaver intensely disliked the title, which was foisted upon him by his editor. In *Barbarians in the Saddle: An Intellectual Biography of Richard M. Weaver*, Joseph Scotchie reports that Weaver almost pulled the book from the press over the title. Weaver's friend Russell Kirk said that *The Adverse Descent* was the title Weaver favored; other scholars say it was *The Fearful Descent*. Whatever it was, Weaver was fortunate that his editor prevailed.

As WEAVER'S FRIEND Eliseo Vivas, a professor of philosophy, noted, Weaver's defining intellectual trait was "audacity of mind." It was audacity of a decidedly contrarian stamp. In the mid-1940s, when Weaver was writing *Ideas*, America was blooming with post-war prosperity. The ideology of progress was underwritten by the joy of victory and the extraordinary dynamo of capitalism suddenly unburdened by the demands of war. Material abundance was rendered even more seductive by a burgeoning technological revolution: cars, radios, gadgets galore. Easier. Faster. Louder. More—above all, more.

Weaver wanted none of it. *Ideas*, he said, was not a work of philosophy but "an intuition of a situation," namely, a situation in which the "world that has lost its center." Weaver traced that loss back to the rise of nominalism in the twelfth century, a familiar pedigree that is both accurate and comical. It is is accurate because the modern world—a world deeply shaped by a commitment to scientific rationality—does have a root in the disabusing speculations of nominalism. It is comical because to locate the source of our present difficulties on so distant and so elevated a plane is simply to underscore our impotence. If William of Occam is responsible for what's wrong with the world, it's time to close up shop all around.

Nevertheless, Weaver's diagnosis struck a chord, or rather many chords. On the strength of *Ideas*, the quirky Yale polemicist Willmoore Kendall declared Weaver "captain of the anti-liberal team"—a team, as Scotchie notes, that was only just coming into its own with figures like Weaver and Russell Kirk and, just over the horizon, William F. Buckley

Jr. and the circle he assembled around *National Review* (a circle that included Weaver).

In fact, though, Weaver was not so much anti-liberal as anti-modern. This shows itself, for example, in his discussion of private property. He praises private property as "the last metaphysical right." But although he clearly appreciates the place of private property in fostering liberty and forestalling the tyranny of the state, his defense is actually highly qualified: "Respecters of private property are really obligated to oppose much that is done today in the name of private enterprise, for corporate organization and monopoly are the very means whereby property is casting aside its privacy." Private property is good, Weaver thinks, so long as it is limited: "The moral solution is the distributive ownership of small properties." Who or what oversees that distribution was not a problem he solved.

Something similar can be said about his discussion of total war, war conducted not just among recognized combatants but against civilians as well. No sane person is "in favor" of war, total or otherwise. But Weaver's laments about the loss of chivalry in war are bootless. Weaver locates the origin of total war in the American Civil War and the North's brutal campaign against the South. But he applies his criticism to other conflicts, for example the firebombing of Dresden and the use of the atomic bomb in Japan. In the posthumously published *Visions of Order* (1964), he argues that the usual justification—that those actions ultimately "saved lives"—has "a fatal internal contradiction," since if one really wanted to save lives one could simply capitulate and stop fighting. Really, though, there is no contradiction. It takes away nothing of the horror of those episodes to say that the real alternative—for example, invading the Japanese islands—would have been even more horrible. The decision about saving lives was made then, in the aftermath of Iwo Jima and Okinawa. The point is that the choices life presents us with, especially in wartime, are often not between good and bad but between bad and worse. That is a central conservative insight, and it is a curious feature of Weaver's thought that, despite his ostensible celebration of the particular over the abstract, he sometimes sacrifices vital human reality for the sake of an abstraction.

WEAVER'S TAXONOMY of decadence is both bracing and over-stated—bracing, perhaps, because overstated. He lamented "the lowering of standards, the adulteration of quality, and, in general, . . . the loss of those things which are essential to the life of civility and culture." Who can disagree? In his opening pages, he notes that "Man is constantly being as-sured today that he has more power than ever before in history, but his daily experience is one of powerlessness." This is certainly true, and it testifies to the accuracy of de Tocqueville's analysis of "democratic despotism"—you'll have noticed that's a theme of this book—which does not tyrannize so much as it enervates and infantilizes. But then Weaver proceeds to argue that if one "is with a business organization, the odds are great that he has sacrificed every other kind of independence in return for that dubious one known as financial. Modern social and corporate organiza-tion makes independence an expensive thing; in fact, it may make common integrity a prohibitive luxury for the ordi-nary man." Is this true?

Weaver acknowledged at the beginning of *Ideas* that lam-entation about "the decadence of a present age is one of the permanent illusions of mankind." But that was a pro forma rider. At the center of his analysis was the insistence that modern man, "like Macbeth," had made an evil decision to trade allegiance to transcendent principles for present gain. From this Faustian bargain all manner of bad things flow.

Weaver warns about "the insolence of material success," the "technification of the world," the obliteration of distinctions that make living "strenuously, or romantically" possible. "Presentism," the effort to begin each day, as Allen Tate put, as if there were no yesterday, has robbed man of his history and therefore his identity as a moral agent. Weaver is particularly harsh on what he regards as the tepid ambitions of the middle class: "loving comfort, risking little, terrified by the thought of change, its aim is to establish a materialistic civilization which will banish threats to its complacency." In a chapter called "Egotism in Work and Art" he launches an extraordinary attack on jazz that presages Allan Bloom's attack on rock music in *The Closing of the American Mind.* Jazz, Weaver wrote, was "the clearest of all signs of our age's deep-seated predilection for barbarism." All this, I think, is not so much wrong as radically incomplete. Weaver speaks of "hysterical optimism," and rightly; it is not, however, the only form of hysteria on offer.

Weaver is often at his best when applying himself to the concrete analysis of language. He understood with rare subtlety that rhetoric (as Aristotle insisted) is an ethical as well as an instrumental discipline. A debasement of language, he knew, was also a debasement of reality. In 1937, when asked how he could worry about the misuse of language when the Japanese were bombing Shanghai, Karl Kraus responded that "If all commas were in the right place, Shanghai would not be burning." An overstatement, perhaps, but one that errs in the right direction. In *The Ethics of Rhetoric,* Weaver has penetrating and original things to say about Lincoln's speeches, Milton's rhetoric, and the legal arguments deployed in the Scopes trial. Particularly noteworthy is his discussion of the way certain words acquire a positive or negative charge that lifts them out of the precincts of ordinary semantics to a realm of moral inviolability. Consider the word "progress." Weaver nominates it as "the god term of the present age" which can "validate almost anything."

> It would be difficult to think of any type of person or of any institutions which could not be recommended to the public through the enhancing power of this word. A politician is urged upon the voters as a "progressive leader"; a community is proud to style itself "progressive"; technologies and methodologies claim to be "progressive"; a peculiar kind of emphasis in modern education calls itself "progressive," and so on without limit.

Thus it is, as Scotchie puts it, that certain words, and by extension the causes to which they are attached, become "unassailable." The word "democracy," Weaver notes, enjoys a similar dispensation. (Friedrich von Hayek, we'll see later in this book, makes a similar point about the misuse of the word "social.")

It works the same way on the negative side of the lexicon: certain terms seem unredeemable. One of the primary "devil terms" in modern times is "prejudice," a term that once meant "prejudgment" but now, as Weaver says his important essay "Life Without Prejudice" (1957), is primarily "a flail to beat enemies." Edmund Burke, we remember from the last chapter, could praise "just prejudice" as that which "renders a man's virtue his habit." For us, the word is synonymous with bigotry. Prejudice in the old sense, Weaver notes, was a "binding element" in society. And that is precisely why—at least, it is one reason why—the attack on prejudice occupies such a prominent place in the strategy of the Left.

> For as long as this integrative power remains strong, the radical attack stands refuted as hopeless. This will explain the

peculiar virulence with which communists attack those transcendental unifiers like religion, patriotism, familial relationship, and the like. It will also explain, if one penetrates the matter shrewdly, why they are so insistent upon their own programs of conformity, levelling, and de-individualization.

"Life without prejudice," Weaver concludes, "were it ever to be tried, would soon reveal itself to be a life without principle."

The late Irving Kristol famously said that a neo-conservative is a liberal mugged by reality. Weaver might be described as a socialist repelled by modernity. You don't have to be Karl Marx to recognize that capitalism is a powerful solvent of tradition. (Think of Joseph Schumpeter's identification of "creative destruction" as the central energy of capitalism.) Moralists have inveighed against luxury ever since there was luxury to tempt us. But capitalism and the free markets which feed it drastically up the ante. Capitalism is an unparalleled engine for the production of wealth. It is also an unparalleled engine for the production of freedom, but that freedom has two faces: increased choice and increased dislocation. Weaver lamented that latter and blamed the former.

WEAVER SAID that his "core belief" revolved around the recognition that "man in this world cannot make his will his law without any regard to limits and to the fixed nature of things." Quite right, and Weaver has penetrating things to say about the "spoiled-child psychology" that underlies the modern culture of entitlement. He is right, too, that modern science and technology present us with formidable moral temptations. But the pretense that we might issue a categorical "no" to modernity would not only be impracticable, it would be immoral—and it would be so on good Weaverian grounds. Richard Weaver was eloquent in warning about the disastrous results of Prometheanism, of attempting to subjugate the world to our will. But part—a large part—of our world today is the world shaped by science. What greater hubris than to think we could dispense with that world in an effort to live "strenuously, or romantically"?

"Art in Crisis"

*[Today] we find a pursuit of illusions of artistic progress,
of personal peculiarity, of "the new style," of "unsuspected
possibilities," theoretical babble, pretentious fashionable
artists, weightlifters with cardboard dumb-bells. . . . What
do we possess to-day as "art"? A faked music, filled with
artificial noisiness of massed instruments; a failed painting,
full of idiotic, exotic and showcard effects, that every ten
years or so concocts out of the form-wealth of millennia
some new "style" which is in fact no style at all since
everyone does as he pleases. . . . We cease to be able to
date anything within centuries, let alone decades, by the
language of its ornamentation. So it has been in the Last
Act of all Cultures.*
—Oswald Spengler, *The Decline of the West*

*Beauty is the battlefield where God and the devil war for
the soul of man.*
—Fyodor Dostoevsky, *The Brothers Karamazov*

A MONG THE MORE remarkable books I first encountered
in graduate school was a blistering polemic called (in
English) *Art in Crisis: The Lost Center*. It was already long
out of print—and more's the pity. There is nothing else quite

like it in the annals of conservative cultural speculation. The author was Hans Sedlmayr, an Austrian art and architectural historian whose primary field of expertise was Baroque architecture. Sedlmayr (1896–1984) was a founding member of the "New Vienna School" of art historians, a group that flourished in the late 1920s and 1930s and included Fritz Novotny and Otto Pächt (whose book *The Practice of Art History* is also a neglected classic). Their chief intellectual inspiration was another Austrian, Alois Riegl (1858–1905), whose idea of *Kunstwollen*—"art will" or "art impulse"— was one of those omnivorous explanatory concepts that set susceptible academic hearts beating faster for two or three generations. Riegl believed that there was an intrinsic evolutionary logic to the development of artistic styles, one whose career (or careers) he and his successors proposed to trace and ruminate about.

It was a fertile idea—fertile, anyway, in the production of papers and books. Sedlmayr edited a collection of Riegl's essays in 1929 and, in 1931, published an essay called "*Zu einer strengen Kunstwissenschaft*"—"Toward a Rigorous Study of Art"—which distinguished between two approaches to the study of art. The first, empirical, approach focused on such pedestrian issues as provenance, chronology, influence, and patronage. The second, more exciting, approach endeavored to ride the wave of the *Kunstwollen*, to intuit the "inner organization" of the work of art. Both approaches, Sedlmayr said, were necessary to the discipline of art history, but the second (surprise, surprise) was "more 'essential' and more 'valuable' than the first."

Many art historians wondered how "rigorous" Sedlmayr's new approach really was. For example, in "The New Viennese School" (1936), Meyer Schapiro acknowledged the "intensity and intelligence" that Sedlmayr and his colleagues brought to the table. But he also complained about Sedlmayr's use of "spiritualistic conceptions and . . . allusions to qualities or causes that we have no means of verifying." Moreover, Schapiro objected, Sedlmayr unfairly deprecated the usual procedures of art history: "Anyone who has investigated with real scruple a problem of art history knows how difficult it often is to establish even a simple fact beyond question." Schapiro scored some palpable hits, above all, perhaps, in his observation that the new Vienners sometimes tended to substitute their discovered "principles" or "structures" for the "work itself." (An objection to which many art historians, Schapiro included, might profitably attend.)

I knew nothing of Sedlmayr's other work when reading *Art in Crisis*—his highly regarded book on Francesco Borromini's churches, for example. Nor did I know that Sedlmayr had joined the fledgling Nazi party in Austria as early as 1932, a moment when the party was still outlawed. Sedlmayr was not a committed Nazi. But he did not behave honorably. He kept his job and flourished professionally during Hitler's rise and throughout the war while Jewish colleagues, including his friend Pächt, lost their positions and (those that were lucky) had to flee the country. Still, Sedlmayr was never a party ideologue in the sense, for example, that Martin Heidegger was. His association with the toxin of Nazism was close enough that he lost his academic position after the war, not close enough to be prosecuted by the oss. Christopher Wood, editor of *The Vienna School Reader* (2003), exhibits a marked distaste for Sedlmayr and what he calls his "bombastic, hectoring, even devious" tone. But Wood acknowledges that Sedlmayr was inspired not by political animus—he was, Wood says, "no revolutionary"—but by "bourgeois and Catholic nostalgia for the Old Europe, the Hapsburg Mitteleuropa, that he had known as a child."

Art in Crisis was published in Germany in 1948 under the title *Verlust der Mitte: Die bildende Kunst des 19. und*

20. *Jahrhunderts als Symptom und Symbol der Zeit*: "Loss of the Center: The Fine Arts of the Nineteenth and Twentieth Centuries as Symptom and Symbol of the Times." The German title is better, or at any rate is a more accurate guide to the book's real subject than "Art in Crisis." Sedlmayr certainly did believe that modern art was in crisis. But in his view the artistic crisis was only a coefficient or manifestation of a much deeper cultural and religious disintegration. In an important sense, *Verlust der Mitte* is not an exercise in art history at all. It uses art, not to make an aesthetic case but in order to illustrate a moral diagnosis. His epigraph—from Yeats's poem "The Second Coming"—presages the book's governing mood: "Things fall apart; the center cannot hold . . ."

In the decade between its original publication and its appearance in English in 1957, *Verlust der Mitte* sold 100,000 copies in Germany and Austria alone. In America, it bombed utterly. In 1996, Stephen J. Tonsor spoke at an event honoring Henry Regnery, who published *Art in Crisis*. Tonsor estimated that the book, which he described as "one of the post-war's most important art-historical discussions and criticisms of artistic modernism," sold "about 250 copies in the United States." Tonsor may be off by a few hundred: no matter, the book in English encountered some hostility but mostly neglect.

No DOUBT Sedlmayr's connection with the Nazis was part of the reason. For example, in a tart, contemptuous, review in *Commentary*, Alfred Werner charged that Sedlmayr's diction was "more reminiscent of Streicher's newspaper, *Der Stürmer*, than serious art history." I do not believe Werner's characterization was fair. If it were, then the rhetoric of moral disapprobation would be forever out of bounds in discussing art. In 1937, the Nazis mounted a show of modernist art and called it "Degenerate Art." They were wrong about the art, but does that mean we are henceforth forbidden from describing any art as "degenerate"? Consider the photographs in Robert Mapplethorpe's notorious "X Portfolio": would "degenerate" be out of place in describing them? Sedlmayr does not, I believe, use the infamous term *"entartete"* ("degenerate") but he freely employs terms from the same lexicon, speaking throughout his book of breakdown, chaos, negation, decline. (A typical section is title "The Chaos of Total Decay.")

In any event, Sedlmayr's discreditable political history was not, I think, the main reason for the failure of *Art in Crisis* in the court of public opinion. The more important reason was his attack on modernism, indeed on modernity itself. Christopher Wood speaks of Sedlmayr's "antimodernist tirade," dismissing *Art in Crisis* as "a neo-Spenglerian, pessimistic, anti-intellectual assault on modern art."

The idea that an incisive, encyclopedic mind such as Sedlmayr's is "anti-intellectual" is the sort of preposterous thought that could only occur to a certain type of intellectual. But Wood is right about the neo-Spenglerian cast of *Art in Crisis*. Spengler's lowering two-volume masterpiece *Der Untergang des Abendlandes*, "The Decline of the West," had mesmerized the post-World War I intelligentsia. (The first volume appeared in 1918, the second in 1922.) Sedlmayr quotes Spengler incessantly. The narrative he presents in *Art in Crisis* assumes rather than argues for Spengler's view of cultural development as a centuries-spanning organic process of youth-maturity-senescence. Sedlmayr also accepts much (though by no means all) of Spengler's seductive interpretations of cultural significances, in particular his understanding of nineteenth-century eclecticism as a symptom of decay. Indeed, the whole realm of medicalized rhetoric—"symptom," "diagnosis," "disease," "prognosis"—is a Spenglerian trope that Sedlmayr adopts wholesale. (It is from Spengler, by the way, not the Nazis, that he takes his vocabulary of decline.)

Where Sedlmayr departs from Spengler most importantly is on the issue of inevitability. For Spengler, the "organic" cultural developments he chronicles are necessary processes. The "phases" of civilization he describes are the products not of human ingenuity but of the operation of "Destiny," "Fate," or some other ineluctable, upper-case inevitability: a force that is as irresistible as it is impersonal and supra-human. Sedlmayr, too, is fond of "phases." *Art in Crisis* is full of them: a section called "From the Liberation of Art to the Negation of Art," for example, traces four phases of the "disease," from 1770 to 1900 and after. Later in the book, he denominates modern art the "fourth phase" of artistic de-velopment, a phase devoted above all to the pursuit of artis-tic and spiritual autonomy. But Sedlmayr softens Spengler's analysis by admitting a place for human initiative. A late chapter carries an epigraph from Christian Morgenstern: "We are at the end . . ." A gloomy thought, though Sedlmayr embraces that ellipsis as an opportunity, not a declaration. "It may be a somewhat questionable proceeding to designate one's own age as the turning point in history," he admits,

> nevertheless it is difficult to shake off the feeling that since 1900 a kind of limit has been reached and that we are faced by something wholly without precedent. Beyond this limit it is difficult to imagine anything except one of two things— total catastrophe or the beginnings of regeneration.

The possibility of humanly directed "regeneration" sounds a distinctly un- (even anti-) Spenglerian note. It is what ulti-mately rescues Sedlmayr's astringent analysis from Wood's charge of Spenglerian pessimism.

Not, I hasten to add, that the picture Sedlmayr paints is cheerful. *Art in Crisis* is primarily a contribution to the library of conservative reaction to the intoxications of the Enlightenment, especially in its French—which is to say, in its extreme, egalitarian, revolutionary—modality. The Enlightenment came bearing the promise of universal emancipation. The promise turned rancid. In the second volume of *The Decline of the West*, Spengler observed that "Every 'Age of Enlightenment' proceeds from an unlimited optimism of the reason . . . to an equally unqualified scepticism." Sedlmayr doesn't quote that passage, but in the final pages of *Art in Crisis* he cites Nietzsche to similar effect: "Enlightenment is always followed by a darkening of men's souls and a pessimistic coloring of life. Towards 1770 (!) you can already note a lessening of joy." Sedlmayr interpolates an exclamation point to underscore the historical marker. He opens *Art in Crisis* by observing that in the years before 1789, "there began a revolution the extent of which was vast, perhaps more vast than we can imagine." The revolution in question was not the political revolution wrought by Robespierre and his colleagues but the "huge inner catastrophe" of which the political detonations were merely a part. "There can be no doubt," Sedlmayr writes with typical portentousness, "that many people really feel that this our age is sick." It is part of his task to show how many disturbing features of our culture that we think of as distinctively modern actually have roots in the nineteenth and even eighteenth centuries.

At bottom, we might best describe *Art in Crisis* as an exercise in cultural or spiritual epidemiology. Sedlmayr's goal is "to interpret," to draw a fever chart of the modern age "through the language of art." But he regards art in this book less as an aesthetic reality than as an exfoliation of spiritual aspiration. This makes *Art in Crisis* a difficult book to classify. It is not really art criticism, though it frequently passes judgment on various works. Nor is it art history, though it draws freely on that discipline. Indeed, Sedlmayr insists *Art in Crisis* is not "in any sense . . . concerned with the history of art as such." He describes it rather as a " 'critique' of the spirit and an attempt to diagnose the age both in its greatness and its wretchedness, as that age is revealed to us in its art." Sedlmayr occasionally dilates on some achievement of modernity, but it is the "wretchedness" that sets his pen moving. Nor is this surprising. It is partly due to the fact that bad news generally makes the most piquant copy. But there is also the contention that failure is more indicative of cultural drift than success. Sedlmayr agrees with the architectural historian Auguste Choisy that "*Ce sont les abus qui caractérisent le mieux les tendances*": "It is the abuses that are the best indicators of trends."

IN SOME WAYS, *Art in Crisis* is a book that was written too early. Sedlmayr focuses more attention on painting than sculpture because, he says, "A meaningless form in sculpture is always in danger of being merely ridiculous." Well, yes, but will it be seen as ridiculous? What, one wonders, would Sedlmayr have to say about the work of Carl Andre and his tile-like squares of metal? It is true that much of the absurdity that we see in the art world today is but a tired rehash of absurdities that surfaced in Surrealism, Futurism, and Dada. Whatever else can be said about them, artists like Duchamp and Dalí really did achieve a limit that cannot be surpassed, but merely recapitulated along a spectrum that starts in naïveté and ends in irony, parody, and camp. Dalí defined Surrealism as "the systematization of confusion." Louis Aragon said it was "the child of raving and darkness"—he meant that as praise—and noted that, far from being merely an art movement, it aspired to be "all-embracing" and sought "transformation of the whole of life." Really, Sedlmayr wrote, Surrealism should be called "sous-realism," since it deals chiefly not with elements that transcend expression but which precede it in the inarticulate basement of life. Surrealism is important not because of its aesthetic achievements but because it is "a movement that unites a number of the basic tendencies of modern art—the love of the illogical, the receptivity for the chaotic, faithfulness in representation together with an icy coldness of finish." With Surrealism, as the art historian Wilhelm Pindar pointed out, "art finally reaches the stage where it is concerned not with that which is beyond the power of language to express but with that which is inexpressible because it is so far below it." What, one wonders, would writers like Sedlmayr and Pindar say about contemporary artists like Gilbert and George, the Chapman brothers, Matthew Barney? (For more on that rogues' gallery, see "Why the Art World Is a Disaster" below.)

Sedlmayr admits that his approach is "somewhat sweeping." But he argues that behind the seemingly chaotic multiplicity of modern artistic expression may be discerned "mighty trends." *Art in Crisis* is an effort to catalogue and assess the meaning of those trends. Sedlmayr pauses now and again to note (as he puts it in his introduction) "the limitations of the thesis." It would, he admits, be mistaken to consider works of art "exclusively as symptoms of mental disorder." He insists, however, that it would also be mistaken to consider works of art "exclusively as examples and transitory points in the development of a style, as the criticism of art on purely stylistic grounds."

Consider, for example, Claude-Nicolas Ledoux's idea of building a house in the shape of a huge sphere. In 1770, Ledoux designed such an edifice (probably then unbuildable) for a bailiff. "Most people," Sedlmayr writes, "have treated this notion as nothing more than a bad joke or a very ordinary piece of lunacy, while the more charitable have looked upon it as an 'experiment with form.' The thing is certainly insane enough, but if it were no more than that, we should hardly be justified in wasting much time over it."

According to Sedlmayr, however, Ledoux's plan is not simply a bold aesthetic *jeu d'esprit*. It is "a symptom of a profound crisis both in architecture and in the whole life of the human spirit." Why? Because, Sedlmayr says, Ledoux's fantasy is part of a larger effort to deny the traditional rootedness of architecture (and of man): it is a rewriting of architecture in the abstract language of geometry. A sphere, resting upon the ground at but a single point, lacks a foundation; top and bottom are interchangeable, or rather are obliterated; its measure is not the needs and limitations of the human body—the traditional measure of architecture—but the fancy of the unfettered imagination. It is in this sense that "a nonsensical idea"—a house in the shape of a sphere—"need by no means be wholly without significance." Sedlmayr reads off—sometimes he reads into—the extravagances of modern artistic expression the spiritual itinerary of the age.

Sedlmayr offers a similar interpretation of the advent and spread of the English landscape garden, one of the several new "master problems" that defined the artistic activity of the eighteenth century. Beginning in about 1720, he points out, the English garden, a "conscious protest against the architectural gardens of France," swept through Europe in a fit of what one nobleman, who had twice ruined himself in an effort to transform his property into a nature preserve, called "Parkomania." What—if anything—should we make of this phenomenon? According to Sedlmayr, it betokened "something much more than a new kind of garden. It implied a revolt against the hegemony of architecture. It implied a wholly new relationship between man and nature and a new conception of art in general." "Romanticism" is the usual shorthand for that novelty, but what Sedlmayr stresses is the pantheistic revolution in religious sentiment that this form of Romantic nature worship implies. "The word 'nature' itself now gained a religious coloring. . . . Nature is raised to the rank of an all-pervading spiritual power. She no longer stands confronting man as an alien thing, man is 'sympathetically' woven into her being."

In part, what Sedlmayr presents in *Art in Crisis* is a chronology of the birth of "the aesthetic" as an independent enterprise, one consciously emancipated from its traditional roots in religion. The term "aesthetic" was born at this time—it was first used in its modern sense by the German philosopher Alexander Baumgarten around 1750. The landscape garden; the architectural monument; the art museum as a dedicated building type; the exhibition as a showcase for technological and engineering prowess—these and other outlets for artistic energy testified to a new relationship not only between man and his handiwork but also between man and the forces that transcend him. The phenomenon of the art museum is a conspicuous case in point.

> Regarded as a temple, the museum is not the temple of any particular God but a Pantheon of Art in which the creations of the most varied epochs and peoples are ranged next to one another with equal claims to our attention. For this to be possible, however, it was first necessary for Heracles and Christ to become brothers and for their divinity to be regarded as a thing of the past, so that they could both be seen in the temple of art, as manifestations of a deity which had swallowed all the others.

It is this aestheticizing impulse that Sedlmayr is everywhere at pains to exhibit and anatomize, showing how it implies, first, the ambition to forge a new autonomy of art and, second, a new autonomy of man. "Man deifies his inventive power," Sedlmayr writes, "with which he hopes both to master nature and to supersede her."

Sedlmayr is often a perceptive critic. The essential aim of Cézanne—whose work, Sedlmayr says, is a "key to understanding modern painting as a whole"—is

> to represent what "pure" vision can discover in the visible world, vision, that is to say, that has been cleansed of all intellectual and emotional adulteration. . . . The magic that pertains to this way of looking at things is that even the most ordinary scene acquires a strange and original freshness, and above all that color released from its task of indicating and identifying objects, gains an intensity that it never previously possessed.

This seems to me to be right. Yet Sedlmayr puts a minus sign next to Cézanne precisely because in his work "mere paint enjoys a quite peculiar supremacy": "In Cézanne an apple has the same physiognomic value as a face."

Sedlmayr takes a similar approach to Goya. The more we study the work of Goya, he says, especially his series called "Dreams" and "Madness"—subjects, Sedlmayr says, that are the "the most essential thing in modern art"—"the more intense grows our conviction that, like Kant in philosophy and Ledoux's architecture, he is one of the great pulverizing destructive forces that bring a new age into being."

THE PROBLEM IS that Goya's art, like Cézanne's, exists not just as a metaphor of the Zeitgeist, but also as an aesthetic object that has its own internal logic. Apart from everything else, Goya produced objects that commandeer attention, that are deeply interesting to look at.

Sedlmayr knows this. But, having surveyed modern art from the perspective of a spiritual diagnostician, he finds it wanting. At the center of *Art in Crisis* is the insight that, in art as in life, the pursuit of unqualified autonomy is in the end a prescription for disaster, aesthetic as well as existential. Sedlmayr writes as an Augustinian Catholic. For him, the underlying motive for the pursuit of autonomy is pride. The "lost center" of his original title is God. Autonomy, for finite, mortal creatures, is a dangerous illusion. "Autonomous man," he writes, "does not and cannot exist—any more than can autonomous art, architecture, painting and so on. It is of the essence of man that he should be both natural and supernatural. . . . Man is fully human only in so far as he is a repository of the divine spirit."

One need not, I think, share Sedlmayr's theological convictions in order to appreciate the power of his strictures about the search for autonomy. "The fact is," he argues, "that art cannot be assessed by a measure that is purely artistic and nothing else. Indeed, such a purely artistic measure, which ignored the human element, the element which alone gives art its justification, would actually not be an artistic measure at all. It would merely be an aesthetic one, and actually the application of purely aesthetic standards is one of the peculiarly inhuman features of the age, for it proclaims by implication the autonomy of the work of art, an autonomy that has no regard to men—the principle of l'art pour l'art." Art has its own aesthetic canons of legitimacy and achievement; but those canons are themselves nugatory unless grounded in a measure beyond art. That is the ultimate, indispensable, lesson of *Art in Crisis*.

Why the Art World Is a Disaster

*It is now that we begin to encounter the fevered quest for
novelty at any price, it is now that we see insincere and
superficial cynicism and deliberate conscious bluff; we meet,
in a word, the calculated exploitation of this art as a means
of destroying all order. The mercenary swindle multiples a
hundredfold, as does the deceit of men themselves deceived
and the brazen self-portraiture of vileness.*
—Hans Sedlmayr, Art in Crisis

It was like entering a cult group.
—Marieluise Hessel, on her introduction to the contemporary
art world in Munich.

*Some of what she said was technical, and you would have
had to be a welder to appreciate it; the rest was aesthetic
or generally philosophical, and to appreciate it you would
have had to be an imbecile.*
—Randall Jarrell, Pictures from an Institution

B ACK IN 2007, a friend telephoned and urged me to travel
to Bard College to see "Wrestle," the inaugural exhibition mounted to celebrate the opening of "css Bard Hessel
Museum," a 17,000-square-foot addition to the college art

museum. It sounded, my friend said, spectacularly awful. She'd just had a call from her husband, a Bard alum, who had zipped through the exhibition while doing some work at the college. Huge images of body parts—yes, *those* body parts—floating on the walls of a darkened room, minatory videos of men doing things—yes, those things—to each other, or to themselves, all of it presented in the most pretentious fashion possible. It really was something . . . special. Well, these folks are not naïfs. They've both been around the avant-garde block and back a few times. If they said an exhibition was ostentatiously horrible, then it was likely to be something worth taking some trouble to avoid—unless, that is, your job description includes regular stints as a cultural pathologist, in which case it is something that duty requires you to inspect, docket, and file away for the instruction and admonition of future generations.

This is my unhappy position. So, one fine May morning I motored up to lovely Annandale-on-Hudson, New York, home of the elite, super-trendy Bard College. Bard is one of those small educational institutions whose ambient wealth has allowed them to substitute avant-garde pretense for scholarly or artistic accomplishment. If your bank account is healthy (comprehensive tuition and fees for entering students in 2011 is $56,962) and young Heather or Dylan is "creative," i.e., not likely to get into a Harvard or Yale or Williams, then Bard is a place you can park them and still look your neighbor in the eye. The college is probably best known for its baton-wielding president, Leon Botstein, who conducts orchestras in his spare time and whom the music critic Tim Page once described as the sort of chap who gives pseudo-intellectuality a bad name. Bard also has the distinction of being, as far as I know, the only college in the United States to honor the memory of Alger Hiss, the perjurer and Soviet spy, by establishing a chair in his memory.

It had been a long time since I had visited Bard. Back in the early 1990s, I ventured into its sylvan purlieus to write about the opening of the Richard and Marieluise Black Center for Curatorial Studies and Art in Contemporary Culture for *The New Criterion*. Now here we had, attached to the old edifice, the Marieluise Hessel Museum of Art. Two Marieluises? It turned out to be like the evening star and morning star of philosophical lore, Hesperus and Phosphorus: two names but one and the same orb—in short, as William Demerast put it in *The Lady Eve*, "It's the same dame." The German-born businesswoman shed the unfortunate (or maybe not) Mr. Black somewhere along the line. Although married again, she is taking no chances and now endows her endowments with her maiden name. Marieluise has been busy. In the early 1990s, when the Black Center opened, her collection of contemporary art consisted of some 550 items. It has grown to 1,700, of which approximately 200 items were on view in "Wrestle."

Although you won't be able to see the show, you need not pine. You haven't missed anything. Have I become jaded? Too many close encounters with Gilbert and George, Matthew Barney, and all the other exotic fauna that populate the galleries and art museums these days? Perhaps. In any event, I thought my friends overstated the awfulness of the exhibition. Don't get me wrong: it was plenty awful. Body parts, "explicit" images, and naughty language galore. The exhibition certainly merited the warning to parents at the entrance. But it wasn't worse than dozens of other exhibitions I've seen, you've seen, we've all seen.

I thought about this as I picked my way through the galleries at the Hessel Museum. A "video installation" by Bruce Nauman in which a man and a woman endlessly repeat a litany of nonsense, tinctured here and there with scatological phrases. Been there. Photographs (in four or five different places) by Robert Mapplethorpe of his S&M pals. Very 1980s. Histrionic photographs by Cindy Sherman of herself looking victimized. Been there, too. Nam June Paik and his video installations. Done that. A big pile of red, white, and blue lollipops dumped in the corner by . . . well, it doesn't much matter, does it? Any more than it matters who was responsible for the room featuring images of floating genitalia or the room with the video of ritualistic homosexual bondage. Ditto the catalogue: its assault on the English language is something you can find in scores, no, hundreds of art publications today: "For Valie Export, the female Body is covered with the stigmata of codes that shape and hamper it." Well, bully for her. "As usual with Gober, the installation is a broken allegory that both elicits and resists our interpretation; that materially nothing is quite as it seems adds to our anxious curiosity." As usual, indeed, though whether such pathetic verbiage adds to or smothers our curiosity is another matter altogether.

No, the thing to appreciate about "Wrestle," about the Hessel Museum and the collection of Marieluise Hessel, and about the visual arts at Bard generally is not how innovative, challenging, or unusual they are, but how pedestrian and, sad to say, conventional they are. True, there is a lot of ickiness on view at the Hessel Museum. But it is entirely predictable ickiness. It's outrage by-the-yard, avant-garde in bulk, smugness for the masses. And this brings me to what I believe is the real significance of institutions like the art museum at Bard, the Hessel collection that fills it, and the surrounding atmosphere of pseudo-avant-garde self-satisfaction. The "arts" at Bard are notable not because they are unusual but because they are so grindingly ordinary. Leon Botstein described Marieluise Hessel as a "risk giver." An essay in the *Bardian*, the college magazine, elaborates on this theme:

> She was drawn to work that challenged and subverted the status quo, work that flaunted [the author means "flouted," but, hey, this is Bard] and struggled with urgent, utopian notions of gender and identity, feminism, and the politics of AIDS, among other issues.

MR. BOTSTEIN and the *Bardian* have it exactly wrong. When it comes to art, Ms. Hessel is neither a risk taker nor a "risk giver." Like Bard itself, she simply mirrors the established taste of the moment. Far from "challenging" or "subverting" the status quo, the 1,700 objects she has accumulated *are* the status quo. And far from "struggling" with questions about gender or feminism or anything else, she has simply issued a rubber stamp endorsing the dominant clichés of today's academic art world. "Academic," in fact, is the *mot juste* for activities as a collector: not in the sense of "scholarly," but rather in the sense that we speak of "academic art," stale, conventional, aesthetically nugatory. A wall full of photographs of two girls does nothing to "interrogate" (a favorite term of art- and lit-crit-speak) identity any more than a mutilated doll forces us to reconsider our usual notions of whatever-it-is those odious objects are supposed to make us reconsider. Really, the only thing exhibitions like "Wrestle," or institutions like the Hessel Museum, challenge is the viewer's patience.

Ms. Hessel once enthusiastically recalled her introduction to contemporary art as a young woman in Munich: "It was like entering a cult group." That cult has long since become the new Salon where the canons of accepted taste are enforced with a rigidity that would have made Bouguereau jealous. The only difference is that instead of a pedantic mastery of perspective and modeling we have a pedantic mastery of all the accepted attitudes about race, class, sex, and politics. Since skill is no longer necessary to practice art successfully, the only things left are 1) appropriate subject matter (paradoxically, the more inappropriate the better) and 2) the right politics.

Again, my point is not to deny the repellent nature of much that was on view in "Wrestle." It deserves its "X" rating, all right. But it has been a long time since shock value had the capacity to be aesthetically interesting—or even, truth be told, to shock. Decades ago, writing about Salvador Dalí, George Orwell called attention to, and criticized, the growing habit of granting a blanket moral indemnity to anything that called itself art. "The artist," Orwell wrote,

> is to be exempt from the moral laws that are binding on ordinary people. Just pronounce the magic word "Art," and everything is O.K. Rotting corpses with snails crawling over them are O.K.; kicking little girls in the head is O.K.; even a film like *L'Age d'Or* [which shows among other things detailed shots of a woman defecating] is O.K.

Orwell was writing in the 1940s. Already that attitude was old hat: it had definitively entered the cultural bloodstream with the Dadaists shortly after the turn of the last century. What those folks didn't know about "challenging" and "subverting" conventional taste and attitudes wasn't worth knowing. In essentials, they pioneered all the tricks on view in "Wrestle"—the sex, the violence, the tedium, the presentation of everyday objects as works of art. The difference is that Duchamp was in earnest: "I threw the bottle rack and the urinal into to their faces as a challenge," Duchamp noted contemptuously, "and now they admire them for their aesthetic beauty."

No wonder he gave up on art for chess. Duchamp mounted a campaign against art and aesthetic delectation. In one sense, he succeeded brilliantly. Only the campaign backfired.

Once the aloof and brittle irony of Duchamp institutionalized itself and became the coin of the realm, it descended
from irony to a new form of sentimentality. I do not have
much time for Marcel Duchamp; in my view his influence
on art and culture has been almost entirely baneful; but it
is amusing to ponder how much he would have loathed
the contemporary art world where all his ideas had been
ground-down into inescapable clichés, trite formulas served
up by society grandees at their expensive art fêtes in the mistaken belief that they are embarked on some existentially or
aesthetically daring enterprise. Perhaps Duchamp, aesthete
that he was, would have savored the comedy. I suspect his
amour-propre would have caused him to feel nausea, not
amusement.

Why is the art world a disaster? The prevalence of exhibitions like "Wrestle," of collectors like Marieluise Hessel, of
institutions like the Hessel Museum and Bard College help
us begin to answer that question. Their very ordinariness
enhances their value as symptoms. In part, the art world is
a disaster because of that ordinariness: because of the popu-
larization and institutionalization of the antics and attitudes
of Dada. As W. S. Gilbert knew, when everybody's some-
body, nobody's anybody. When the outré attitudes of a tiny
elite go mainstream, only the rhetoric, not the substance, of
the drama survives.

That's part of the answer: the domestication, the normalization, of deviance, and its subsequent elevation as an
object of aesthetic—well, not delectation, exactly: perhaps
veneration would be closer to the truth. But that is only part
of the puzzle.

There are at least three other elements at work. One is the
unholy alliance between the more rebarbative and hermetic
precincts of academic activity and the practice of art. As
even a glance at the preposterous catalogue accompanying

"Wrestle"—accompanying almost any trendy exhibition these days—demonstrates, art is increasingly the creature of its explication. It's not quite what Tom Wolfe predicted in *The Painted Word* (1975), where in the gallery-of-the-future a postcard-sized photograph of a painting would be used to illustrate a passage of criticism blown up to the size of its inflated sense of self-worth. The difference is that the new verbiage doesn't even pretend to be art criticism. It occupies a curious no man's land between criticism, political activism, and pseudo-philosophical speculation: less an intellectual than a linguistic phenomenon, speaking more to the failure or decay of ideas than to their elaboration. Increasingly, the "art" is indistinguishable from the verbal noise that accompanies it, as witness the little red band that surrounded the catalogue for "Wrestle." This "work" was by Lawrence Weiner and read: "An Amount of Currency Exchanged from One Country to Another." The point to notice is the usurpation of art by these free-floating verbal clots, full of emotion but utterly lacking in what David Hume called "the calm sunshine of the mind."

A SECOND ELEMENT that helps to explain why the art world is a disaster is money—not just the staggering prices routinely fetched by celebrity artists today, but the bucket-loads of cash that seem to surround almost any enterprise that can manage to get itself recognized as having to do with "the arts." The presence of money means the presence of "society," which goes a long way toward explaining why yesterday's philistine is today's champion of anything and everything that presents itself as art, no matter how repulsive it may be. If tout le monde is going to an opening for Matthew Barney at the Guggenheim, you can bet your bottom black tie that the nice lady next door who gave MOMA $10 million will be there, too. The vast infusion of money into the art world in recent decades has done an immense amount to facilitate what Hilton Kramer aptly called "the revenge of the philistines."

A third additional element in this sorry story has to do with the decoupling of art-world practice from the practice of art. Ponder the objects that were on view in "Wrestle": almost none has anything to do with art as traditionally understood: mastery of a craft in order to make objects that gratify and ennoble those who see them. On the contrary, the art world has wholeheartedly embraced art as an exercise in political sermonizing and anti-humanistic persiflage, which has assured the increasing trivialization of the practice of art. The object is to assault the viewer, not please him. For those who cherish art as an ally to civilization, the disaster that is today's art world is nothing less than a tragedy. But this, too, will pass. Sooner or later, even the Leon Botsteins and Marieluise Hessels of the world will realize that the character in Bruce Nauman's "Good Boy, Bad Boy" was right: "this is boring."

Architecture & Ideology

"The problem of architecture as I see it . . . is the problem
of all art—the elimination of the human element from the
consideration of form."
—Professor Otto Silenus, in Evelyn Waugh's *Decline and Fall*

This meticulous observance of "pure styles" is a mark
of failing energy in imagination; it is a mark, also, of an
inadequacy in thought: of a failure to define the nature of
style in general. We cling in architecture to the pedantries
of humanism, because we do not grasp the bearing upon
architecture of the humanist ideal.
—Geoffrey Scott, *The Architecture of Humanism*

I WAS DELIGHTED to learn that my presence at a Yale symposium about the American architect Peter Eisenman and
the Luxembourg-born architect Léon Krier was to be under the aegis of my late friend Brendan Gill. Brendan was
a distinguished alumnus of Yale—I trust other alumni will
forgive that pleonasm—and he was also widely admired as
a keen, lively writer about architecture for *The New Yorker*.

Brendan was a merry soul. It is pleasing to speculate about
what his reaction would have been to the news that Robert
A. M. Stern, the Dean of the School of Architecture, had decided not only to ask me to introduce this symposium, but

also to denominate me, if but momentarily, the Brendan Gill Lecturer. I suspect that his response would have been one of amusement—spiced, perhaps, with a soupçon of anxiety.

Since I happened to be in New Haven while this exhibition of Mr. Eisenman's and Mr. Krier's work from the 1970s and 1980s was being installed, I took advantage of the coincidence to get a glimpse of the exhibition as it went up. It is one of the privileges of being a critic that one often has the opportunity to drop in as an exhibition is being mounted. There is always a certain excitement, a certain freshness, about seeing an exhibition in this state of morning dishabille, as it were. The bustle of technicians fixing labels, touching up the paint, making some late decisions about exactly how that last row of pictures should be hung is somehow more energizing than distracting. It's like a glimpse backstage at a theatrical performance, which to my mind tends rather to enhance than dissipate the magic of the performance.

I thought about Brendan as I picked my way gingerly among the ladders, drills, track-lighting, and masking tape. I wish that he could have accompanied me. He would, I think, have had a smile for the images on the wall and a twinkle in his eye for the symposium as a whole. Brendan liked handsome pictures, and he had a healthy appetite for incongruity. He would not have been disappointed on either score.

The welcoming image in the exhibition is a copy of one of Mr. Krier's classical fantasies. It is a sort of acropolis populated by friends and patrons besporting themselves in contemporary garb: Puvis de Chavannes with couture by Ralph Lauren, sets by Winckelmann. It would, I think, have brought Brendan up short. "Do you suppose it is meant seriously?" he might have whispered, amusement once again competing with anxiety.

Now, Brendan liked his bit of kitsch as much as the next chap, but he preferred it light and gently self-mocking. There is a mocking quality to some of the images on view in this exhibition; there is certainly a mocking quality in some of the architectural visions that the exhibition represents; but it is a mockery directed outward, toward the viewer, toward the public, not inward toward the maker. The great social theorist Phineas Taylor Barnum is alleged to have remarked that "There's a sucker born every minute." Although a proof of this proposition awaits definitive formulation, "Eisenman, Krier: Two Ideologies" deserves an honored place in the annals of corroborative incident.

Still, there are a lot of fetching images on view in this exhibition. Mr. Krier is more than an accomplished architectural draftsman: he is a brilliantly evocative artist whose classicizing fantasies are a delight to the eye and a spur to the imagination. His drawings are something more—something other, at any rate—than attractive building instructions or architectural elevations. They are tranquil portraits of—I was going to say of a vanished world, but perhaps it would be more accurate to say that they are reconstructions of a world that never quite existed, indeed that never could exist, but whose beauty, whose seductiveness, lies precisely in that mixture of impossibility and exquisite delineation.

Mr. Eisenman of course does not go in much for seducing his viewers—not, anyway, with promises of any normal gratification. But considered simply as drawings—that is, considered apart from any alleged connection with the art of architecture—the plans and sketches for the unbuilt "House IV" possess their own beauty and fascination. It is naturally a very different sort of fascination from that exerted by Mr. Krier's drawings. They are cooler, less sumptuous, less immediately welcoming than Mr. Krier's classical essays. They bear the stamp not of an artist's hand but of a puzzle-maker's ingenuity, and they do this by design. Mr. Krier elaborates a way of life; Mr. Eisenman analyzes—or seems to analyze—a geometry. His drawings are fiercely, indeed ostentatiously, cerebral. It is, from one point of view, good fun and, it should be acknowledged, Mr. Eisenman expresses his vision with considerable elegance. A cube is presented; it is bisected; it is hollowed out; the cube is rotated; inverted; elaborated and transformed by a series of algorithms. This prodigy, Mr. Eisenman tells us, is a house. Some people believe him. He says "House IV" is "an attempt to alienate the individual from the known way in which he perceives and understands his environment." Rich Canadians stand in awe and shovel money his way. Universities appoint him to the faculty. Learned seminars are devoted to dissecting his importance. How it would have gratified Mr. Barnum.

Alice Roosevelt Longworth famously said that "If you can't say something good about someone, sit right here by me." I confess that I have always harbored a sneaking fondness for Alice. But by and large Brendan belonged to the opposite school. He tended to look on the bright side. He much preferred liking things to disliking them. I have no doubt that he would have found a good deal to like in "Eisenman, Krier: Two Ideologies." In purely visual terms there is a good deal to like. But I suspect that, like me, he would have greeted the proposition that this was an exhibition whose chief concern was with architecture with a certain scepticism.

Why the scepticism? I believe that the subtitle of this symposium—"Two Ideologies"—may have a useful clue to at least part of the answer. It is, I think, a spectacularly apt subtitle. For with these two architects we really are dealing not simply with radically different approaches to architecture but with two opposing ideologies.

The literature accompanying this symposium suggests that the planners were interested chiefly in exploring that opposition—exploring, that is to say, the discontinuities that define Mr. Eisenman's and Mr. Krier's relationship to the tradition of modernism and to each other. I will have something to say about that in due course. First I invite you to ponder what it might mean to say that an architect espouses an ideology.

Of course architects, like lesser mortals, might espouse or exhibit an ideology in their capacity as individual political agents. But what does it mean to say that an architect, considered in his capacity as an architect, espouses an ideology? Think about it: Did Brunelleschi have an ideology? Did Alberti? Did Stanford White? They certainly had opinions about what made good architecture: they embraced some things and disparaged others. But having an opinion is not the same thing as espousing an architectural ideology.

MODERNISM was notoriously an architecture that never left home without a manifesto, and doubtless some practitioners of modernist architecture would count as ideological architects. Or one might point to Albert Speer whose grandiose neo-classicism was self-consciously put in the service of an ideology. It is perhaps significant in this context that Mr. Krier has had some admiring things to say about Speer's architecture—not, I hasten to add, because of its association with the Nazis but because of its effort to revivify, in hypertrophied form, a certain version of neo-classicism.

But what, to step back for a moment, is an ideology? We live at a time when we are regularly assured that "everything is political," that everyone and everything has an ideology, that no point of view is "innocent," that "truth" is merely an honorific conferred by power, and so forth. But let's leave that self-contradictory, mind-numbing lit.-crit.-shtick to one side. It doesn't bring us any closer to understanding the title "Eisenman, Krier: Two Ideologies."

The word *idéologie* seems to have been coined by the French nobleman Destutt de Tracy in 1796. Destutt, a follower of the materialist philosopher Condillac, had set out to describe the process by which ideas came to consciousness. He was a sort of proto-sociologist. But although the word, like so many dubious intellectual imports, is of French origin, it did not acquire its full quota of owlishness until it was adopted and groomed by the Germans. Marx and Engels did more than anyone to popularize the term. It was while at school with the Marxists that the word "ideology" turned nasty and developed teeth. Characteristically, the word acquired a dual meaning: overtly, it was just a fancy term for describing someone's world view, but by insinuation it also cast a negative penumbra, a suggestion of rigidity or "false-consciousness," as the Marxists say. More and more, "an ideology" was understood to describe an unfortunate piece of mental—and even moral—baggage that one's opponents labored under but which did not much bother right-thinking—by which I mean Left-leaning—souls.

The word "ideology" has never quite lost its Marxist accent; it continues to carry with it the hint of subterranean forces at work—forces that only the initiated are in a position to discern and emancipate themselves from. Indeed, that aura of impermeable knowingness is an important reason that "ideology" is such a popular word in the academy. Still, continual use has smoothed some of its rough edges. One can thus have a title like "Eisenman/Krier: Two Ideologies" without people thinking you are being rude.

In *The Origins of Totalitarianism*, Hannah Arendt observes that an ideology differs from a simple opinion in that an ideology claims to possess "the key to history" or "intimate knowledge" of "hidden universal laws." Dilute this a bit further and you wind up with ideology in the sense we have it here: "Eisenman/Krier: Two Ideologies"—that is, two efforts to recast architecture on the basis of a specialized program or agenda that takes its cue as much from extra-architectural considerations as from architectural ones.

What is the nature of those programs or agendas? In the case of Mr. Eisenman, I believe, it revolves largely around an ambition to uncover a hitherto concealed "essence" of architecture. In the case of Mr. Krier—at least in his work during the years that this symposium focuses on—the ideology revolves around an attempt to redefine architecture as a sort of classicizing mythopoesis or mythmaking.

LET's START with Mr. Eisenman. "House IV" is one of six similarly abstract houses that he designed in the 1960s and 1970s. The fact that they are known only by Roman numerals adds to their forbidding aura. A book called *Houses of Cards*, published in the late 1980s, is devoted to these works. In an essay he published in this volume, Mr. Eisenman writes that "the essence of the act of architecture is the dislocation of an ever-reconstituting metaphysic of architecture."

In case that was unclear, Mr. Eisenman goes on to explain that the designs for the six houses were all "governed by the intent to define the act of architecture as the dislocation of consequent reconstitution of an ever-accruing metaphysic of architecture."

At this stage of his career, anyway, Mr. Eisenman was very fond of the word "metaphysic." In the course of his essay, readers are introduced not only to the "metaphysic of architecture" but also to the "metaphysic of the center," the "metaphysic of the house," even the "metaphysic of dining."

It would, I think, be a mistake to regard such formidable phrases as extraneous verbal curlicues. The point is that experience of Peter Eisenman's architecture is partly a rhetorical experience. Architecture is not itself a verbal medium, as Mr. Eisenman sometimes pretends, but his own architectural efforts are incomplete without the accompanying text. When we encounter a stairway that leads nowhere, as we do at the Wexner Arts Center in Columbus, Ohio, we need his help to understand that we are being given a lesson in linguistic futility. Otherwise we might foolishly conclude that it was just a stairway that led nowhere and wonder about the sanity of the chap who paid the architect's bill.

Mr. Eisenman was once a recherché taste. But he has, in recent years, become something of a celebrity, and so his little lessons have become quite familiar. For the benefit of those who have not experienced his act, however, I feel I should provide at least one full-fledged example. Regarding the "metaphysic of dining," Mr. Eisenman tells us that "House III" and "House IV" explore

> an alternative process of making occupiable form, . . . a process specifically developed to operate as freely as possible from functional considerations. From a traditional point of view, several columns "intrude on" and "disrupt" the living and dining areas as a result of this process. . . . Nonetheless, these dislocations . . . have, according to the occupants of the house, changed the dining experience in a real and, more importantly, unpredictable fashion.

Being of a charitable disposition, I do not propose to analyze this passage. Instead, I present it as an artwork in its own right, something that is better admired for its autonomous beauty than picked over for its meaning. Such passages are best regarded as rhetorical adjuncts of Mr. Eisenman's drawings and buildings: frames without whose support his work could not even appear to us *as* architecture. Still, it does seem worth noting that although the occupants of Mr.

Eisenman's houses may have found that his provocatively placed columns have changed—even changed "unpredictably"—their experience of living and dining, Mr. Eisenman does not say that their experience was made any more pleasant. Far from it. One of the main goals of Mr. Eisenman's architecture is to subvert anything so bourgeois as comfort or intelligibility. As he puts it, his houses

> attempt to have little to do with the traditional and existing metaphysic of the house, the physical and psychological gratification associated with the traditional form of the house, . . . in order to initiate a search for those possibilities of dwelling that may have been repressed by that metaphysic.

With respect to leaving behind "physical and psychological gratification," I think we can judge Mr. Eisenman's houses an unqualified success. As for "dwelling"—well, the word has a gratifying Heideggerian ring to it. But what about the "repressed possibilities" of dwelling? Could it be that there are some things that should be repressed? Might it be the case that, if there are such things as repressed possibilities of dwelling, it is to our benefit that they *stay* repressed? I suppose it could be said that Mr. Eisenman exposed one repressed possibility of dwelling when he left a few holes in the second-story floor of one of his houses. In that case, one repressed possibility was a broken leg or a broken neck, and the occupants of the house, as we read in an article about Mr. Eisenman in *The New York Times*, quickly saw to it that this "possibility of dwelling" was firmly re-repressed through the expediency of some metal grates fitted over the holes.

LET US TURN NOW to Mr. Krier. At first blush, he seems to present a kinder, gentler face to the world than Mr. Eisenman. At least, it is a less cerebral face. Mr. Krier's stairways lead somewhere, his floors are solid, his façades have the pleasing aspect of old friends. He offers a Masterpiece-Theatre sort of coziness: stately homes, lots of pillars and classical cornices, and one assumes that the servant problem is well under control. If Peter Eisenman is engaged in a search for the essence of architecture, Mr. Krier is engaged in a search for its Arcady, a dreamy version of its idealized form.

Although the portion of the Yale exhibition devoted to Mr. Krier's work is centered on The Atlantis Project, an unbuilt, classically decorated retreat for artists and intellectuals, it includes a wide range of drawings by Mr. Krier. Most pertain to unbuilt projects. Of course, many visionary architects have specialized in unbuilt projects: one thinks of Ledoux, Boulée, Piranesi, and others. Furnishing the imagination with possibilities—even, if I may so put it, impossible possibilities—has been a fertile source of architectural activity since the Tower of Babel—or perhaps even the bowers populating the Garden of Eden. Still, Mr. Krier embraces the unbuilt with a special passion.

A COMMON THREAD running through many of his projects is rejection: rejection not only of modernist architecture but of modern reality. It's a small-is-beautiful, natural materials, brown-rice, and no-curtain-wall sort of philosophy—attractive to elites who can afford to dream those dreams and why not? Some twenty years ago, Mr. Krier famously summed up this ethic of rejection when he declared: "A responsible architect cannot possibly build today. . . . Building can only mean a greater or smaller degree of collaboration in a civilized society's process of self-destruction." Mr. Krier has apparently repudiated that statement. Nevertheless, it underscores a permanent temptation to which his approach to architecture is susceptible. Nor was that statement a solitary aberration. "I can only make Architecture," he said in another manifesto-like statement from the 1970s, "because I do not build. I do not build because I am an Architect."

With those declarations in mind, it is interesting to consider the developments that Mr. Krier collaborated on in Seaside, Florida, and Poundbury, England: do such New Urbanist experiments count as upper-case-A Architecture, lower-case-a architecture, or something else entirely? And what about Mr. Krier? Was he an upper-case-A or lower-case-a architect while he was working on those projects? Maybe he wasn't an architect at all, but something else entirely? And here's a further worry: if only those who do *not* build can make Architecture, what about those who *have built*? Can they go back to being upper-case-A Architects after a certain period of abstinence? Or is being an upper-case-A Architect like virginity: a quality that, once lost, is gone forever?

I do not pretend to know the answers to these questions. But I raise them because I think they point to an element in Léon Krier's work that has not perhaps been sufficiently noticed. Mr. Krier has often been described as an historicist; he is that. But he is an historicist with a powerful commitment to purity, to an idealism that is moral as much as architectural. Throughout Mr. Krier's work there is a conscious effort to evoke a more humanized future by reimagining the past. Mr. Krier dislikes the word "utopian." But there is a reason that one finds it cropping up so often in discussions of his work. In the face of an unsatisfactory reality—a reality populated by ugly buildings, too many people, and pollution: in other words, our reality—he composes highly personal versions of tradition that seek more to liberate the imagination than to describe a definite task. One attractive side of this vision is to be found in all those pretty pictures of classically faced buildings. I have not myself been to Seaside or Poundbury, but I am willing to believe that those boutique showpieces are plenty *mignon*, too.

But in fact those developments represent Mr. Krier in a conciliatory, compromising mood. And according to some reports, he was not at all happy with the results at Poundbury: too many concessions to vulgarity. In any event, more typical—more typical of the work highlighted by this symposium, anyway—are fantasies like The Atlantis Project or his plan to scratch Washington, D.C. and turn it into four Georgetown-sized villages in which pedestrian traffic would be moderated by such expedients as flooding the Washington Mall.

If there seems to be a touch of megalomania about such projects, well, Mr. Krier once spoke of facing up to "the colossal and almost inhuman task of global ecological reconstruction." Around the same time, he also remarked that the criterion for his work is contained in a question: "If I had to design the whole world, what would I do?" This was a contingency that Mr. Krier, only half-jokingly, described as "not improbable."

I HAVE REHEARSED what I take to be certain central aspects of Mr. Eisenman's ideology and Mr. Krier's ideology in order to delineate the basic shape or thrust of their architectural vision. I have left a lot out of account. For example, there are other aspects to Mr. Eisenman's activity besides the search for the essence of architecture. A sceptical observer, noting such things as the holes in the floors of his house, the small windows at ankle level in offices he designed, the stairways that go nowhere, the plans he offered for Ground Zero after 9/11 that included offices buildings that looked like half-squashed paper bags, might wonder whether Mr. Eisenman was really in earnest.

Years ago, Philip Johnson extolled postmodernism for having insinuated "the giggle" into architecture. Is it possible that Mr. Eisenman—who after all is a late beneficiary of

Philip Johnson's activities as an architectural impresario—is it possible that he, too, is a giggle-making postmodernist? Only, having found the all slots for cheerful historical pastiche occupied, he took the next best opening and specialized in angry-looking send-ups of Corbusier and Terragni? Is Mr. Eisenman, too, in the business of purveying architectural spoofs? Perhaps, like other sensible people, he knows deep down that Jacques Derrida is a French fog-making-machine whose opinions about language and architecture are no less risible than they are mystifying? I do not know the answer to these questions but I mention them as possibilities worth considering.

Mr. Krier is a bit harder to get in focus. Having started his professional life as a disciple of James Stirling, he seems to have vacillated between the role of architectural gadfly or prophet—"Repent! The end of the curtain wall is nigh!"—and the role of pragmatic urban planner who is trying to get the Prince of Wales's business done.

It was one of the assumptions of the Yale symposium that in the 1970s and 1980s Mr. Eisenman and Mr. Krier were both, in their disparate ways, reacting against modernism. Maybe they were. But I am not sure how illuminating that observation is. I mean, at least since Robert Venturi inverted Mies van der Rohe and proclaimed the gospel of "Less is a bore," elite architects have been hopping onto the anti-modernist bandwagon faster than you can say Colin Rowe. And some of them have done hugely attractive work.

But Mr. Eisenman and Mr. Krier stand out or stand apart from most anti-modernist architects, and so I am not sure how instructive it would be to explore their "dissimilar perceptions of history," as the program for the Yale symposium invited us to do.

How else can we understand their activity? One possibly fruitful parallel that occurred to me comes from the world of ethology, of animal behavior. Readers of Konrad Lorenz's fascinating books on the subject will remember his discussion of what he calls a "vacuum activity." A vacuum activity is instinctual behavior that occurs when an animal, deprived of its normal surroundings and objects, nevertheless "goes through the motions" of some activity typical of its species. Lorenz provides several examples from the bird kingdom. Many city dwellers who own dogs will have witnessed another example. Long deprived of bones and dirt, a city-living dog will pretend to bury a nonexistent bone in nonexistent dirt in the corner of a room. Burying bones is instinctive behavior for dogs, and a bone-less, dirt-less life is just not to be borne. After a certain period of time sans bones and sans dirt, this behavior "discharges" itself, in Lorenz's term, and we find Fido pawing earnestly at the carpet in the corner of the living room.

I wonder whether the intriguing concept of a vacuum activity sheds some light on the relevant work of Mr. Eisenman and Mr. Krier. After all, much of what we were presented with in this exhibition was unbuilt—surely a frustrating contingency for men whose profession is building things. Just as a dog "buries" a nonexistent "bone," so Mr. Eisenman "designs" a "house" and Mr. Krier "plans" a fantasy-island hideaway.

I am sorry that we cannot engage Konrad Lorenz as a consultant in this case. I suspect he might discover some useful extensions to his idea of a vacuum activity. Is there, for example, such a thing as a half-vacuum activity—just a bit of air hissing in—in which, for example, a dog has a bone but no dirt, or an architect builds a house that turns out to be uninhabitable? I do not know. It is a question that demands more research, and probably a government grant. I cannot help thinking that the idea of the vacuum activity may be illuminating for architectural ideologies in which futility is budgeted in as either a basic design element or as a necessary adjunct of its impracticality.

The issue of futility brings me—a bit late admittedly—to my own title. I've settled here on "Architecture & Ideology." Originally, though, I had something more baroque. When I accepted Dean Stern's invitation to participate in the Yale symposium, he instantly asked for a title for my remarks. After a bit of cogitation, I wrote back and offered "Is There Architecture After Modernism?" I thought that might be appropriate for a discussion of work that is not only self-consciously anti-modernist but that also raises the question of the future of architecture, in one instance by subverting traditional architectural practice, in the other by fetishizing it. As an afterthought, I told Dean Stern that I'd considered proposing, in deference to Mr. Eisenman, something like—please note the parentheses—"(Re)positioning Architecture: (Post)modernism, (Re)presentation, and the Discourses of (Dis)play." Dean Stern replied that he favored the longer title—it was, he suggested, "more provocative." I saw his point. "Is There Architecture After Modernism?" is moderately provocative because it raises the possibility that there isn't any architecture after modernism, which is clearly absurd. But the longer title has the advantage of total unintelligibility, which I know is in some circles a powerful recommendation.

Still, that original title was not merely flippant. The first bit poses what I think is a serious question. My answer to the question is "No, there isn't architecture after modernism—if by 'modernism' we understand not a certain denuded style of building but rather the social, economic, and political givens of contemporary life." Various English statesmen, from Gladstone to Sir William Harcourt, have been credited with the observation that "We are all socialists now." Alas, you might say—well, I would say "alas." But there it is. That is simply a statement of how things are. You might lament it but you cannot change it.

Similarly, there is an important sense in which we are all modernists now, Mr. Krier as much as Gordon Bunshaft. It doesn't matter whether you favor curtain walls or Corinthian columns, jeweled concrete or cedar shakes. The issue is not modernism or anti-modernism but good architecture versus bad architecture. If the architecture we have been accustomed to calling modernist errs in the direction of severity and hyper-rationalism, much of the architecture that has arisen to challenge it has erred in the direction of silliness, grim or fatuous as the case may be.

Which is worse? Stock in the modernist enterprise has been unnaturally depressed for some time now, and so it is worth reminding ourselves that there are plenty of great modernist success stories—the Yale Art Gallery by Louis Kahn, for example, or the Yale Center for British Art, its younger cousin across the street.

I BELIEVE THAT if we are to get a fruitful perspective on the opposition named in the title "Eisenman/Krier: Two Ideologies," we need to put that opposition in a wider context. One way of doing that allows me to introduce the hero of this lecture, the English architect and architectural historian Geoffrey Scott. Most people interested in architecture will know of Scott. He is the author of a deservedly famous book. *The Architecture of Humanism* was first published in 1914 and instantly attained the status of a classic. I bring up *The Architecture of Humanism* because, although it is in one sense well known, its fundamental messages seem to have been forgotten. It is the old story of familiarity breeding, if not contempt, exactly, then at least neglect.

It might seem odd to introduce Geoffrey Scott into a discussion of work by Peter Eisenman and Léon Krier. After all, the ostensible subject of *The Architecture of Humanism* is Renaissance architecture. But Scott's subtitle—"A Study in the History of Taste"—points to the book's larger purview. Although its subject is Renaissance architecture, its pertinence extends to the practice and appreciation of architecture generally.

Scott has two sets of lessons for us. The first revolves around his distillation of Vitruvius's principles of architecture. Vitruvius had a clutch of seven or eight; Scott, quoting the Renaissance poet Henry Wotton, boils them down to three: Commodity, Firmness, and Delight—or as we might put it, comfort and serviceability, craftsmanship and solidity, and beauty. These are the principles that must be observed in order to achieve what Wotton called "well-building."

Scott's second set of lessons revolves around the series of "fallacies" he enumerates. Especially important in this context are the Romantic Fallacy, whose most typical form, Scott tells us, is "the cult of the extinct," and the fallacies detailed in a chapter called "The Academic Tradition." Scott was himself an apostle of traditional architectural order. But he noted that, although order is a good, it is not by itself sufficient for good architecture. "Many of the ugliest patterns and most joyless buildings," he wrote, "possess order in a high degree; they exhibit fixed and evident ratios of design." But because they lack the animating leaven of taste, they fail.

What is the gravamen of taste? In a word, it is the body. Again and again Scott came back to the importance of the human body as the indispensable measure in architecture. The needs and dispositions of the human spirit incarnate— which means both a body in space and a body registering, contemplating space—provide the measure of that bedrock architectural value, the appropriate.

Scott speaks partly as an historian of architecture, partly as a custodian of the humanist values that were articulated with luxurious richness in Renaissance architecture. Which is why the lasting value of his book is not as an antiquarian relic but as an ever contemporary inspiration. The humanist values for which Scott enlists architecture are as pertinent today as they were in 1914—or, for that matter, 1419. All of us have heard trendy architects and their apologists natter on about Michel Foucault, the advent of the "post-human," and the impossibility of coherence or stability. But that is the twittering of sterility and exhaustion. As Scott noted,

> space affects us and can control our spirit. . . . The architect models in space as a sculptor in clay. He designs his space as a work of art; that is, he attempt through its means to excite a certain mood in those who enter it.

That is as true for us as it was for Brunelleschi or Alberti. And like them, we too possess what Scott calls "the humanist instinct," which "looks in the world for physical conditions that are related to our own, for movements which are like those we enjoy, for resistances that resemble those that can support us, for a setting where we should be neither lost nor thwarted."

Catering to that "humanist instinct" in the medium of space is the vocation of architecture. There is an aesthetic component to this project: a component satisfied in the pleasing arrangement of masses, lines, shadows, and spaces. But the essential neediness and incompleteness of the human condition guarantees that architecture can never be judged by aesthetic criteria alone. "Architecture," as Scott put it, "is subservient to the general uses of mankind." We approach architecture with what Scott, echoing the famous Kantian formula, calls a "disinterested desire for beauty," but this desire is tethered by continual reference to the quotidian inventory of physical, psychological, and social imperatives.

If we compare Scott's humanism with the ideologies of Mr. Eisenman and Mr. Krier, we may distill several principles or, if that seems too grand a term, several admonitions. One is what I like to refer to as the Amis principle, after the British novelist Kingsley Amis. It reads: "Nice things are nicer than nasty ones." A simple principle, that—but consider how often it has been forgotten or indeed deliberately sabotaged by people who believe that notoriety can successfully substitute for genuine artistic accomplishment.

This leads naturally to my second admonition, which I take from Alberti: "Never let greed for glory," Alberti says at the end of Book 9 of *On Architecture*, "impel you to embark rashly on anything that is unusual or without precedent." That is a sentiment that might profitably be chiseled into the lintel over the entrance of Paul Rudolph's Art and Architecture Building at Yale.

The third admonition concerns what we might call the "pudding test": architecture must be not only looked at but lived with, indeed lived in, and so what works marvelously on paper may fail utterly on the street. The proof of architecture is concrete, not abstract. Seductive theories do not necessarily produce gratifying buildings.

The fourth admonition concerns what we might call novelty architecture. When someone erects a hot dog stand in the shape of a giant hot dog, the result may be in bad taste— maybe comic bad taste—but no great harm is done. The problem is that more and more architecture is coming to resemble novelty architecture. I don't mean that architects are slavishly mimetic. But novelty architecture comes in several varieties. Is a building that allegedly illustrates linguistic vertigo any less preposterous than the hot dog stand? How about something that could have come from the set for *Ben Hur*? Novelty architecture has a place; even Geoffrey Scott would admit that, I think. Only we need to keep it in its place: roadside refectories, amusement parks, universities, and other retreats from the serious business of life.

THE LAST ADMONITION I will mention is perhaps the most important. It concerns the question of essence, the ambition to exhibit or explore "the essence of architecture"—as if a house stripped bare somehow revealed the inner reality of a house. It is one of the virtues of the humanist instinct to recognize that the human world is—*essentially* is, if you like—something more than a distillation of essences. It is, on the contrary, a world of appearances: of how things look and comport themselves. This is something that our culture, and our architecture, has largely lost sight of, to our very great diminishment. The philosopher Roger Scruton has dilated on this point in his writings about architecture. "There is," Scruton writes, "no greater error in the study of human things than to believe that the search for what is essential must lead us to what is hidden." Scruton is hardly an aesthete: indeed, he follows Ruskin in insisting that art and culture are "not detachable, in the last analysis, from piety." But part of that piety is acknowledging our deep submission to the superficial, to the realm of appearance. This is the profound wisdom contained in Oscar Wilde's apparently flippant remark that only a very shallow person does not judge by appearances.

There was a large retrospective, even autumnal, ingredient in Yale's celebration of work by Peter Eisenman and Léon Krier. We were invited to look back a couple of decades or more to explore the work of two energetic architects whose words and whose work helped set the agenda for important aspects of contemporary architectural theory and practice. It is, in all senses of the word, heady stuff, full of breath-taking ideas. My question: Are they, for all that, *good* ideas? Well, I will leave you all to answer that question—or to leave it unanswered if that course seems more expedient. Leaving it unanswered, I suspect, is what Brendan Gill would have done, if for no other reason than that he wanted to keep the fun of architecture going as long as possible.

Fun is nice. I like fun. But fun remains most fun when it keeps to its appropriate place. The ambition to transform all of life into a playground is a prescription for the ruin of fun. Brendan knew this, too, fortunately. I am convinced that he would have approved of my concluding quotation, from the nineteenth-century American historian William Hickling Prescott. "The surest test of the civilization of a people," Prescott wrote, ". . . is to be found in their architecture, which presents so noble a field for the display of the grand and the beautiful; and which, at the same time, is so intimately connected with the essential comforts of life." It's a lot to live up to. But the alternative is having a lot to live down.

Part Three

Friends of Humanity

*Bertie in particular sustained simultaneously a pair of
opinions ludicrously incompatible. He held that in fact
human affairs were carried on after a most irrational
fashion, but that the remedy was quite simple and easy,
since all we had to do was to carry them on rationally.*
—J. M. Keynes, on Bertrand Russell

*Oh, tell me, who first declared, who first proclaimed that
man only does nasty things because he does not know
his own real interests; and that if he were enlightened,
if his eyes were opened to his real normal interests, man
would at once cease to do nasty things, would at once
become good and noble because, being enlightened and
understanding his real advantage, he would see his own
advantage in the good and nothing else. . . . Oh, the babe!
Oh, the pure, innocent child!*
—F. Dostoevsky, *Notes from the Underground*

IN FEBRUARY OF 1793, a lapsed Presbyterian minister
named William Godwin published his *Enquiry Concerning
Political Justice*, an answer—so he believed—to the hitherto
intractable problem of human happiness. Overnight, this
plump compendium of Enlightened opinion transformed

Godwin, then in his late thirties, from an obscure scribbler of atheistic leanings into an international celebrity. Wherever advanced thinking flourished, there were Godwin and his wife, the feminist writer Mary Wollstonecraft, celebrated. "I was nowhere a stranger," he boasted to his diary, "I was received everywhere with curiosity and kindness"—not to mention (he might have added) worshipful adulation.

The following year, his didactic novel *Caleb Williams, or Things as They Are*—a fictionalized dramatization of the egalitarian ideas that fueled the Enquiry—seemingly cemented the fame. Godwin's many acolytes gleefully identified themselves as "Godwinites"; they began referring to "The Grand Master," "The Philosopher," an appellation formerly reserved for Aristotle. "No work in our time," Hazlitt wrote in 1815, looking back on the comet of Godwin's fame, "gave such a blow to the philosophical mind of the country [as did the *Enquiry*]. . . . Truth, moral truth, it was supposed, had here taken up its abode." Intellectuals and literary types were particularly susceptible. Robert Southey and Wordsworth enthused wildly over Godwin, as did Coleridge, who dedicated an "ardent lay" to the man who "Bade the bright form of Justice meet my way—/And told me that her name was HAPPINESS."

Of course, sudden intoxications have a way of turning crapulous without warning. Such was the fate awaiting the reputation of Godwin and his gospel. Published when the public's infatuation with the French revolutionary "experiment" was at high tide, Godwin's *Enquiry* formed a perfect obligato to the incessant clamorings for "liberty, equality, fraternity." It was just at that dawn when (said Wordsworth) it was "bliss . . . to be alive." Yes, well: tell it to Robespierre. Within a couple of years the Terror had translated the famous slogan into tyranny, usurpation, and panic. Then there was the war between England and France. Godwin's flame guttered as suddenly as it had ignited. Hazlitt, himself a one-time worshipper, mournfully registered the change: "no one was more talked of, more looked up to, more sought after. . . . Now he has sunk below the horizon, and enjoys the serene twilight of a doubtful immortality."

Like many, Hazlitt was more disappointed than disabused. Whatever eclipse Godwin suffered in the court of public opinion, his fame, Hazlitt thought, "can never die." If his eminence seemed "posthumous," it was with the venerable majesty that marks eternal intellectual monuments. In 1812, the nineteen-year-old Shelley, freshly rusticated from Oxford, showed that the *Enquiry* still had the power to ensorcell. He thrilled to Godwin's paeans on behalf of radical equality, the abolition of private property, the tyranny of marriage as only an aristocratic heir to an estate worth £6000 per annum (more than £300,000 today) could do.

For his part, Godwin was only too happy to avail himself of loans and gifts from his new disciple. Matters cooled markedly when Shelley ran off with Godwin's sixteen-year-old daughter Mary (the future author of *Frankenstein*) without first disencumbering himself of his wife, Harriet. Godwin refused to see them (though he graciously continued to accept Shelley's largess). Fortunately, Harriet soon obliged everyone by committing suicide. Before long Shelley had set up house for all involved, and Godwin was proudly writing friends that Mary was about to marry "the heir to a baronetcy."

The Shelley circus to one side, Hazlitt was right about the fate of Godwin's ideas. They suffered a temporary setback because of the Terror and the war with France: the rude intrusion of violence will do that to Enlightened moral ideas. But this was a matter of hibernation, not extinction. In many respects—in their overall drift if not in detail or rhetorical temperature—Godwin's ideas, with or without Godwin's name attached, continue to fire the imagination of . . . let's call them "idealists" or "Friends of Humanity" down to this day.

ALTHOUGH IT IS a work of nearly 800 pages in its modern editions, Godwin's *Enquiry* is nevertheless an impatient work—impatient, that is, about the human condition. Hazlitt said that Godwin's fault was "too much ambition. . . . He conceived too nobly of his fellows." That is one way of putting it. But the question remains whether such overestimation is a form of laudable generosity or culpable blindness.

Every philosophy has its master words and concepts. Chief among Godwin's is "benevolence." What his philosophy teaches, Godwin says, is a "system of disinterested benevolence." Hitherto "the whole structure of human society" has been "a system of the narrowest selfishness." That spirit of selfishness results above all from the institution of private property. Inherently, human beings are "formed to glow with benevolence." But laws, governments, institutions—all the apparatuses designed to protect and perpetuate private property and, hence, inequality—have dimmed the glow. Since "The Characters of Men Originate in Their External Circumstances" (as Godwin denominates one of his early sections), all we need to do is reform the "external circumstances" of society and, presto (or possibly allegro non troppo), men's characters will also improve. Sound familiar? Here is the crux: Abolish private property, and mankind, finally awakened to its true interests, will cease to plot and hoard and accumulate. The worker's paradise, Comrade, is just around the corner.

I know: it sounds . . . preposterous. It *is* preposterous. But I have provided the merest bald summary. Let Godwin put some flesh on the bones:

The spirit of oppression, the spirit of servility, and the spirit of fraud, these are the immediate growth of the established administration of property. They are alike hostile to intellectual improvement. The other vices of envy, malice, and revenge are their inseparable companions. In a state of society where men lived in the midst of plenty, and where all shared alike the bounty of nature, these sentiments would inevitably expire. The narrow principle of selfishness would vanish. No man obliged to guard his little store, or provide with anxiety and pain for his restless wants, each would lose his individual existence in the thought of the general good. No man would be an enemy to his neighbours, for they would have no subject of contention; and of consequence philanthropy would resume the empire which reason assigns her. Mind would be delivered from her perpetual anxiety about corporal support; and be free to expatiate in the field of thought which is congenial to her.

In other words, the *Enquiry* is, par excellence, an Enlightenment product: contemptuous of the past and its institutions, boundless in its optimism and faith in the transformative power of reason.

Godwin's attack on selfishness went deep. The institution of marriage, he points out, is only an extension of the institution of private property. It, too, is an unjust "monopoly." When it comes to relations between the sexes, Godwin says, reason tells us that "no ties ought to be imposed upon either party, preventing them from quitting the attachment, whenever their judgement directs them to quit it." (Unless, of course, his daughter Mary be involved.) Godwin pondered the matter and concluded that "The abolition of the present system of marriage appears to involve no evils." Any children, he thinks, will be cared for by the benevolence of individuals or society as a whole. And the issue of sexual passion and jealousy barely makes it onto his radar.

But "it may happen that other men will feel for her the same preference that I do."

> This will create no difficulty. We may all enjoy her conversation; her choice being declared, we shall all be wise enough to consider the sexual commerce as unessential to our regard. It is a mark of the extreme depravity of our present habits, that we are inclined to suppose the sexual commerce necessary to the advantages arising from the purest friendship.

It was next to this paragraph, it pains me to report, that a previous reader of a library copy of the *Enquiry* inscribed the indelicate objection "horseshit."

WE ALL FROWN on the defacement of library books. But the impulse in this instance is perhaps understandable. In any event, Godwin does not confine his speculations to mundane matters like property and marriage. In an (admittedly conjectural) appendix on "Health and the Prolongation of Human Life," he dilates on his belief in the "omnipotence of mind." It works like this: Cheerfulness, he argues, is a habit "peculiarly favorable to corporeal vigor"; "the surest source of cheerfulness is benevolence"; and since his philosophy taught benevolence for breakfast, as it were, one may look forward not simply to better health among Godwinites but to "a total extirpation of the infirmities of our nature." It is one version of mind over matter.

One might worry that greater longevity would lead to overpopulation. Not so. Men in the future "will probably cease to propagate," Godwin reasons, partly because people will live so long that the population won't need topping up often, partly because "One tendency of a cultivated and virtuous mind is to diminish our eagerness for the gratification of the senses."

True political justice is not just a matter of individual gratification, of course. As individual characters become increasingly benevolent, so will the character of society as a whole. Godwin admits that he is going a bit out on a limb here, but he speculates that there are many "other improvements" that "may be expected" when society finally catches up with his philosophy.

> There will be no war, no crimes, no administration of justice, as it is called, and no government. Beside this, there will be neither disease, anguish, melancholy, nor resentment. Every man will seek, with ineffable ardour, the good of all. . . . Men will see the progressive advancement of virtue and good, and feel that, if things occasionally happen contrary to their hopes, the miscarriage was a necessary part of that progress.

I hope you will agree that the historian Gertrude Himmelfarb exercised remarkable understatement when she described Godwin's political vision as "the utopia to end all utopias."

WHICH IS NOT, of course, to suggest that there were not other, equally fervent, Friends of Humanity competing with Godwin for that trophy. Consider, for example, Marie-Jean-Antoine-Nicolas Caritat, the Marquis de Condorcet (1743–1794). Condorcet, the philosopher Stuart Hampshire eulogized, was "a man of gentle and ardent disposition . . . with a passionate hatred of injustice . . . the type of the philosopher-reformer of his time." Indeed. Condorcet was a mathematician of some note, one of the "Encyclopedists" who gathered around Voltaire, a true son of the Enlightenment. He espoused (with some provisos) the cause of egalitarianism, abominated religion, and hoped to see the end of the French monarchy. While serving as a member of a sub-committee of the Committee of Public Safety, Condorcet voted against the proposed Jacobin constitution. He also voted against executing the king. These were tactical errors. Condorcet was a firm Friend of Humanity. But, as the philosopher David Stove observed, his opponents, who were "even firmer Friends of Humanity, outlawed him and hunted him down, and he died in prison in 1794." During the six months he was in hiding, Condorcet dashed off his most famous work, the *Sketch for a Historical Picture of the Progress of the Human Mind.* It was posthumously published, at government expense, in Year III, i.e., 1795.

It is not surprising that the Revolutionary government approved of Condorcet's work. The man himself might have been unsound, but his ideas—well, they speak for themselves. Most of the *Sketch* deals with the benighted past: "The Eighth Stage: From the invention of printing to the time when philosophy and the sciences shook off the yoke of authority"—that sort of thing. Condorcet does not really come into his own until he gets to the tenth and last "stage," which deals with "the future progress of the human mind."

Like Godwin, Condorcet foresaw all manner of glorious things awaiting humanity now that the "priests and despots" were on their way out. Enlightenment had dawned, was dawning, and inequality, both among nations and, to a large extent, among individuals, would soon be a thing of the past. "Already in Great Britain," Condorcet noted, "friends of humanity have set us an example" in their trade policies. He envisioned a number of things—state-funded pension programs, for example—which have duly materialized.

But free trade, pension schemes, and such were only the tip of the Enlightened Iceberg. Condorcet cherished "a hope that is almost a certainty" that the eradication of inequality would bring about "the absolute perfection of the human race" ("*perfectionnement même de l'espèce humaine*"). The triumph of Enlightenment principles, he said, will lead "almost every man" to cultivate the "habits of an active and enlightened benevolence" Like Godwin, again, Condorcet was an "externalist": he thought that the source of mankind's imperfections lay not in human nature but in the outward circumstances of society. Tidy up society and you can say goodbye to irritating things like selfishness. "What are we to expect," he asked,

> from the perfection of laws and public institutions . . . but the reconciliation, the identification of the interests of each with the interests of all? . . . Is there any vicious habit, any practice contrary to good faith, whose origin and first cause cannot be traced back to the legislation, the institutions, and prejudices of the country wherein this habit, this practice, this crime can be observed?

Sounds pretty up-to-date, doesn't it?

SINCE BAD THINGS are the fault of society, education is the solution to just about every evil. Godwin sounds pretty up-to-date in this regard as well. Education will lead to "the complete annihilation" of the age-old prejudices that nurtured the inequality of the sexes. A little more education and wars will disappear. Education will lead to the obliteration of national animosities "one by one." Advances in education will also result in a sort of scientific esperanto which will make "knowledge of the truth easy and error almost impossible," thus promoting even further the cause of equality. "We may conclude"—which is to say, Condorcet *does* conclude—"that the perfectibility of man is limitless" (*indéfinie*). Not content with longer life, better health, an end to infectious diseases, Condorcet ends with a Godwinian glimpse of the day when the philosopher will dwell in "an Elysium created by reason" and "death will be due only to extraordinary accidents or to the decay of the vital forces, and that ultimately the average span between birth and decay will have no assignable value."

There are many many possible responses to the Godwin-Condorcet version of human destiny. The Victorian critic Leslie Stephen touched on a few when, in an essay on Godwin's novels, he cited his subject's "frigid dogmatism" and "singular incapacity for even suspecting the humorous or fanciful aspects of life." He even allowed himself the phrase "superlative bore." But perhaps the most devastating response came from a studious, Cambridge-educated curate and professor named Thomas Robert Malthus. Malthus, whom we will meet again below in "What's Wrong With Benevolence," was well acquainted with the rosy, Enlightened view of human nature so vividly espoused by Godwin and Condorcet, among many others. Malthus's father had harbored similar views. Indeed, in 1766 he even endeavored to engage Rousseau, then visiting England, as the future tutor for his new-born son. A gracious providence intervened, but one wonders what Malthus and the paterfamilias of whole-wheat, "man-was-born-free" optimism would have made of each other.

Godwin and Condorcet saw splendid vistas opening up for humanity once it had dispensed with the albatross of religion, conventional morality, and private property. Malthus detected a few flies in the ointment. These he enumerated in *An Essay on the Principle of Population*, the first edition of which was published in 1798.

On Population became one of the most influential books of the nineteenth century. It had two additional distinctions. It was among the most reviled books of its era. It was—and is—also among the most widely misunderstood.

Malthus wrote *On Population* as an anti-utopian attack on Enlightenment optimism and the "systems of equality" (i.e., what we would call "socialism" or "communism") which that optimism promulgated. The subtitle of the first edition clarifies Malthus's intentions: Population "as it affects the future improvement of Society, with remarks on the speculation of Mr. Godwin, Mr. Condorcet, and other writers."

THERE ARE MANY ironies attached to the history and reception of *On Population*. One has to do with a persistent popular misunderstanding. Everyone learns about gloomy "Malthusian" prognostications in school. These involve warnings about the alleged difference between the rate at which the food supply and the population grow. Malthus is presented as the Jeremiah of overpopulation, even a covert advocate of contraception, warning that, unless humanity acts fast, it will over-breed and run out of food.

In fact, Malthus issued no such warnings. And he was certainly no advocate of birth control (a species of "vice" that he congregated under the heading of "improper arts"). What Malthus calls the "principle of population" was (in the philosopher David Stove's phrase) a "steady-state" theory. It holds that, for any body of organisms, the population is always at or near the limit of the food supply. At nature's table, Malthus says, all the places are always filled. Hence, to the extent that the equality heralded by Godwin, Condorcet, et al., was achieved, "distress for want of food would be constantly pressing on all mankind." The relative impoverishment of some would be replaced by the absolute impoverishment of all.

Malthus wrote *On Population* as a political tract. But a large part of its fame is due to its place in the history of biology. For it was the principle of population that gave Darwin and A. R. Wallace the mechanism that propelled the process of natural selection. *That* evolution occurred they knew from the fossil record and comparative anatomy. But by what means did it operate? What was the motor? This is where the principle of population came in. In his autobiography, Darwin recalls reading Malthus in 1838. "It at once struck me that under these circumstances favorable variations would tend to be preserved, and unfavorable ones to be destroyed. The result of this would be the formation of new species. Here, then, I had at last got a theory by which to work."

The principle of population was an essential part of what is perhaps the most successful biological theory ever formulated. It is a further irony, then, that the principle is not true, at least as regards human beings. It deserved, and received, criticism from many quarters. For one thing, Malthus contrasts the rate at which population increases with the rate at which food increases; but his theory ignores the fact that food consists of organic populations, i.e., stuff that according to his principle is also supposed to increase "arithmetically." In later editions of his book, Malthus so modified what he said about the principle of population that he abandoned it in fact if not in words.

What he did not abandon was his hostility to the utopian theories formulated by Godwin, Condorcet, and other champions of Enlightenment. At the center of those theories is the cheery conviction that mankind is essentially rational, benevolent, and self-sacrificing. In the abstract, it is a gratifying picture; the problem is reality: human beings are not like that. As Malthus observes, "The substitution of benevolence, as the master-spring and moving principle of society, instead of self-love, appears at first sight to be a consummation devoutly to be wished. . . . But alas! That moment can never arrive." On the contrary, the exaltation of benevolence is a prescription for misery, for in suppressing self-interest one also suppresses the force through which mankind has achieved whatever moral and intellectual triumphs it can claim.

Private property is indeed an impediment to universal benevolence; but universal benevolence is no more than a phantom. As Malthus observes, "To the laws of property and marriage, and to the apparently narrow principle of self-interest which prompts each individual to exert himself in bettering his condition, we are indebted for all the noblest exertions of human genius, for everything that distinguishes the civilised from the savage state."

LIKE MOST such schemes of universal benevolence, the Godwin-Condorcet brand of utopia is essentially disestablishing of the past and its legal, economic, and religious institutions. But it is one of the bitterest lessons of history that, although human institutions are often the cause of "much mischief to society," they are, Malthus noted, "light and superficial in comparison with those deeper-seated causes of evil which result from the laws of nature and the passions of mankind." Abolish private property and the result would be not the extinction but the enhancement of selfishness: "Were there no established administration of property, every man would be obliged to guard with force his little store. Selfishness would be triumphant. The subjects of contention would be perpetual."

The moral? In part, that Friends of Humanity are no friends of humanity. It is easy to smile at the musings of a Godwin or a Condorcet. But it is worth recalling how many progeny they have spawned—not only Marx, Lenin, Stalin, and other such thoroughgoing Friends of Humanity, but also myriad contemporary well-wishers who, though less rigorous, nevertheless combine the emotion of benevolence with imperative moralism. They want to "spread the wealth around." They want the creators of wealth to "pay their fair share." Etc., etc. It is a combination that promises paradise but in fact, as David Stove put it, "is infallibly and enormously destructive of human happiness." Reflecting on the sudden eclipse of Godwin's reputation, Hazlitt asked: "Were we fools then, or are we dishonest now?" Either way, the answer, alas, is Yes.

The Death of Socialism

*Those who dare to undertake the institution of a people
must feel themselves capable, as it were, of changing
human nature, of transforming each individual . . . into
a part of a much greater whole, . . . of altering the
constitution of man for the purpose of strengthening it.*
—Jean-Jacques Rousseau, 1762

We are all socialists nowadays.
—Albert Edward, Prince of Wales, 1895

*The most important political event of the twentieth century
is not the crisis of capitalism but the death of socialism.*
—Irving Kristol, 1976

WHAT IS SOCIALISM? In part, it is optimism translated
into a political program. Until he took up gardening,
Candide was a sort of proto-socialist; his mentor Pangloss
could have been one of socialism's founding philosophers.
Socialism is also unselfishness embraced as an axiom: the
gratifying emotion of unselfishness, experienced alternately
as resentment against others and titillating satisfaction with
oneself. The philosophy of Rousseau, which elevated what
he called the "indescribably sweet" feeling of virtue into
a political imperative, is socialism in ovo. "Man is born

free," Rousseau famously exclaimed, "but is everywhere in chains." That heart-stopping conundrum—too thrilling to be corrected by mere experience—is the fundamental motor of socialism. It is a motor fueled by this corollary: that the multitude unaccountably colludes in perpetuating its own bondage and must therefore be, in Rousseau's ominous phrase, "forced to be free."

We owe the term "socialism" to some followers of Robert Owen, the nineteenth-century British industrialist who founded New Harmony, a short-lived utopian community on the banks of the Wabash in Indiana. Owen's initial reception in America was impressive. In an 1825 address to Congress, Joshua Muravchik reports in *Heaven on Earth: The Rise and Fall of Socialism* (2002), Owen's audience included not only congressmen but also Supreme Court justices, cabinet members, President Monroe, and President-elect John Quincy Adams. Owen described to this august assemblage how his efforts to replace the "individual selfish system" with a "united social" system would bring forth a "new man" who was free from the grasping imperatives that had marred human nature from time immemorial. (And not only human nature: the utopian socialist Charles Fourier expected selfishness and cruelty to be obliterated from the animal kingdom as well: one day, he thought, even lions and whales would be domesticated.)

The starry-eyed aspect of socialist thinking did not preclude a large element of steel. As Muravchik points out, the French Revolution was "the manger" of socialism. It was then that the philosophy of Rousseau emerged from the pages of tracts and manifestos to strut and fret across the bloody field of history. The architects of the revolution invoked Rousseau early and often as they set about the task of "changing human nature," of "altering the constitution of man for the purpose of strengthening it."

This metamorphosis does not come easily. Human nature is a recalcitrant thing. It is embodied as much in persistent human institutions like the family and the church as in the human heart. All must be remade from the ground up if "Liberty, Equality, and Fraternity" are at last to be realized. Since history (the revolutionaries thought) is little more than an accumulation of errors, history as hitherto known must be abolished. The past, a vast repository of injustice, is by definition the enemy. Accordingly, the revolutionists tossed out the Gregorian calendar and started again at Year One. They replaced the Genesis-inspired seven-day week with a ten-day cycle and rebaptized the months with names reflecting their new cult of nature: *Brumaire* (fog), *Thermidor* (heat), *Vendémiare* (wind), etc. A new religion was born, as imperious as it was jealous. It is significant that the socialist mentality is usually also an atheistic mentality, where atheism is understood not so much as the disbelief in God as the hatred of God—an attitude as precarious logically as it has been destructive in practice. There is an important sense in which religion as traditionally understood reconciles humanity to imperfection and to failure. Since the socialist sets out to abolish failure, traditional religion is worse than de trop: it is an impediment to perfection. ("Criticism of religion," Marx said, "is the prelude to all criticism.") In 1793, the churches were closed to worship and ransacked for booty. The anticlericalism that had been a prominent feature of revolutionary sentiment grew increasingly vicious. Muravchik describes so-called "revolutionary marriages" in which priests and nuns were tied together naked and drowned. Rousseau was always going on about establishing the "reign of virtue." His far-seeing disciple Maximilien Robespierre spoke more frankly of "virtue and its emanation, terror."

It is one of the great ironies of modern history that socialism, which promises a more humane, caring, and equitable society, has generally delivered a more oppressive and mis-managed one. Socialism's motto—Muravchik optimistically offers it to us as socialism's "epitaph"—turns out to be: "If you build it, they will leave."

IF, ONE MUST ADD, they are allowed to leave. As Murav-chik reminds us in his excellent survey of socialist personali-ties and socialist experiments, encouraging dissent is never high on a socialist's agenda. The socialist pretends to have glimpsed paradise on earth. Those who decline the invitation to embrace the vision are not just ungrateful: they are trai-tors to the cause of human perfection. Dissent is therefore not mere disagreement but treachery. Treachery is properly met not with arguments but (as circumstances permit) with various degrees of ostracism, legal penalties, not to mention the guillotine, the concentration camp, the purge.

In tracing "socialism's phenomenal trajectory," *Heaven on Earth* tells the "story of man's most ambitious attempt to supplant religion with a doctrine about how life ought to be lived that claimed grounding in science rather than rev-elation." It is, to say the least, a cautionary tale. Muravchik provides a devastating anatomy of the socialist dream—a dream that with clocklike regularity becomes a nightmare. Sometimes the nightmare is the tepid one of bland and soul-less conformity. Often, it is far nastier. If, as Muravchik sug-gests, "socialism was . . . the most popular political idea ever invented," it is also undoubtedly the bloodiest. Of course, many who profess socialism are decent and humane people. And it is worth noting that socialism comes in mild as well as tyrannical versions. Muravchik, who was once a socialist himself, pays frequent homage to the generous im-pulses that lie behind some allotropes of the socialist enter-prise. Nevertheless, he acknowledges that "regimes calling themselves socialist have murdered more than one hundred million people since 1917." Why? Why is it that "the more dogged the effort to achieve" the announced goals of socialism, "the more the outcome mocked the human ideals it proclaimed"? And why is it that conservatives, who by and large have agreed with Samuel Johnson that "A decent provision for the poor is the true test of civilization," have regularly been demonized as uncaring brutes?

A large part of the answer lies in the intellectual dynamics of utopianism. "Utopia" is Greek for "nowhere": a made-up word for a make-believe place. The search for nowhere inevitably deprecates any and every "somewhere." Socialism, which is based on incorrigible optimism about human nature, is a species of utopianism. It experiences the friction of reality as an intolerable brake on its expectations. "Utopians," the philosopher Leszek Kolakowski (about whom more below in Chapter 16) observed in "The Death of Utopia Reconsidered," "once they attempt to convert their visions into practical proposals, come up with the most malignant project ever devised: they want to institutionalize fraternity, which is the surest way to totalitarian despotism."

There was also the intervention of Marx. Intellectually, Marxism is the most highly developed—as well as the most influential and most murderous—form of socialism the world has seen. But Kolakowski is surely correct that Marxism's influence, far from depending on its alleged "scientific character," depends "almost entirely [on] . . . its prophetic, fantastic, and irrational elements." Marxism says that as capitalist societies develop, most people are hounded into abject poverty while a tiny coterie of capitalists thrive. This scenario is presented, *à la* Hegel, as a "dialectical" inevitability. But in fact capitalism has always made societies richer, much richer. Capitalists may get rich, but their workers become more prosperous than their grandparents could have ever imagined possible.

Whether or not this is a "necessary" concomitant of market forces, it is an historical fact. The curious thing is that this phenomenon, which any dispassionate observer might count as a refutation, leaves the true-believing Marxist entirely unruffled. Whatever else one can say about it, Marxism is surely one of the most impervious systems of thought ever devised. It is also one of the most protean. It has always, as Kolakowski notes, been able to change "content from one situation to another and [crossbreed] with other ideological traditions." In part, this is a testimony to its intellectual adaptability; in part, it is simple mendacity. As Marx himself explained in an 1857 letter to Friedrich Engels about an election prediction he had made, "It's possible that I shall make an ass of myself. But in that case one can always get out of it with a little dialectic. I have, of course, so worded my proposition as to be right either way."

Muravchik begins his account of the career of socialism with figures like François-Noël Babeuf and Sylvain Maréchal, whose radical egalitarianism and endorsement of violence helped set the tone—and the murderous program—of the French Revolution. Maréchal, who took to signing himself l'HSD (l'Homme Sans Dieu, the man without God), was above all an apostle of radical egalitarianism: equality understood not as a legal postulate but as an existential imperative. "If there is a single man on earth who is richer and more powerful than his fellows," he wrote, "then the equilibrium is broken: crime and misfortune are on earth." It is imperative, Maréchal said in his *Manifesto of Equals*, to "remove from every individual the hope of ever becoming richer, or more powerful, or more distinguished by his intelligence." Tough work, that removal, but the promised rewards were great: really establish equality, Maréchal argued, and the result would be "the disappearance of boundary marks, hedges, walls, door-locks, disputes, trials, thefts, murders, all crimes . . . courts, prisons, gallows, penalties, . . . envy, jealousy, insatiability, pride, deception, duplicity, in short all vices." Of course, until that happy day arrives there will be plenty of "trials, thefts, murders, . . . courts, prisons, gallows, penalties" in order to hasten the institution of equality.

Babeuf, who called himself "Gracchus" Babeuf after the legendary Roman land reformer, also put radical equality at the center of his revolutionary program. Since nothing institutionalized inequality more than private property, he reasoned, private property and its distillate, money, must go. Babeuf looked forward to the "general overthrow of the system of private property" as an "inevitable" adjunct of revolution. "Society," he said, "must be made to operate in such a way that it eradicates once and for all the desire of a man to become richer, or wiser, or more powerful than others." Like Maréchal—like Robespierre whom he admired as a "regenerator" who "mow[ed] down all that impeded him"—Babeuf (who also called himself "the Marat of the Somme") believed that "in order to govern judiciously it is necessary to terrorize the evilly disposed, the royalists, papists and starvers of the public. . . . [O]ne cannot govern democratically without this terrorism." If the cost of paradise was unfortunately high, it was as nothing compared with the envisioned benefits. "I don't think it is impossible," Babeuf enthused to his wife, "that within a year, if we carry out our measures aright and act with all necessary prudence, we shall succeed in ensuring general happiness on earth."

TODAY, BABEUF is little more than a footnote to the history of tyranny. As with many extremists, the very extravagance of his pronouncements is implicitly taken as a license to dismiss him or deprecate his importance. What fundamentally challenges the status quo is defanged by the rhetoric of extremism: what is extreme is also exceptional, a special case, i.e., not really threatening. But this line of reasoning misunderstands the threat posed by radicals like Babeuf. His extremism was not limited to acts perpetrated in the late eighteenth century. It lived on in the murderous socialist programs he helped to inspire. Babeuf's importance in the history of socialism was underscored by Marx and Engels. In *The Holy Family*, their first work together, they fondly note that Babeuf's attack on private property "gave rise to the communist idea." (The essence of Communism, Marx correctly observed, can be summed up in a single phrase: the abolition of private property.) Babeuf's importance was reaffirmed in the founding manifesto of the Comintern in 1919, whose authors saw themselves as "the direct continuators of the heroic endeavors and martyrdom of a long line of revolutionary generations [starting] from Babeuf." In our own day, the Frankfurt-school Marxist Herbert Marcuse has championed Babeuf's thought as a tool to battle the seductive evils of advanced capitalism.

Muravchik ranges confidently through the history of socialism, neatly weaving biography, anecdote, and political commentary into a fascinating chronicle of disappointed idealism. A large part of *Heaven on Earth* is given over to the rise and eventual foundering of what we might call "soft socialism." Muravchik patiently details the experiments of utopians like Robert Owen, Marxist reformers like Eduard Bernstein (a protégé of Engels), the trade-union movements of Samuel Gompers and George Meany, and mid-twentieth-century redactions of the socialist impulse in Clement Attlee's Labour government, Julius Nyerere's Tanzania, and the Israeli kibbutz.

Perhaps his most illuminating pages are devoted to the careers of Mussolini and of Engels. We tend to think of fascism as the antithesis of socialism or Marxism. But as

Muravchik reminds us, there are in fact deep continuities between them. Mussolini began as a disciple of Lenin and did not so much repudiate Marxism-Leninism as become a self-declared "heretic." Thus one of Mussolini's groups of thugs called itself the Cheka, after Lenin's secret police. As Muravchik observes, "However fierce they grew in their antipathy to communism, the fascists never ceased mimicking it, implicitly underscoring their claim to be the true or superior heirs to the same legacy." (Something similar can be said of Hitler, whose party, after all, was called National Socialism. It is true that Hitler was adamantly anti-Communist; at the same time, he acknowledged that he had "learned a great deal from Marxism.")

Most of us think of Engels as the junior partner in the conglomerate of Marxism, Inc. In some ways that perception is accurate. But Muravchik shows that Engels's contribution to the formation of Marxist doctrine was much larger than is usually recognized. The well-to-do son of a German textile manufacturer, Engels beavered diligently for decades in the Manchester office of Ermen & Engels in order to earn enough money to support his comrade-in-arms. (Engels was always sending Marx money; when he finally retired from the family firm, he made Marx an annuity of £350—several times more than the average family lived on but not enough for Marx, who always adjusted his spending to a level above what his benefactors supplied.) Engels was an indefatigable publicist. It was Engels, for example, who suggested the title "Communist Manifesto" for their jointly authored "confession of faith." When Marx finally, after innumerable delays, managed to complete the first volume of that great reader-proof tome *Das Kapital*, Engels flogged it everywhere, taking it upon himself to write ten separate reviews of the book. He also completed volumes two and three of the book, working up Marx's scattered notes into something resembling a consecutive argument. More substantively, Engels's 1844 "Outlines of a Critique of Political Economy" articulated many central points of the doctrine we have since learned to call Marxism, above all the thesis that the evolution of capitalism necessarily leads to cutthroat competition among capitalists and poverty and dehumanization for the majority of the populace. Marx himself called it "a work of genius" and incorporated many of its central arguments into his later work.

MURAVCHIK'S ARGUMENT has two aspects. Like many other disabused commentators, he presents a sobering chronicle of socialism's delusions and crimes. He reminds us—if we still need reminding—of the central role that the "annihilation . . . of reactionary races" (Marx), the "extermination" of enemies (Lenin) has always played in "really existing" Marxism. Muravchik also presents the cheering news that daybreak has come at last, that we have finally awakened from the long dream of socialist utopia. It is difficult to argue with the first part of his argument. What about the second? It is certainly significant that the Soviet Union imploded and that its last leader, Mikhail Gorbachev, should have acknowledged that Communist claims about economic progress had been "pure propaganda." Perhaps it is also significant that Tony Blair in Britain should have campaigned on the slogan "Labour is the party of business." But I cannot help receiving the news of socialism's death with a certain scepticism. For one thing, Communism is still alive and well in several countries, including the world's largest. Then, too, the fact that an idea has been thoroughly discredited intellectually does nothing to render it impotent. It is part of the perversity of human nature that discredited ideas are often the most successful ideas.

254

Finally, I see little evidence that socialism's fundamental tenet—namely, the ideal of equality—is on its way to the dustbin of history. Think of Barack Obama's ambition to "fundamentally transform the United States of America," part of which transformation was to be accomplished by "spreading the wealth around." The wheels of egalitarianism may grind away more slowly in liberal democratic countries than in Communist ones, but grind away they do. It would be pleasant to think that in leaving history's bloodiest century behind, we have also left behind the passions that sparked its unprecedented carnage. But time and again history has taught us that the hunger for equality is among mankind's most brutal passions. It is for this reason that I believe the philosopher David Stove was correct when he identified "bloodthirstiness" as a central ingredient in the psychology of egalitarianism. Socialism will be conquered to the extent that egalitarianism is conquered. In the meanwhile, I fear that Stove is correct that "very far from communism being dead, as some foolish people at present believe, we can confidently look forward to bigger and better Marxes, Lenins, Stalins, Maos, Kim Il-sungs, Pol Pots, Ceausescus, Baader-Meinhofs, Shining Paths, and all the rest."

The Power of James Burnham

*I put for a general inclination of all mankind, a perpetual
and restless desire of power after power, that ceaseth only
in death.*
—Thomas Hobbes, *Leviathan*

*The common-place critic . . . believes that truth lies in the
middle, between the extremes of right and wrong.*
—William Hazlitt, "On Common-Place Critics"

*Americans have not yet learned the tragic lesson that the
most powerful cannot be loved—hated, envied, feared,
obeyed, respected, even honored perhaps, but not loved.*
—James Burnham, *Containment or Liberation?*

"WHO IS James Burnham?" How often did I field
variants of that question while pondering this essay! My informal survey suggests that almost no one under
the age of sixty has even heard of him ("James who?").
And for most people over that magic age, Burnham is but
an attenuated presence, a half-remembered, even vaguely
embarrassing fashion that has failed to return—fins on the
back of a model that was discontinued long ago for lack
of sales. "Ah, yes," speak the glimmers of remembrance,

"author of *The Managerial Revolution*"—Burnham's first and most famous book, published in 1941—"ardent Cold Warrior, helped organize the Congress for Cultural Freedom (remember that?), and . . . wasn't he a supporter of Joseph McCarthy?" The answer to that last question is No—more on this below—but even the hint of an adumbration of a suspicion of "McCarthyite" leanings is sufficient to expel one from the ranks of civilized recollection, as Burnham learned to his cost.

The most notable exception to the oblivion surrounding Burnham is among people associated with *National Review*, the conservative fortnightly that Burnham helped start in 1955 when he was fifty. For more than two decades, Burnham enlivened the magazine's pages with his spare but unsparing prose and editorial intelligence. He ranged widely, dilating on everything from foreign policy—his specialty—to (early on) the movies. William F. Buckley Jr., the founding editor and perpetual *genius loci* of *NR*, called Burnham "the number one intellectual influence on *National Review* since the day of its founding." In a just world, that would be patent enough for continued interest and recognition. But in this world, the combination of Burnham's ferocious intellectual independence and unclubbable heterodoxy long ago consigned him to the unglamorous limbo that established opinion reserves for those who challenge its pieties too forcefully.

IN 2002, Daniel Kelly published *James Burnham and the Struggle for the World*, a meticulous and thoughtful biography of this sage political gadfly. If any book could resuscitate Burnham's reputation, this was it. But Burnham is too idiosyncratic, too polemical, and too faithful to the dictates of intellectual integrity to enjoy anything like a general renaissance. As I write, in the summer of 2011, all of Burnham's ten or so books are listed as "Out of Print" or being of "Limited Availability," i.e., more limited than available.

I should acknowledge that until reading *James Burnham and the Struggle for the World*, I, too, belonged to that unfortunate multitude which recognized "James Burnham" as but a name. I am deeply grateful to Kelly for dispelling my ignorance. For James Burnham (who died in 1987 after a decade's incapacity) was an astonishing writer. Subtle, passionate, and irritatingly well-read, he commanded a nimble style that was sometimes blunt but unfailingly eloquent. Burnham was above all a rousing writer. Immanuel Kant paid homage to David Hume for awakening him from his "dogmatic slumbers" about metaphysical questions. Burnham performed a similar service for the politically complacent. If he occasionally exaggerated the extent or imminence of the evils he described—Burnham was liberally endowed with what Henry James called "the imagination of disaster"—he was fearless in opposing and exposing the totalitarian temptation. Which is to say that he was fearless in opposing and exposing the most corrosive, most addictive, most murderous ideology of our time: Communism.

Today, Burnham is best known—to the extent that he is known at all—as an anti-Communist crusader. He was that. But he did not confine his criticism to Communism. On the contrary, he understood that the impulse to totalitarian surrender comes in many guises. The "managerial revolution" that he warned about was a revolution that aimed to repel freedom for the sake of bureaucratic efficiency and control. That revolution has not—not yet—succeeded in the monolithic fashion that Burnham envisioned. He did not, as his subtitle promised, so much tell us "What Is Happening in the World" as what might happen should certain tendencies be left unchecked. But who can gaze upon the ever-increasing routinization of life and regulation of individual liberty in our society without acknowledging the pertinence of Burnham's gloomy analysis?

Over his long career, Burnham changed his mind about many things. He went from being a sort of philosophical aesthete to having a serious infatuation with Trotskyism—a form of Marxism peculiarly seductive to intellectuals—emerging in the 1940s as a prominent spokesman for an astringent species of democratic realism. But throughout the evolution of his opinions Burnham remained unwavering in his commitment to freedom. This commitment had two sides: an infrequently exercised celebratory side, which he reserved for freedom's genuine triumphs, and an oppositional side, which he lavished with cordial hostility on those opinions, policies, sentiments, and personalities that worked to stymie freedom.

This dual commitment made Burnham an equal-opportunity scourge. He was almost as hard on what Tocqueville called democratic despotism—the tendency of democracies to barter freedom for equality—as he was on Communism. Burnham was a connoisseur of insidiousness, of the way benign—or seemingly benign—intentions can be enlisted to promulgate malevolent, illiberal policies. He descried this process as accurately in Western democracies as he did in Communist tyrannies, and he was tireless in his excoriation of what he called "that jellyfish brand of contemporary liberalism—pious, guilt-ridden, do-goody—which uses the curious dogma of 'some truth on both sides' as its principal sales line." Would that Burnham were with us today!

Kelly observes that Burnham was "the living embodiment of what would later come to be known as political incorrectness." Kelly is right. Consider, to take just one example, Burnham's observation that most African nations were really "half-formed pseudo nations." Now, as then, that is indisputably the case, but how many accredited intellectuals have the forthrightness to apprise Robert Mugabe of that inconsiderate fact? (Burnham was refreshing on many subjects, not least the United Nations and its disapproving resolutions about U.S. policy: "Why in the world," he wondered, "should any sensible person give a damn what some spokesman for cannibalistic tribes or slave-holding nomads thinks about nuclear tests?")

IT WOULD BE EASY to multiply such crisp interventions. Nevertheless, I hesitate to apply the label "politically incorrect" to so insightful and spirited a critic as James Burnham. In many quarters, calling someone "politically incorrect" has become a popular method of discounting his opinions without the inconvenience of allowing them a hearing. It is a clever, if cowardly, rhetorical trick. It allows you to ignore someone by the simple expedient of declaring his arguments to be beyond the pale, "extreme"—that is, unworthy of a place in the forum of public exchange. At bottom, the procedure is a form of political ostracism. The goal is to silence someone not by forbidding him to speak but by denying him an audience. This technique is especially effective with writers, like Burnham, who specialize in telling truths that most people would rather not hear.

James Burnham cut an odd figure in the world of intellectual polemics. He impressed his peers as both unusually pugnacious and curiously disengaged. His background had a lot to do with the mixture. The eldest of three sons, he was born in 1905 to a prosperous Chicago railway executive. His father, Claude, was a classic American success story. At fourteen, he was a poor English immigrant delivering newspapers at the head office of James J. Hill's Great Northern Line. Two decades later he was a vice-president of the Burlington and Quincy Railroad (among other lines), traveling with his family in a private railway car. In later life, Burnham objected to the description of his father as a "minor railway magnate," but the epithet does seem to cover the facts.

Even moderate wealth can be a segregating force, and it was one factor that set Burnham apart from many of his fellows. Religion was another. Burnham's father (who died of pneumonia in his late forties in 1928) was Protestant but his mother, in Kelly's phrase, was a "rigorous Catholic." Burnham grew up Roman Catholic in a world still mildly suspicious of Papist influence. Society did not snub the Burnhams, exactly, but neither did it welcome them without reserve. And if Catholicism was grounds for distance, so was culture. The Burnhams were a cultivated family. Art, literature, and argument were staple goods in the Burnham household. Young James was musical, like his mother, and delighted throughout life in playing the piano. He enjoyed an expensive education. When the Burnhams understood that their local parochial schools discouraged their charges from applying to Ivy League colleges, they decided to send James and his brother David to the Canterbury School, a tony Catholic institution in New Milford, Connecticut.

Burnham performed well, brilliantly in English and math, and matriculated at Princeton in 1923. He majored in English, graduated at the top of his class, and went to Balliol to study English and medieval philosophy. Among his teachers were an unknown professor of Old English called J. R. R. Tolkien—I wonder if Burnham ever recorded his opinion of Hobbits? I doubt that it was flattering—and the suave Jesuit philosopher Martin D'Arcy. D'Arcy had a magnetic effect on non-believers such as Evelyn Waugh. But while Burnham gloried in theological argument, D'Arcy did nothing to salvage Burnham's religious commitments, which he shed without noticeable struggle while at Balliol.

Being an ex-Catholic is not the same thing as being a non-Catholic, and an ex-Catholic with a taste for theological argumentation is a decidedly strange hybrid. Burnham did not return to the Church until the very end of his life, but his Catholic upbringing and intellectual training served to inflect his intelligence in distinctive ways. In 1929, he went to teach philosophy at New York University—a task he discharged for some two decades—and Burnham stood out not only because of his brilliance but also because of his tone, a combination of passion, polish, and polemic. One of Burnham's students, Joseph Frank, the future biographer of Dostoevsky, remembered him as "very sophisticated, very serious, and very intense."

AMONG BURNHAM'S early colleagues at NYU was the philosopher Philip E. Wheelwright, whose book *The Burning Fountain: A Study in the Language of Symbolism* made a deep impression on generations of students. (I encountered it myself in college.) Wheelwright had been one of Burnham's teachers at Princeton. The two had corresponded for some time about starting a new literary-philosophical magazine, and in January 1930 (one year after the debut of Lincoln Kirstein's *Hound & Horn*) the first issue of *Symposium: A Critical Review* appeared. The first issue of the quarterly contained essays by John Dewey, Ramon Fernandez (the French literary critic who is probably best known today for his cameo appearance in Wallace Stevens's poem "The Idea of Order at Key West"), and the philosopher Morris R. Cohen. Burnham contributed a long review of I. A. Richards's *Practical Criticism*. It is a canny essay. Burnham judged Richards's book to be "the most considerable and the most formidable study of poetry . . . which has appeared in America during the past year." But he also noted that he could "not help feeling . . . that Mr. Richards's Defense of Poetry is more 'inspired,' more 'stirring,' and more *desperate* than any Sidney's or Shelley's."

To those of us who, however ardent may be our affection for poetry, do not look to it so entirely for the organization of our lives, Mr. Richards defense may seem most damaging to poetry itself; and poetry may appear through his efforts, as in the old twist of Pope's, faint with damned praise.

That is pretty good stuff.

Symposium had a run of three years. It was an impressive, if sometimes discursively academic, achievement. Burnham and Wheelwright snagged essays by Lionel Trilling (on D. H. Lawrence), Frederick Dupee (on Edmund Wilson's *Axel's Castle*), Allen Tate (on Emily Dickinson), and Sidney Hook (on Marxism). Ezra Pound wrote for *Symposium*, as did Herbert Read, J. Middleton Murry, Harold Rosenberg, and G. Wilson Knight. The first bit of Ortega y Gasset to appear in English—a portion of *The Dehumanization of Art*—appeared in *Symposium*, as did important essays on Eliot (a major influence on Burnham's thinking at the time), Valéry, and other modernist figures.

In general, the magazine lived up to its announced ambition "not to be the organ of any group or sect or cause," which may be one reason that Burnham let it fold in 1933. In one of the last issues, Burnham contributed a long review of Trotsky's *History of the Russian Revolution*. He was deeply impressed—that "remarkable book," the reading of which was "an exciting experience," had strengthened his conviction that "a major transition [was] taking place" in the world. As for the lineaments of that transition—perhaps "revolution" would be the apter term—Burnham was more and more coming to see it in Marxist terms.

Whatever the internal logic that propelled Burnham toward Marxism in the 1930s, there were also two important external factors. One was the Depression. Burnham looked around and saw the institutions of American society in crisis. The liberal nostrums seemed useless at best, malevolent at worst. (Burnham loathed the paternalistic, big government policies of Roosevelt, describing the New Deal as "Fascism without shirts.") The second factor was the philosopher Sidney Hook, who was Burnham's entrée into the world of "pragmatic" Marxism, Marxism (or so Hook thought at the time) with a human face.

Burnham was an idiosyncratic Marxist. It's not that he lacked fervency. On the contrary, as Kelly reports, he fell "head-over-heels" for Marxism and "labored mightily for the Trotskyist cause." Under Hook's guidance, he joined the American Workers Party and petitioned, agitated, organized, and above all wrote to further its aims. He helped edit and contributed innumerable broadsides to publications like *The New Militant, Socialist Appeal,* and *The New International.* His efforts did not go unnoticed. Before long he was in regular correspondence with "the Old Man," with Trotsky himself, and although they never met Burnham became a trusted lieutenant in Trotsky's left-wing anti-Stalinist movement.

At the same time, Burnham always regarded the utopian strain of Marxism with a suspicion bordering on contempt. He had too low—too accurate—an opinion of human nature to be seduced by the promise of perfection. And while he did not repudiate violence, he was always alert to Marxism's—to any bureaucracy's—sweet tooth for totalitarian strategies. Burnham was also a social oddity among the comrades. In 1934, after getting married, he moved from Greenwich Village to Sutton Place, where he entertained in a style appropriate to that address. (For her part, his wife always seemed to regard her husband's adventures with Trotskyist radicalism with bemused distaste.) It is likely, as Kelly notes, that Burnham was "the only Trotskyist to own a tuxedo." When he summered with his family in Biarritz, he perused Marx and Engels during the day and played *chemin de fer* at night. His acquisition of a summer house in Kent, Connecticut, completed the contrast.

OF COURSE, Burnham was hardly the only privileged benefi- ciary of capitalism to embrace Communism while holding fast to his bank account. But his intellectual independence made him an unreliable militant. Burnham happily im- mersed himself in Aquinas, Dante, and the Renaissance one moment, Marx and bulletins from comrade Trotsky the next. It was a giddy but unstable amalgam. Unwilling, as Kelly puts it, to sacrifice intellect to militancy, Burnham became an increasingly restless recruit. The break came in 1939 when the Soviets, fortified by the Hitler-Stalin Pact, at- tacked Poland. Trotsky justified the action as a step toward the abolition of private property (and how!), but Burnham saw it for what it was: a brutal land grab by a totalitarian power. He wrote as much and in short order found himself expelled from the Socialist Workers Party and the object of Trotsky's rage: overnight Burnham went from being a fa- vored if sometimes wayward collaborator to being an "ed- ucated witch-doctor," "strutting petty-bourgeois pedant," and (the *coup de grâce*) an "intellectual snob." Burnham's response was to gather his correspondence with Trotsky and dump it into the incinerator.

By the end of the 1930s, Burnham was a minor but respected public intellectual. In 1938, he began a long as- sociation with *Partisan Review*, the premier intellectual organ of the anti-Stalinist Left. But he did not become an intellectual celebrity until 1941, when *The Managerial Revolution: What Is Happening in the World* became a runaway bestseller—much to the surprise of its publisher and the chagrin of the several houses that had turned it down. Written at the moment when Hitler's army seemed poised to overrun Europe, the book is a grim exercise in dystopian prognostication. It is not, I think, one of Burnham's better books. As he himself later admitted, it is full of "remnants of Marxism," above all the depressing aroma of economic determinism and praise for the superiority of central planning. But *The Managerial Revolution* certainly is a bold, an impressive book. Its vision of the rise of an oligarchy of experts and alignment of world powers into three competing super-states made a deep impression on many readers, not least on George Orwell.

Orwell wrote about Burnham at least three times, reviewing *The Managerial Revolution* in 1944 and then in long essays about his work in 1946 and 1947. As Kelly notes, Orwell found *The Managerial Revolution* both "magnetic and repellent." Orwell criticized Burnham for "power worship," for being "fascinated by the spectacle of power" (and hence contenting himself with analyzing rather than condemning Hitler's early military successes). Burnham's essential intellectual failing, Orwell thought, was in "predicting a continuation of the thing that is happening." Nazi power is on the rise, *ergo* it will continue irresistibly; American capitalism is in crisis, *ergo* it will necessarily disintegrate—except that the rude, unkempt force of reality intervenes, transforming those *ergos* into "might have beens."

With hindsight, we can see that Orwell was right that Burnham underestimated "the advantages, military as well as social, enjoyed by a democratic country." His neat, schematic intelligence lulled him into believing that the (apparently) better organized nation was going to be the victorious nation. Burnham undervalued the advantages of the ad hoc, the unexpected reversal, the sudden inspiration. His "besetting sin," Orwell said, is to overstate his case: "He is too fond of apocalyptic visions, too ready to believe that the muddled processes of history will happen suddenly and logically." (Orwell makes the arresting observation that, during the Second World War, the smarter Brits were often the more pessimistic: "their morale was lower because their imaginations were stronger.") At the same time, Orwell repeatedly underscored Burnham's "intellectual courage" and willingness to deal with "real issues." And it is clear that, whatever his criticisms, Orwell was deeply influenced by *The Managerial Revolution*. In 1984, he adopted wholesale Burnham's idea that the world was reorganizing itself into three rival totalitarian states. *The Managerial Revolution* itself appears in Orwell's novel under the title *The Theory and Practice of Oligarchic Collectivism*.

FROM 1939 TO 1941, the Communists worked mightily to keep America "neutral." Good Trotskyist that he aspired to be, Burnham, too, was opposed to America's entry into the war. His opposition persisted after his break with Trotsky. But it did not survive Pearl Harbor. The Japanese attack on the Pacific fleet precipitated a political metanoia. Overnight, Burnham became a vociferous supporter of all-out war against the Axis powers.

This hardening, or clarifying, is evident in his next book—considered by many critics to be his best—*The Machiavellians: Defenders of Freedom*. Published in 1943, *The Machiavellians* is ostensibly an exposition of, and homage to, some modern followers of Machiavelli. Its larger purpose is to distinguish between the sentimental and the realistic in politics. Dante (in *De Monarchia*), Rousseau, and the architects of the French Revolution are prime examples of the former: they represent "politics as wish": noble, optimistic, ultimately futile (indeed, ultimately "reactionary and vicious" in Burnham's judgment).

Machiavelli and his heirs belong to the latter camp. They saw things as they really were and faced up to unpleasant facts about human nature. Because they saw humanity as it was—in its imperfection, its treachery, its unceasing desire for power—they were the true friends of liberty. They did not exchange real freedoms for pleasant-sounding but empty idealities. They understood that all political freedom is imperfect freedom, won through struggle, preserved with difficulty, constantly subject to assault and diminution.

Burnham's political thought is often described as "hard-boiled." *The Machiavellians* is the cauldron in which the promised firmness is achieved. "All societies," he writes, "including societies called democratic, are ruled by a minority." Although the minority, the ruling "élite," naturally seeks to legitimize its power in the eyes of society, in the end "the primary object of every élite, or ruling class, is to maintain its own power and privilege," an aim that is sought largely on "force and fraud." Burnham had high hopes for "an objective science of politics"; at the same time he believed that "logical or rational analysis plays a relatively minor part in political and social change." The true friends of freedom budget heavily for the imperfection of humanity and acknowledge the relative impotence of reason in political affairs. Above all, they understand that the possession of power is inseparable from its intelligent exercise.

Regarded as an item in the evolution of Burnham's thought, *The Machiavellians* is perhaps most important not for its exposition of power politics but for its implicit recognition of the value of freedom, "that minimum of moral dignity which alone can justify the strange accident of man's existence." As the 1940s and the Second World War unfolded, Burnham came more and more to understand that the preservation of freedom was primarily a salvage operation. And as the war hurried to its end, he looked on aghast as the West timidly made concession after concession to the Stalinist tyranny. In 1944, Burnham wrote a paper on postwar Soviet ambitions for the Office of Strategic Services. In 1947, an expanded version of this document appeared as *The Struggle for the World*. It is with this book, I believe, that Burnham comes into his own, for it is here that he first clearly articulates the opposition between the West as a precious heritage to be defended and Communism as a murderous tyranny to be defeated.

WAS BURNHAM'S OPPOSITION "oversimplified," as many critics charged? Doubtless it was. But it was also right in essentials and was, moreover, a salutary corrective to the naïve—and therefore deluded—advice of good-hearted liberals. Burnham understood with searing clarity two fundamental facts. First, that Communism was an expansionist ideology bent on world domination. And, second, that its triumph would entail the destruction of every liberty, intellectual as well as political, that we in the West held sacred and yet (perilously) took for granted—above all "the absolute value of the single human person."

It is worth underscoring this point. Communism, Burnham saw, was opportunism elevated to a position of absolute power. Unchecked, no human good, not even the commitment to truth, can withstand its assault. Anyone who has leafed through Marxist-inspired writings will remember attacks on "mechanical logic." But this, Burnham notes, is at bottom an attack on "the rules of objective inference and proof, the rules that permit us to test for truth and falsity." The alternative, what is called "dialectical logic," is simply a device that declares "whatever serves the interest of communist power is true."

In terms of foreign policy, the fight against Communism required neither appeasement—appeasement was merely a prelude to capitulation—nor containment—containment was merely appeasement on the installment plan. What was required was a concerted campaign to undermine, to roll back, the Communist juggernaut.

In domestic terms, the fight against Communism had to begin with the recognition that Communists used and abused democratic freedoms in order to destroy them. Their aim was the subversion of democracy. Therefore, Burnham argued, their capacity to subvert must itself be subverted. In the end, he thought, this meant that Communism would have to be outlawed. In the near term, it required that serious restraints be placed upon Communist sympathizers and agents. Would this be a violation of their civil rights—the right to free speech, for example? Doubtless it would. But, Burnham argued,

> Democracy in practice has never, and could never, interpret the right of free speech in an absolute and unrestricted sense. No one, for example, is allowed to advocate, and organize for, mass murder, rape, and arson. No one feels that such prohibitions are anti-democratic. But why not? Why cannot some purist tell us that any restriction whatsoever is, logically, counter to the absolute democratic principle of free speech?

Burnham's point was that because "Communism, in democratic nations, makes use of free speech in order to abolish free speech," its own right of free speech had to be curtailed. (Burnham stressed later that great care would have to be taken to avoid lumping real Communists together with "socialists, liberals, honest progressives" and other "legitimate" critics and reformers.)

Burnham's point, as pertinent today as when he uttered it, is that free speech cannot be understood in isolation, but only in the context of that which makes it possible, that is, in the context of democratic government and the functioning social community that supports it. "The principles of an organized society," he argued, cannot be interpreted in such a way as to make organized society impossible. . . . Any individual right or freedom is properly extended only to those who accept the fundamental rules of democracy. How . . . could any society survive which deliberately nursed its own avowed and irreconcilable assassin, and freely exposed its heart to his knife?

The publication of *The Struggle for the World* happened to coincide with President Truman's speech announcing what came to be known as the Truman Doctrine, according to which the U.S. sought to "support free peoples who are resisting attempted subjugation by armed minorities or by outside pressures." This coincidence garnered a great deal of publicity—much of it negative—for the book. It also aroused the interest of the fledgling Central Intelligence Agency. Burnham, recommended by his Princeton classmate Joseph Bryant III, worked as a consultant to the Political and Psychological Warfare division (which Bryant headed) of the Office of Policy Coordination, a semi-autonomous covert branch of the agency. He took a leave from NYU— to do "research" the university explained—and moved to Washington.

Perhaps Burnham's greatest contribution while working for the CIA was to help found the Congress for Cultural Freedom. This organization, covertly funded by the CIA, was established to provide a liberal anti-Communist alternative to the Communist-controlled propaganda initiatives for "peace and friendship." The liberal element of the Congress cannot be overemphasized: this was an effort to win over the liberal intelligentsia—forgive the pleonasm—to the cause of anti-Communism. Accordingly, in 1950 at the Congress's inaugural conference in Berlin, patrons and speakers included Bertrand Russell, John Dewey, Benedetto Croce, Karl Jaspers, Jacques Maritain, Herbert

Read, A. J. Ayer, Ignazio Silone, Sidney Hook, and Arthur M. Schlesinger Jr. Burnham was one of the few hard-liners. In his talk, Burnham tackled head on "neutralism"—what we have come to call "moral equivalence"—the "denunciation on equal terms of American and Soviet barbarism." Burnham admitted the demotic nature of American pop culture. But tawdriness was better than tyranny: Coca-Cola might be bad, he said, but "not quite in the same league with Kolyma," the notorious Siberan home to many labor camps.

BURNHAM'S TENURE with the CIA (which, we tend to forget, was and is a deeply liberal institution) came to an end over the issue of "McCarthyism." Burnham was ambivalent about the Wisconsin Senator: he was not, he explained, a McCarthyite but an "anti-anti-McCarthyite." He understood that anti-McCarthyism was often "a screen and cover for the Communists and . . . a major diversion of anti-Communist efforts." Reflecting on the phenomenon after McCarthy's death, Burnham noted that

> McCarthy became the symbol through which the basic strata of citizens expressed their conviction . . . that Communism and Communists cannot be part of our national community, that they are beyond the boundaries: that, in short, the line must be drawn somewhere. This was really at issue in the whole McCarthy business, not how many card-carrying members were in the State Department . . . The issue was philosophical, metaphysical: what kind of community are we? And the Liberals, including the anti-Communist Liberals, were correct in labeling McCarthy the Enemy, and in destroying him. From the Liberal standpoint—secularist, egalitarian, relativist—the line is not drawn. Relativism must be Absolute.

Burnham's stand on McCarthy precipitated his deportation to political Siberia. Overnight, this influential public commentator became persona non grata. Philip Rahv, his colleague at *Partisan Review*, put it well: "The Liberals now dominate all the cultural channels in this country. If you break completely with this dominant atmosphere, you're a dead duck. James Burnham had committed suicide." The irony is that Burnham, so astute about the workings of power, should have become a casualty of this skirmish: one might have expected him to negotiate the battlefield more cannily.

IT WAS *National Review* that rescued Burnham and provided him a home for his intellectual energies and platform for broadcasting his insights in the final decades of his career. "Every aspect of the magazine interested him," William F. Buckley Jr. recalled at the magazine's 25th Anniversary Banquet. "Its typography—just for instance." But also its coverage of culture, the length of its book reviews, and, above all, its stance with respect to America's foreign policy. Burnham saw with ferocious clarity that, as he put it in *Suicide of the West: The Definitive Analysis of the Pathology of Liberalism* (1964), civilizations generally collapse because of internal failures, not attacks from outside. "Suicide," he wrote "is probably more frequent than murder as the end phase of a civilization." Contemplating the expansionist threat of Soviet Communism, Burnham warned that "The primary issue before Western civilization today, and before its member nations, is survival."

In some ways, *Suicide of the West* is a period piece. A product of the Cold War, many of its examples are dated. But in its core message it is as relevant today as ever. The field of battle may have changed; the armies have adopted new tactics; but the war isn't over: it is merely transmogrified. Indeed, what Burnham had to say about Communism applies, *mutatis mutandis*, to Islamofascism. It is amusing to contemplate what James Burnham would have had to say about liberals who unwittingly collude with that murderous ideology by denoucing the made-up sin of "Islamophobia." (Burnham, I suspect, would have agreed with me that the charge of "Islamophobia" is incoherent: a "phobia" is an irrational fear; what could be more rational that fearing the effects of militant Islam?) In the subtitle to *Suicide of the West*, Burnham promised "the definitive analysis of the pathology of liberalism." At the center of that pathology is an awful failure of understanding which is also a failure of nerve, a failure of "the will to survive." Burnham admits that his invocation of "suicide" may sound hyperbolic. "'Suicide,' it is objected, is too emotive a term, too negative and 'bad.'" But it is part of the pathology that Burnham describes that such objections are "most often made most hotly by Westerners who hate their own civilization, readily excuse or even praise blows struck against it, and themselves lend a willing hand, frequently enough, to pulling it down."

Burnham offered this still-pertinent reflection about facing down the juggernaut of Communism: "just possibly we shall not have to die in large numbers to stop them: but we shall certainly have to be willing to die." The issue, Burnham saw, is that modern liberalism has equipped us with an ethic too abstract and empty to inspire real commitment. Modern liberalism, he writes,

> does not offer ordinary men compelling motives for personal suffering, sacrifice, and death. There is no tragic dimension in its picture of the good life. Men become willing to endure, sacrifice, and die for God, for family, king, honor, country, from a sense of absolute duty or an exalted vision of the meaning of history. . . . And it is precisely these ideas and

institutions that liberalism has criticized, attacked, and in part overthrown as superstitious, archaic, reactionary, and irrational. In their place liberalism proposes a set of pale and bloodless abstractions—pale and bloodless for the very reason that they have no roots in the past, in deep feeling and in suffering. Except for mercenaries, saints, and neurotics, no one is willing to sacrifice and die for progressive education, medicare, humanity in the abstract, the United Nations, and a ten percent rise in Social Security payments.

In his view, the primary function of liberalism was to "permit Western civilization to be reconciled to dissolution," to view weakness, failure, even collapse as not as a defeat but "as the transition to a new and higher order in which Mankind as a whole joins in a universal civilization that has risen above the parochial distinctions, divisions, and discriminations of the past." It's a mug's game, worthy of those "friends of humanity" we discussed in a previous chapter. Like the poor, they seem always to be with us. Which is another reason the teachings of James Burnham are as relevant today as they were when Nikita Khrushchev came to the U.N. to bang his shoe on the table and warn the West that "we will bury you." "But," says the Friend of Humanity, "that didn't happen. Don't you see, we overreacted?" Which reminds me of an observation by the great Oxford don Benjamin Jowett: "Precautions are always blamed," he said. "When successful, they are said to be unnecessary." James Burnham would have liked Jowett.

What's Wrong with Benevolence

*The most melancholy of human reflections, perhaps, is
that, on the whole, it is a question whether the benevolence
of mankind does most good or harm. Great good, no
doubt, philanthropy does, but then it also does great evil.
It augments so much vice, it multiplies so much suffering,
it brings to life such great populations to suffer and to be
vicious, that it is open to argument whether it be or be not
an evil to the world, and this is entirely because excellent
people fancy they can do much by rapid action—that they
will most benefit the world when they most relieve their
own feelings.*
—Walter Bagehot

Benevolence is the heroin of the Enlightened.
—David Stove

WHAT JAMES BURNHAM anatomized as "the pathology
of liberalism" in the last chapter has a complicated
and often ironical symptomatology. "It is," Burnham reflects,
"as if a man, struck with a mortal disease, were and to say
and believe, as the flush of fever spread over his face, 'Ah, the
glow of health returning!'" Consider, to take one example,
the place of benevolence in the economy of liberal ideology.

As we saw in a previous chapter when considering some Friends of Humanity like William Godwin and Condorcet, benevolence is a curious mental or characterological attribute. It is, as the philosopher David Stove observes in *What's Wrong with Benevolence: Happiness, Private Property, and the Limits of Enlightenment* (2011), less a *virtue* than an *emotion*. To be benevolent means—what? To be disposed to relieve the misery and increase the happiness of others. Whether your benevolent attitude or action actually has that effect is besides the point. Yes, Stove says, "benevolence, by the very meaning of the word, is a desire for the happiness, rather than the misery, of its object." But here's the rub: "the fact simply is that its actual effect is often the opposite of the intended one. The adult who had been hopelessly 'spoilt' in childhood is the commonest kind of example; that is, someone who is unhappy in adult life because his parents were too successful, when he was a child, in protecting him from every source of unhappiness."

It's not that benevolence is a bad thing per se. On the contrary, it's just that, like charity, it works best the more local are its aims. Enlarged, it becomes like that "telescopic philanthropy" Dickens attributes to Mrs. Jellyby in *Bleak House*. Like other such benefactors, Mrs. Jellyby's philanthropy is more ardent the more abstract and distant its objects. Africa excites her benevolence. When it comes to her own family, however, she is indifferent to the point of callousness.

Barbara Tuchman made a kindred point in *The Proud Tower*: "Humanitarian instincts grow fiercer in proportion to the distance by which their causes are removed and it is always easier to build Jerusalem in Africa than at home." The sad truth is that theoretical benevolence is compatible with any amount of practical indifference or even cruelty. You feel kindly towards others. That is what matters: your feelings. The *effects* of your benevolent feelings in the real world are secondary. Rousseau was a philosopher of benevolence. So was Karl Marx. Yet everywhere that Marx's ideas have been put into practice, the result has been universal immiseration. His intention was the benevolent one of forging a more equitable society by abolishing private property and, to adapt President Obama's famous phrase, by "spreading the wealth around." Every Marxist society has spread it wide and spread it thin. Hence Ronald Reagan's observation that the nine most terrifying words in the English language are "I'm from the government, and I'm here to help."

An absolute commitment to benevolence, like the road that is paved with good intentions, typically leads to an unprofitable destination. My epigraph from the great nineteenth-century English essayist Walter Bagehot underscores the point: it is a melancholy occupation, observed Bagehot, to ask whether the benevolence of mankind actually does more good than ill. It makes the purveyor of benevolence feel better—where by better I mean more smug and self-righteous. But it is unclear whether the objects of benevolence are any better off.

Just so with the modern Welfare State: a sterling incarnation of the sort of abstract benevolence Stove anatomizes. It doesn't matter that the welfare state actually creates more of the poverty and dependence it was instituted to abolish: the intentions behind it are benevolent. Which is one of the reasons it is so seductive. It flatters the vanity of those who espouse it even as it nourishes the egalitarian ambitions that have always been at the center of Enlightened thought. This is why Stove describes benevolence as "the heroin of the Enlightened." It is intoxicating, addictive, expensive, and ultimately ruinous.

The intoxicating effects of benevolence help to explain the growing appeal of politically correct attitudes about everything from "the environment" to the fate of the Third World. Why does the consistent failure of statist policies not disabuse their advocates of the statist agenda? One reason is that statist policies have the sanction of benevolence. They are "against poverty," "against war," "against oppression," "for the environment." And why shouldn't they be? Where else are the pleasures of smug self-righteousness to be had at so little cost?

The intoxicating effects of benevolence also help to explain why unanchored benevolence is inherently expansionist. The party of benevolence is always the party of big government. The imperatives of benevolence are intrinsically opposed to the pragmatism that underlies the allegiance to limited government.

STOVE'S ARGUMENT is that the union of abstract benevolence, which takes mankind as a whole for its object, with unbridled moralism is a toxic, misery-producing brew. "It is only the combination of these two elements," Stove observes in a powerful essay called "Why You Should Be a Conservative,"

> which is so powerful a cause of modern misery. Either element on its own is almost always comparatively harmless. A person who is convinced that he has a moral obligation to be benevolent, but who in fact ranks morality below fame (say), or ease; or again, a person who puts morality first, but is also convinced that the supreme moral obligation is, not to be benevolent, but to be holy (say), or wise, or creative: either of these people might turn out to be a scourge of his fellow humans, though in most cases he will not. But even at the worst, the misery which such a person causes will fall incomparably short of the misery caused by Lenin, or Stalin, or Mao, or Ho Chi Minh, or Kim Il-sung, or Pol Pot, or Castro: persons convinced both of the supremacy of benevolence

among moral obligations, and of the supremacy of morality among all things. It is this combination which is infallibly and enormously destructive of human happiness.

Of course, as Stove goes on to note, this "lethal combination" is by no means peculiar to Communists. It provides the emotional fuel for utopians from Robespierre to the politically correct bureaucrats who preside over more and more of life in Western societies today. They mean well. They seek to boost all mankind up to their own plane of enlightenment. Inequality outrages their sense of justice. They see tradition as the enemy of innovation, which they embrace as a lifeline to moral progress. They cannot encounter a wrong without seeking to right it. The idea that some evils may be ineradicable is anathema. The notion that the best is the enemy of the good, that many choices are to some extent choices among evils—such proverbial wisdom seems quaintly out of date. The result is a campaign to legislate virtue, to curtail eccentricity, to smother individuality, to barter truth for the current moral or political enthusiasm.

For centuries, political philosophers have understood that the lust for equality is the enemy of freedom. That species of benevolence underwrote the tragedy of Communist tyranny. The rise of political correctness has redistributed that lust over a new roster of issues: not the proletariat, but the environment; not the struggling masses, but "reproductive freedom," gay rights, the Third World, diversity training, and an end to racism and xenophobia. It looks, in Marx's famous mot, like history repeating itself as farce. It would be a rash man, however, who made no provision for a reprise of tragedy.

The attitude of abstract benevolence is all but ubiquitous in modern Democratic societies. Although of relatively recent vintage, it has insinuated itself deeply into the tissues of the body politic. Back in 1794, James Madison acidly observed that "I cannot undertake to lay my finger on that article of the Constitution which granted a right to Congress of expending, on objects of benevolence, the money of their constituents." How far we have come! The modern Welfare State has left Madison far behind. It represents the triumph of abstract benevolence. Its chief effects are to institutionalize dependence on the state while also assuring the steady growth of the bureaucracy charged with managing government largess. Both help to explain why the Welfare State has proved so difficult to dismantle.

Is there an alternative? Here Stove turns to Thomas Malthus and his famous Essay on Population. The key passage, which I quoted above in "Friends of Humanity," is that "we are indebted for all the noblest exertions of human genius, for everything that distinguishes the civilized from the savage state," to "the laws of property and marriage, and to the apparently narrow principle of self-interest which prompts each individual to exert himself in bettering his condition" (my emphasis). Stove observes that Malthus's arguments (one might quote Adam Smith to the same effect) for the genuinely beneficent effects of "the apparently narrow" principle of self-interest "cannot be too often repeated."

In *Utilitarianism*, John Stuart Mill argued that "justice" required everyone to be "as strictly impartial as a disinterested and benevolent spectator" about his own happiness. But Mill's great critic, James Fitzjames Stephen, is the wiser psychologist: "If this be so, I can only say that nearly the whole of nearly every human creature is one continued course of injustice, for nearly everyone passes his life in providing the means of happiness for himself and those who are closely connected with him, leaving others all but entirely out of account." And this, Stephen argues, is as it should be, not merely for prudential but also for moral reasons:

The man who works from himself outwards, whose conduct is governed by ordinary motives, and who acts with a view to his own advantage and the advantage of those who are connected with himself in definite, assignable ways, produces in the ordinary course of things much more happiness to others . . . than a moral Don Quixote who is always liable to sacrifice himself and his neighbors. On the other hand, a man who has a disinterested love of the human race—that is to say, who has got a fixed idea about some way of providing for the management of the concerns of mankind—is an unaccountable person . . . who is capable of making his love for men in general the ground of all sorts of violence against men in particular.

The partisans of limited government are suspicious of moral Don Quixotes. They want to preserve a space for private initiative. But private initiative is by its nature inequitable. Some individuals will succeed better than others. That indeed is the point: to encourage innovation and hard work by crowning it with success. Writing in 1800, Thomas Jefferson extolled that "wise and frugal Government, which shall restrain men from injuring one another, [but] shall leave them otherwise free to regulate their own pursuits of industry and improvement, and shall not take from the mouth of labor the bread it has earned." Ronald Reagan echoed Jefferson's admonitory observation when he noted that "Democracy is less a system of government than it is a system to keep government limited, unintrusive: A system of constraints on power to keep politics and government secondary to the important things in life, the true sources of value found only in family and faith." A thoroughly benevolent government, on the contrary, puts government first precisely because it regards equality and security as more important than family, faith, or liberty.

The larger the stage upon which the melodrama of benevolence operates, the more dangerous its potential. This is something that Henry Kissinger acknowledged when, writing about the new tendency to subject national politics to international tribunals, he warned about the "risk [of] substituting the tyranny of judges for that of governments." "Historically," he noted, "the dictatorship of the virtuous has often led to inquisitions and even witch-hunts." The "dictatorship of the virtuous" is a reign created by and supported by an imperious benevolence.

The elevation of benevolence from a private practice to a social imperative is not only at odds with traditional virtues like industry and thrift. It is also at odds with the habit of liberty. (Curiously, the apotheosis of benevolence also has the unfortunate side effect of blighting the everyday action of benevolence.)

Friedrich Hayek (about whom more below) said that one of the "main points" of his argument in *The Road to Serfdom* concerned "the psychological change," the "alteration of the character of the people," that extensive government control brought in its wake. The alteration involves a process of softening, enervation, infantilization even: an exchange of the challenges of liberty and self-reliance—the challenges, that is to say, of adulthood—for the coddling pleasures of dependence. Breaking with that drift becomes more and more difficult the more habituated to dependence a people becomes.

Difficult, but not impossible. It is too early to say for certain, but, writing this in late summer of 2011, I like to think there are signs that more and more people are waking up to the wisdom of Madison's observation, in *Federalist* 44, that "in the last resort a remedy must be obtained from the people who can, by the election of more faithful representatives, annul the acts of the usurpers."

Malcolm Muggeridge's Journey

*I came to Carthage, where I found myself in the midst of
a hissing cauldron of lusts. I had not yet fallen in love,
but I was in love with the idea of it, and this feeling that
something was missing made me despise myself for not
being more anxious to satisfy the need. I began to look
around for some object for my love, since I badly wanted
to love something.*
—St. Augustine, *Confessions*

*Diversion is the only thing that consoles us in our
wretchedness, and yet diversion is itself the greatest of
our miseries. For it is diversion above all that keeps us
from seriously taking stock of ourselves and so leads us
imperceptibly to perdition.*
—Pascal, *Pensées*

MARCH 2003 marked the centennial of the British
writer, television personality, and moral and religious gadfly Thomas Malcolm Muggeridge. The "Thomas,"
which Muggeridge never used, was after Thomas Carlyle.
Carlyle's fulminations against modernity, the "cash nexus,"
materialism, etc., greatly impressed Muggeridge père, a factory clerk and earnest Fabian reformer in Croydon, south

of London. H. T. Muggeridge was the overwhelming influence on Malcolm's early life, and so it was only natural that Carlyle's animadversions should greatly impress him, too. The third of five boys, Malcolm once claimed that Carlyle was the greatest influence on his literary style. I doubt that. But Muggeridge did become an accomplished fulminator, sometimes of conspicuous, even Carlylean, gloominess. If he never produced anything to equal Carlyle's great historical works, he did rival the sage of Chelsea in the ferocity of his denunciations—also his enthusiasms—and may have outdone Carlyle in the deployment of gleefully deflationary wit. He certainly wrote more digestible prose.

Muggeridge is not much of a presence today, though his anniversary did spark a minor recrudescence of Muggeridgiana. A painstaking and informative biography by Gregory Wolfe, originally published in 1995, was re-issued with a brief new preface, in 2003. (Richard Ingrams's shorter, more sprightly life, also published in 1995, is unfortunately out of print). There was a sudden spate of panels, symposia, and conferences devoted to "St. Mugg"—as the cartoonist Wally Fawkes ("Trog") once denominated him—as well as sundry essays with titles like "Malcolm Muggeridge's Journey."

It was a brief and haphazard revival, however, and more's the pity. Muggeridge is a tonic force, well worth resuscitating. He could be crankish. Sometimes he was downright absurd. But, at least until the last decade of his life, when his powers guttered, he was rarely *merely* crankish. Often he was incandescently perceptive. Above all he provided an intelligent admonitory voice, a voice against the grain of received opinion, urging caution, broadcasting unwelcome truths, nudging his interlocutors beyond the warm circle of their self-absorption.

In his heyday, which stretched from the 1930s through the 1960s and into the 1970s, Muggeridge was a formidable figure. He commanded prodigious literary and rhetorical gifts. He knew everyone: the infamous as well as the famous. He traveled everywhere: teaching in India and Egypt as a young man, on assignment in Moscow, Washington, New York, Berlin, Tokyo . . . In World War II, Muggeridge was a spy with MI6, stationed in Mozambique. He was, according to one biographer, an "outstanding secret agent," through whose ministrations a German U-boat was captured. Muggeridge was also a nimble public performer, quick with a comeback, heedless of sacred cows. His enemies (never in short supply) belabored his inconsistencies, his "contradictions"; he gloried in them.

Over the course of his long career (he died in 1990 at eighty-seven), Muggeridge published a clutch of novels. In 1931, his play, *Three Flats*, was performed in London. (George Bernard Shaw, who had already read the work, was in the audience opening night.) "From earliest childhood," Muggeridge noted, "it always seemed to me that the only thing worth doing in life was to write."

But Muggeridge was not really Muggeridge in his purely literary efforts. His best work was in the realm of journalism, taking that term in its highest and broadest sense. Muggeridge wrote about virtually every signal public event and personality from around 1930 through the 1970s. And yet he invariably interwove description with introspection. Reporting the news was part of assembling his autobiography. By the same token, his autobiographical writings— published are a volume of diaries and *Chronicles of Wasted Time*, a two-volume memoir that takes Muggeridge through World War II—are instinct with the news and personalities of the day.

Muggeridge seems to have written for just about every important English paper and journal, including *The Spectator, Encounter, The Listener, The New Statesman, The*

Manchester Guardian (where he became chief leader writer at twenty-seven), *The Telegraph* (where he was deputy editor for a spell), and *Punch*, which he edited for nearly five years in the 1950s. Muggeridge also wrote for many American publications. He had a column at *Esquire*—a publication that once mattered—and his work would regularly turn up in *The New Republic*, *The New York Review of Books*, *The Saturday Evening Post*, and other illustrious venues. By late 1940s he was a familiar figure on BBC radio. By the late-1950s he was ubiquitous on BBC television, where his cantankerous wit, oddly patrician appearance (replete with cigarette-and-holder for histrionic effect), and braying, Cambridge-trumps-Croydon accent transfixed audiences. A patent of his celebrity came in 1968 when his wax figure was unveiled at Madame Tussaud's, sharing a room with Elizabeth Taylor, Charles de Gaulle, Alfred Hitchcock, and the Beatles, among others.

IN HIS PROSE, Muggeridge tended to proceed by imbrication, layering his analysis of appearance, character, and achievement—the whole set firmly in the context of world events—to produce memorable, often devastating, portraits. In 1956, after the Suez crisis, Muggeridge had this to say about Prime Minister Anthony Eden:

> His somehow slightly seedy good looks and attire, his ingratiating smile and gestures, the utter nothingness of what he had to say—did it not all provide an outward and visible manifestation of an inward and invisible loss of authority and self-confidence? Yes, it was entirely fitting that this tedious, serious Etonian, on whose lips were the last dying echoes of the late nineteenth-century concept of progress without tears, should have had his moment in the middle of the turbulent and cruel twentieth century. He was a Disraeli

hero who had moved into a service flat. . . . As has been truly said, . . . he was not only a bore, he bored for England.

Has Eden's essential fecklessness ever been more piquantly sketched? Can anyone who has heard of the man who not only "bored, but bored for England" forget the characterization?

Deflationary finales were one of Muggeridge's specialties. After World War II, he went to Tokyo and witnessed a public appearance by the Emperor: a "nervous, shy, stuttering, pathetic figure, formerly god."

There was a large streak of the contrarian in Muggeridge. If all good society were united in believing "X," he was likely to give "not-X" a sympathetic airing. It was part of his lifelong campaign against highminded earnestness—which is not, I hasten to add, the same thing as a campaign against seriousness. Sometimes, it is true, Muggeridge was merely impish. It was part of what made him an effective television performer. An interview with Salvador Dalí began with this exchange:

MUGGERIDGE: I know we're supposed to discuss modern art, and I expect we shall, but first of all may I say I'm fascinated by your moustaches. Might I ask what happens to them at night?
DALÍ: They droop.

When the evangelist Billy Graham replied to a question by saying that "Only God could answer that one," Muggeridge instantly interjected: "And we haven't got him in the studio, or"—casting his eyes upwards—"have we?"

Muggeridge was a complex, many-sided creature. He was a driven man, plagued by insomnia, night fears, and nameless yearnings for surcease. His joking, bad-boy antics were played partly for laughs, for "ratings." But they also, I believe, had a more serious purpose. In the mid-1950s, when the scandal about Princess Margaret and Group Captain Townsend was fresh, he wrote a couple of exasperated pieces about the royal family. The title of the first, "Royal Soap Opera," epitomizes his point.

Muggeridge's criticism seems anodyne by today's standards. But it caused a furor at the time. The BBC banished him (temporarily) from its airwaves. The *Sunday Express* thundered that Muggeridge had "earned the contempt of all Britain." A stranger spat at him in Brighton; his cottage at Robertsbridge was defaced with slogans by empire loyalists; a neighbor told him he was no longer welcome to walk across his fields: the wages of candor. In the United States, Muggeridge was interviewed by Mike Wallace. He dispensed his usual quota of pleasantries. Wallace quoted the British MP Michael Astor's remark that Muggeridge's "genius is for disliking [his] fellow human beings."

> Well, if my fellow human beings were all Astors, there might be some element of truth in that, but fortunately for us all, the Astor family is a large one, but not so large that it's occupied the whole human race.

That sort of thing keeps people entertained. But Muggeridge also went on to make this serious point.

> The essence of a free and civilized society is that everything should be subject to criticism, that all forms of authority should be treated with a certain reservation, and . . . that once you have produced . . . a totally conformist society in which there were no critics, that would in fact be an exact equivalent of the totalitarian societies against which we are supposed to be fighting a cold war.

It is worth noting that in suggesting that "all forms of authority should be treated with a certain reservation," Muggeridge is not denying the legitimacy of authority—what we might call the authority of authority. On the contrary, he hoped that constructive criticism would help bolster the claims of authority. He knew too well what happened when authority collapsed. It is one of the main themes of *The Thirties* (1940), perhaps his most comprehensive piece of social observation. Reviewing the book, George Orwell described this tart moral and political portrait of the decade as "brilliant and depressing." Like many readers, Orwell thought the book too negative—a sobering judgment from the author of *1984*—but he subscribed to its main lesson, that "We are living a nightmare precisely because we have tried to set up an earthly paradise."

Muggeridge was weaned on well-scrubbed attempts to set up an earthly paradise. It was a main plank of the Fabian creed: to dispense with the burdensome scaffolding of the past, its selfish institutions, its superstitions, its allegiance to outmoded vices like competition and greed. Love, harmony, brotherhood—an end to the depredations of inherited wealth, inherited . . . anything. Onwards, upwards, unfettered progress forever and ever. Not only was Muggeridge raised in that creed, he also married into it. Kitty Dobbs was the beautiful, freethinking niece of Sidney and Beatrice Webb; in marrying her, he noted many years later, he was marrying into "a sort of aristocracy of the Left."

Muggeridge's great gift as a political commentator was a nose for spurious idealism. Like nearly every right-thinking (which meant left-leaning) person, the young Muggeridge regarded the Soviet Union as the first chapter of the new utopia. When he went there as Moscow correspondent for

The Manchester Guardian in the early 1930s, disabusement was almost immediate. As a leader writer, Muggeridge had tapped out "Many an uplifting sentence . . . expressing the hope that moderate men of all shades of opinion would draw together, and that wiser counsels might yet prevail." In Moscow, he discovered that "moderate men of all shades of opinion had a way of disappearing into Lubyanka Prison, never to be seen again." Muggeridge saw the future, and—unlike Lincoln Steffens a decade earlier—he saw that it was hell on earth. Russia, he understood, was in the process of becoming "a huge and centrally organised slave state." It wasn't long before he was writing to his aunt-by-marriage Beatrice about his

> overwhelming conviction that the [Soviet] Government and all it stands for, its crude philosophy (religion if you like) is evil and a denial of everything I care for in life. . . .
>
> Why should uncle Sidney say . . . "I indignantly repudiate the slander that there is forced labour in the Soviet Union" when every single person in Russia knows there is forced labour . . . ?

A glimpse of Stalin's Russia spurred Muggeridge's political awakening. It is to his everlasting credit that he had the wit to see through his Fabian "ideals" and the courage to broadcast the horrors going on around him. In the beginning, at least, he was almost alone. Western intellectuals flocked to the workers' paradise that Stalin had created and "they were one and all utterly delighted and excited by what they saw there."

> Clergymen walked serenely and happily through the anti-god museums, politicians claimed that no system of society

could possibly be more equitable and just, lawyers admired Soviet justice, and economists praised the Soviet economy.

As for the Webbs and their starry-eyed ideal of universal brotherhood, Muggeridge summed it up in a dismissive BBC broadcast after their deaths. Comparing Beatrice to Don Quixote, he wrote that "she finished up enmeshed in her own self-deception, adulating a regime [the USSR] which bore as little relation to the Fabian Good Life as Dulcinea del Toboso to the Mistress of Don Quixote's dreams."*

MUGGERIDGE WAS one of the first—perhaps he was the first—Western journalist to expose the awful brutality of Soviet totalitarianism. He was equally prescient about Hitler, early on warning against the British policy of appeasement. In addition, Muggeridge had the rare perspicacity to understand that left-wing tyranny is no less murderous than the right-wing variety. Reporting from Berlin in 1933, he wrote that "It's silly to say that the Brown terror is worse than the Red Terror. They're both horrible."

It is one thing—an important thing—to proclaim the bestiality of Communism or Nazism. It is quite another to discern the ways in which liberalism itself nurtures unfreedom. By the 1950s, Muggeridge had come to believe that liberalism is "the destructive force of the age." In part, his criticism was reminiscent of Tocqueville's. Unchecked, the impulse to equality became an impulse to homogeneity: the drive for

---

* "I listened to the broadcast with growing horror, incredulity, and anger," responded the chairman of the BBC. "The Webbs were personal friends of mine. . . . [N]obody can doubt that they were great public servants; after all they were buried in Westminster Abbey. . . ." *After all,* indeed. Some things never change.

democracy involved a democratic despotism that did not, to quote Tocqueville once again, so much tyrannize as infantilize. "The welfare state," Muggeridge observed, "is a kind of zoo which provides its inmates with ease and comfort and unfits them for life in their natural habitat."

But Muggeridge's brief against liberalism went deeper. Liberalism, he thought, illustrated the paradox of good intentions, whereby the opposite of what was intended comes to pass. Consider education. Scratch a liberal, and he shouts "Education!" Whatever social or political problem society confronts, good liberals huddle together and decide "What's needed is more and better education." (Obligatory codicil: "And the money—i.e., your money—to pay for it.") Is crime a problem? Education is the answer. Poverty? Education is the answer. War, violence, sickness, unkindness, death? Education, education, education. If only, the liberal muses, everyone were awakened to his or her own true interests, all the world's problems could be solved. But this notion, Muggeridge saw, is an illusion. Liberalism proposes what is unattainable:

> that we little men and women should live in amity together on our minute corner of the universe for the few score years vouchsafed us, of our own volition seeking one another's good and sharing equitably in the material things which satisfy our needs and desires. This is a fantasy. This, in human terms, cannot be. Therefore, the effect of believing in it is constantly tearing the world to pieces.

On the question of liberalism, as indeed on much else, Muggeridge's thinking was close to that of Dostoevsky, one of his favorite authors. He understood that some men (and women) do nasty things not because they are ill-informed but simply because they are nasty. I quote this passage from

Dostoevsky's *Notes From the Underground* in an earlier chapter. It gets to the nub of Muggeridge's criticism of liberalism. "Oh, tell me," Dostoevsky wrote,

> who first declared, who first proclaimed that man only does nasty things because he does not know his own real interests; and that if he were enlightened, if his eyes were opened to his real normal interests, man would at once cease to do nasty things, would at once become good and noble because, being enlightened and understanding his real advantage, he would see his own advantage in the good and nothing else. . . . Oh, the babe! Oh, the pure, innocent child!

The point, which Muggeridge saw, is that evil is not something an especially plush government program is going to eliminate. Evil is irremediable. In *Varieties of Religious Experience*, William James made a critical distinction. "There are," James wrote,

> people for whom evil means only a mal-adjustment with things, a wrong correspondence of one's life with the environment. Such evil as this is curable, at least in principle, upon the natural plane. . . . But there are others for whom evil is no mere relation of the subject to particular outer things, but something more radical and general, a wrongness or vice in his essential nature, which no alteration of the environment, or any superficial rearrangement of the inner self, can cure, and which requires a supernatural remedy.

Muggeridge dissented sharply from the liberal's cheery vision of universal brotherhood because he saw that it is based on an abbreviated view of human nature. "If," Muggeridge wrote, "you envisage men as being only men, you are bound to see human society . . . as a factory farm in which the only consideration that matters is the well-being of the livestock and the prosperity or productivity of the enterprise." Liberalism is like utilitarianism in proposing to superintend happiness. But the happiness on offer is the blunt palliative of animal satisfaction: satiety, not joy.

In 1938, Muggeridge published *In a Valley of This Restless Mind*. It was commissioned to be a survey of contemporary religious ideas. What turned out was an odd but powerful sort of spiritual autobiography, a portrait of existential anguish and bewilderment that begins "Looking for God, I sat in Westminster Abbey and watched sightseers drift by." Pascal, another Muggeridge favorite, characterized the human condition as bounded by "inconstance, ennui, inquiétude"—fickleness, boredom, and restlessness. Restlessness was Muggeridge's constitutional affliction, boredom his overpowering fear. *Valley* is an sly acknowledgment of that fact, part ventriloquizing credo, part disaffected satire.

> "What are you interested in?" asks the literary editor.
> I said I was interested in Lust and in Money and in God.
> "I've seen a book lying about that might be suitable. Short notice if worth it."

In a favorable review of the book, Evelyn Waugh noted that "what Mr. Muggeridge has discovered and wishes to explain is the ancient piece of folk-wisdom that Lust and Love are antithetical and that Lust is boring." Muggeridge's life is an illustration of the Pascalian insight that restlessness is a secret friend of boredom, feeding on what it abominates in order to sustain itself. Which is to say that what is boring may also be addictive.

TODAY, to the extent that he is known at all, Malcolm Muggeridge is more notorious than famous. He is remembered less for the truths he communicated than for the life that he led. He is the Libertine Who Found God, a latter-day St. Augustine who lingered in the flesh pots before turning to denounce them and embrace religion. Muggeridge lingered longer and more assiduously than most. He was an ambitious smoker, heavy drinker, and tireless adulterer. (His wife Kitty, it is worth noting, also pursued numerous adulterous liaisons; her last child, Charles, was fathered by one of her lovers.) According to Richard Ingrams, by the 1960s Muggeridge's behavior towards women

> had become embarrassing and frequently outrageous. BBC colleagues called him "The Pouncer." Patricia, [his friend] Claud Cockburn's wife, compared him to a Russian peasant, describing an incident when during a dinner party she went upstairs to make a phone call and was pursued by Malcolm who began to assault her. Outraged, Patricia struck out at him with the telephone, knocked him down and flew into a panic, convinced that she had killed him.

By the mid-1960s, Muggeridge had said goodbye to all that, giving up smoking first, then booze, then womanizing. Plagued by digestive problems, he also became a vegetarian. In 1982 he entered the Roman Catholic Church. His enemies, and even his friends, were not edified. They saw in him the aging reprobate who, stymied by flagging appetite, rails against the sins of his youth and cravenly turns to religion. The fact that Muggeridge launched Mother Teresa as a celebrity in the late 1960s, devoting a television show and book to her life and work, seemed to underscore the divide between Muggeridge the worldly wit and Muggeridge the retiring ascetic.

What this familiar criticism overlooks is the extent to which Muggeridge had always been a deeply religious character, a "pilgrim." As an adolescent, he would secretly read the Bible—secretly, because he knew his father would not have approved. At Cambridge, he seriously contemplated a religious vocation. His diary is full of entries minuting his religious fears, cravings, and exaltations. Muggeridge understood that the merely human is at best the nearly human. At the same time, his revulsions are at odds with the ampleness of the faith he proclaimed. In an interview from the 1960s, Muggeridge said that he "saw life as an eternal battle between two irreconcilable opposites, the world of the flesh and the world of the spirit." Yet "God made the world and saw that it was good." It seems a pity that this robust soul should have mistaken affirmation for indulgence.

Leszek Kolakowski
& the Anatomy of Totalitarianism

It's possible that I shall make an ass of myself. But in that case one can always get out of it with a little dialectic. I have, of course, so worded my proposition as to be right either way.
—Marx to Engels, 1857

What socialism implies above all is keeping account of everything.
—V. I. Lenin, 1917

Le coeur a ses raisons que la raison ne connaît point.
—Pascal, *Pensées*

THE POLISH PHILOSOPHER Leszek Kolakowski was just a few months shy of his eighty-second birthday when he died in July 2009 at his home in Oxford. For anyone inclined to despair that we live in intellectually diminished times, Kolakowski provided a glittering counterexample. He was an intellectual giant. What is even more extraordinary, he was an intellectual giant whose accomplishments were widely celebrated. Kolakowski died full of honors as well as years. The coveted if often risible MacArthur "genius" award: he got that. The Kluge Prize for lifetime achievement

in the humanities—a cool $1 million for that bijou: Kola-
kowski got that, too. Then there were the innumerable degrees honoris causa and lesser awards, honors, lectureships,
and sundry recognitions. He received, and deserved, them
all.

Born in Radom, in eastern Poland, in 1927, Kolakowski
was a boy of twelve when the Nazis stormed into Poland. "I
remember the destruction of the Warsaw Ghetto," he writes
in "Genocide and Ideology" (1978), "which I saw from outside; I lived among Poles who were active in helping Jews
and who risked their lives every day trying to save those
few who could be saved from the inferno." In 1945, the war
over, he joined the Communist Party: the Communists were
anti-fascist, weren't they? (Were they?) He studied and then
taught philosophy in Warsaw, where he also edited a scholarly journal.

Maturity begot doubts; doubts brought forth criticism;
criticism was a dangerous commodity in Soviet-controlled
Poland. In 1954, Kolakowski was accused of "straying
from Marxist-Leninist ideology." (True, all too true.) In
1966, after delivering a speech commemorating the tenth
anniversary of the "October thaw," he was expelled from
the Party with all the usual ceremony. The state-controlled
press launched a series of attacks on the renegade. He was
removed from his university chair for "forming the views of
the youth in a manner contrary to the official tendency of
the country." In 1968, he went into exile. His works were
promptly enrolled in the Index of forbidden authors and,
until 1981, could be neither referred to nor cited officially.

After leaving Poland, Kolakowski taught at several Western universities, including McGill, Yale, the University of Chicago (for more than a decade he was part of the Committee
on Social Thought), and, at Oxford, as a fellow of All Souls.
Throughout the 1980s, he aided and abetted the Solidarity

movement, which was instrumental in ridding Poland of its Communist oppressors.

IT WOULD BE an injustice, however, if this impressive inventory were to obscure one of Kolakowski's most conspicuous gifts: I mean his sense of humor. Consider, for example, this title: "A Comment on Heidegger's Comment on Nietzsche's Alleged Comment on Hegel's Comment on the Power of Negativity." This orotund pseudo-scholarly rubric neatly ushers Kolakowski into a serious point. In a famous interview with *Der Spiegel* published in 1976 shortly after his death, Heidegger was at pains to exonerate himself from his association with the Nazis. Among other things, he suggested that anyone who had ears to hear would know that he had criticized the Nazi regime in his lectures on Nietzsche and the Will to Power. "It probably takes an ear subtler than mine," Kolakowski notes, "to hear this criticism." Indeed, he shows that Heidegger "obliquely but clearly" expressed his commitment to German imperialism in those lectures.

While on the subject of humor, I should also direct readers to Kolakowski's book *The Key to Heaven: Edifying Tales from Holy Scripture to Serve as Teaching and Warning.* You will never regard the story of Job (or Noah, Lot's wife, Sarah and Abraham, or Jacob and Esau) in quite the same light. ("In the highest sphere of heaven stood an elegant bar where Jehovah was wont to receive the reports of His scouts . . .") Kolakowski's philosophically-tinctured sense of humor shows itself throughout his work. I also recommend "The General Theory of Not-Gardening," reprinted in *Modernity on Endless Trial* (1990), in which Kolakowski unfolds Marxist, Psychoanalytical, Existentialist, Structuralist, and Analytic Philosophical theories that explain why "you must not garden." The take-away comes under the rubric of what Kolakowski somewhere called "The Law of the Infinite Cornucopia," according to which the desire for belief generates an unending plethora of supporting arguments.

Despite his eminence, however, Kolakowski has largely escaped, at least in America, the dubious accolades of celebrity. Jacques Derrida has much greater brand recognition, as do Michel Foucault and, probably, Richard Rorty and others further down the intellectual food chain. Kolakowski inhabits a different order of distinction.

A couple of years before Kolakowski's death, Oxford University Press published a new omnibus edition of *Main Currents of Marxism*, all three volumes in one. The only addition was a brief new preface by the author. Although only a few pages long, the preface is valuable for three things. It reminds us straightaway—this emerges as a theme of the book—that Marxist doctrine, by calling for the abolition of private property and the more or less total subordination of the market to state control, provided "a good blueprint for converting human society into a giant concentration camp."("[T]he abolition of the market," Kolakowski comments elsewhere, "means a gulag society.") Kolakowski also makes the important point that, notwithstanding the collapse of the Soviet Union, Marxism is still eminently worth studying, not least because its aspirations continue to percolate in the dreams of various utopian planners. (You needn't go to China or even Cuba: just look at the increasingly pink and authoritarian complexion of the European Union.) Moreover, as Kolakowski puts it in his introduction to *My Correct Views on Everything* (2005),

> Communism was not the crazy fantasy of a few fanatics, nor the result of human stupidity and baseness; it was a real, very real part of the history of the twentieth century, and we cannot understand this history of ours without understanding communism. We cannot get rid of this specter by saying it

was just "human stupidity," or "human corruptibility." The specter is stronger than the spells we cast on it. It might come back to life.

Finally, Kolakowski's new preface contains an arresting aside about the book's publication history. Written in Polish between 1968 and 1976 "when their publication in Poland could only be dreamed of," the three volumes of *Main Currents* were first published in Paris by the Institut Littéraire from 1976–78 and were circulated underground in Poland. They were not published legally in Poland until 2000. In the intervening years the book has been translated into many languages, including Chinese. In French, however, only the first two volumes, which take the story of Marxism through the death of Lenin, have been published. The third volume, which deals with Stalinism and its allotropes—including New Left thinkers like Louis Althusser and Sartre—is still waiting for a French translation. Why? Perhaps, Kolakowski speculates, because its publication "would provoke such an outrage among French leftists that the publishers were afraid to risk it." I wish that some public-spirited soul would publish a French version so that we could make the experiment.

THE PHILOSOPHER David Stove once observed that, "as an item on the intellectual agenda, Marxism is scarcely even a joke. . . . Marxism is a fearful social—and police—problem, but so is the drug trade. It is a fearsome political problem, but so is Islamic fundamentalism. But an intellectual problem Marxism is not, any more than the drug trade or Islamic fundamentalism." Kolakowski has devoted the 1500 pages of *Main Currents of Marxism* as well as a dozen or more essays to Marxism, its genesis, its permutations, its horrifying record of mass murder. In an essay in *My Correct Views on Everything* called "What is Left of Socialism?" (1995), he apostrophizes Karl Marx as "a powerful mind, a very learned man, and a good German writer" ("good," I feel constrained to add, in the way the curate's egg was good: *The Communist Manifesto*, the *Theses on Feuerbach*, *The German Ideology* contain some powerful rhetoric, but have you looked into *Das Kapital* or the *Grundrisse* lately?).

Yet I suspect that Kolakowski would have agreed with Stove. He did not endorse Marxism as an intellectual phenomenon. Rather, he took it seriously as a product of human spiritual striving. This involved him in a complicated historical itinerary. Looking for the origin of the dialectic, Kolakowski took readers back to "the soteriology of Plotinus," providing a lofty vantage point from which to regard the sage who assured his audience (in the endlessly quoted snippet from the *Theses on Feuerbach*) that "hitherto, philosophers have only interpreted the world; the point is to change it." Meister Eckhart and Nicholas of Cusa loom as large in Kolakowski's exposition of Marx as do the proletariat, the labor theory of value, and the "contradictions of capitalism." He does not give Marxism the benefit of the doubt, exactly, but he does give it the benefit of patient scrutiny and the highest level of historical intelligence.

The results of that scrutiny are devastating. Notwithstanding its pretensions to "science" (perhaps the most grotesque aspect of Marxism's intellectual pretension—remember, for example, Engels' insistence that social laws were no less objective than geological deposits), Marxism has proven to be completely barren as an instrument of social understanding or prediction. This does not mean, as Kolakowski points out, that Marx's theories have not been useful. It's just that their usefulness has been confined entirely to providing "a set of slogans that were supposed to justify and glorify communism and the slavery that inevitably goes with it."

All of Marx's major predictions have turned out to be wrong. He said that societies based on a market economy would suffer spiraling class polarization and the disappearance of the middle class. Every society lucky enough to enjoy the fruits of a market economy shows that Marx was wrong about that. He predicted the growing immiseration and impoverishment of the working class in capitalist societies. (Actually, he didn't merely predict that it would happen, he predicted that it would happen necessarily and *inevitably*—thanks, Hegel.) The opposite has happened. Indeed, as Kolakowski notes, "in the second edition of *Capital* Marx updated various statistics and figures, but not those relating to workers' wages; those figures, if updated, would have contradicted his theory." *Contradicted*, Comrade. Dialecticians like Hegel and Marx pretend that a contradiction is as much an intellectual commendation as a refutation. It's merely pretense, though. A simpler, but more profound philosopher, David Hume, had the right attitude when he complained of "the custom of calling a *difficulty* what pretends to be a *demonstration*, and endeavoring by that means to elude its force and evidence."

Marx further predicted the inevitable revolution of the proletariat. Mark that, *inevitable*. This is the very motor of Marxism. Take away the proletarian revolution and you neuter the theory. But there have been no proletarian revolutions. The Bolshevik revolution, as Kolakowski points out, "had nothing to do with Marxian prophesies. Its driving force was not a conflict between the industrial working class and capital, but rather was carried out under slogans that had no socialist, let alone Marxist, content: Peace and Land for Peasants." Marx said that in a capitalist economy, untrammeled competition would inevitably squeeze profit margins: eventually—and soon!—the economy would grind to a halt and capitalism would collapse. Take a look at capitalist economies in the hundred and fifty years since Marx wrote: have profit margins evaporated? Marx thought that, when they matured, capitalist economies would hamper technical progress and Communist societies would support it: the opposite is true.

No, Marxism has been as wrong as it is possible for a theory to be wrong. Addicted to "the self-deification of mankind," it continually bears witness to what Kolakowski calls "the farcical aspect of human bondage." Why then was Marxism like moral catnip—not so much among its proposed beneficiaries, the working classes who bore the brunt of its immiserating effects, but among the educated elite? Why?

Well, beguiling simplicity was part of it. "One of the causes of the popularity of Marxism among educated people," Kolakowski notes, "was the fact that in its simple form it was very easy." Marxism—like Freudianism, like Darwinism, like Hegelianism—is a "one-key-fits-all-locks" philosophy. All aspects of human experience can be referred to the operation of a single all-governing process, which thereby offers the illusion of universal explanation.

Marxism also spoke powerfully to mankind's unsatisfied utopian impulses. How imperfect a construct is capitalist society: how much conflict does it abet, how many desires does it leave unsatisfied! Can we not imagine a world beyond those tensions and conflicts in which we could realize our full human potential without competition, without scarcity, without want? A society in which, as Marx famously put it in *The German Ideology*, the alienating "division of labor" has been overcome and anyone can "do one thing today and another tomorrow, to hunt in the morning, fish in the afternoon, rear cattle in the evening, and be a critic after dinner, just as I have a mind."

Sure, we can imagine that, but there is a reason that "utopia" means "nowhere." Kolakowski shows how Marxism speaks powerfully to those unrealized, and unrealizable, utopian dreams. Marxism, he wrote, was the "greatest fantasy" of the twentieth century, not because it offered a better life but because it appealed to apparently ineradicable spiritual cravings.

> The influence that Marxism has achieved, far from being the result or proof of its scientific character, is almost entirely due to its prophetic, fantastic, and irrational elements. Marxism is a doctrine of blind confidence that a paradise of universal satisfaction is awaiting us just around the corner. Almost all the prophecies of Marx and his followers have already proved to be false, but this does not disturb the spiritual certainty of the faithful, any more than it did in the case of chiliastic sects. . . . In this sense Marxism performs the function of a religion, and its efficacy is of a religious character. But it is a caricature and a bogus form of religion, since it presents its temporal eschatology as a scientific system, which religious mythologies do not purport to be.

Of course, it is not just to mankind's spiritual cravings that Marxism appeals. It also speaks to its inherent thuggishness.

This point cannot be emphasized too much. These days, Stalin and Stalinism are in bad odor. But we forget the romance that Western intellectuals indulged for this mass murderer. We also tend to overlook the fact that thuggishness is an integral, not an accidental, feature of Marxism. Marx spoke of the "dictatorship of the proletariat." What did he mean by "dictatorship"? Lenin explained. "Dictatorship," he wrote in 1906, "means unlimited power based on force, and not on law."

In case that was not sufficiently compelling, Lenin added the word "scientific": "The scientific term 'dictatorship' means nothing more nor less than authority untrammelled by any laws, absolutely unrestricted by any rules whatever, and based directly on violence."

In 1917, Lenin got the chance to show the world what this theory would look like when put into action. "He created a system," Kolakowski observes, "in which, depending on the whim of a local party or police authority, any criticism might be regarded as counter-revolutionary and expose its author to imprisonment or death." Hence, as we've seen in earlier chapters, the importance of terror, an essential ingredient in the revolutionary's utopian program at least since Robespierre spoke of "virtue and its emanation, terror." "The courts," Lenin wrote in 1922, "must not ban terror . . . but must formulate the motives underlying it, legalize it as a principle, plainly, without any make-believe."

The crucial thing to bear in mind, however, is not the brutality of Communist rule—what we might call "really existing Marxism"—but its spuriousness and contempt for law. This is what distinguishes ordinary despotism from its totalitarian counterpart. "A law," Kolakowski notes, "may provide draconic penalties for small offenses without being specifically totalitarian; what is characteristic of totalitarian law is the use of such formulas as Lenin's: people may be executed for expressing views that may 'objectively serve the interests of the bourgeoisie.' This means that the government can put to death anyone it chooses; *there is no such thing as law*; it is not that the criminal code is severe, but that it has no existence except in name" (my emphasis).

In other words, the very arbitrariness of Communist rule is a coefficient of its ambition to total control of life. Lenin said that what socialism implies above all is "keeping account of everything." Everything was subject to regulation from above because nothing had significance apart from the diktats of the Party. In this sense, Marxism is a solution in which the idea of intrinsic value dissolves into absolute expediency. For the Communist there is no such thing as impartiality or disinterestedness because there is no such thing as an independent object of value. Nothing has inherent significance because everything acquires value from its function in the impersonal engine of utopia.

STALIN ONCE REMARKED that the death of an individual is a tragedy, but the death of a million is a statistic. What he neglected to add is that, for the Communist, there is no such thing as the individual. By the same token, there is no such thing as independent judgment—scholarly, judicial, or even aesthetic judgment. Our postmodern literary critics are fond of declaring that "there is no such thing as"—take your pick: intrinsic value, objectivity, disinterestedness, impartiality, even truth. It landed them in a cloud-cuckoo-land of self-contradictory nihilism. But Marx and Lenin got there before them. For the Marxist, art and literature are not human pursuits guided by their own rules of achievement but rather instruments to be used for the shifting and arbitrary ends of the Party. "Down with non-partisan writers!," Lenin wrote in 1905, "Down with literary supermen! Literature must become part of the common cause of the proletariat, 'a cog and a screw' of one single great Social-Democratic mechanism set in motion by the entire politically conscious vanguard of the entire working class!"

The key issue is not partisan politics but rather the subordinating of intellectual life generally to non-intellectual, i.e., political imperatives. "The greatest danger," Kolakowski wrote in "What Are Universities For?,"

> is the invasion of an intellectual fashion which wants to abolish cognitive criteria of knowledge and truth itself. . . .
> The humanities and social sciences have always succumbed to various fashions, and this seems inevitable. But this is

probably the first time that we are dealing with a fashion, or rather fashions, according to which there are no generally valid intellectual criteria.

Indeed, it is this failure—the colonization of intellectual life by politics—that stands behind and fuels the degradation of liberal education. The issue is not so much—or not only—the presence of bad politics as the absence of non-politics in the intellectual life of the university.

Sidney Hook described *Main Currents of Marxism* as "magisterial." Quite right, too. In its nimble mastery of intellectual history and generous humanity, the book has no equal. Kolakowski's survey of Marxist thought is breathtaking in its sweep—from the Bible and the Greeks through the web of nineteenth-century socialist thought and the florid dissemination of Marxist and quasi-Marxist ideas in the "new-age" redoubts of the twentieth century, Kolakowski has provided the definitive account of a spiritual-political itinerary gone terribly wrong.

But what impresses one about *Main Currents of Marxism* is not only Kolakowski's breadth or learning but also his economy. This is a book from which the reader benefits from the author's great powers of distillation. It is a long book. In the hands of most writers, it would have been much longer. Kolakowski has an uncanny ability to seize upon and express the essential features of the doctrines he discusses. No doubt this is partly a matter of talent. It is also a testament to the huge labor, not only of reading but also of sifting and synthesizing, that went into the book. Kolakowski gives us not his first thoughts but his considered judgments, honed of the superfluous. Anyone who reads these sobering volumes will come away with not only an understanding of the intellectual and spiritual precursors of Marxism, but also a good grasp of the essentials of "classical" Marxist doctrine and its hybridization in the Soviet Union, the Frankfurt School, and other left-wing impulses. Writing about the amorphous New Left of the 1960s, for example, Kolakowski notes that although

> the ideological fantasies of this movement . . . were no more than a nonsensical expression of the whims of spoilt middle-class children, and while the extremists among them were virtually indistinguishable from Fascist thugs, the movement did without doubt express a profound crisis of faith in the values that had inspired democratic societies for many decades. . . . The New Left explosion of academic youth was an aggressive movement born of frustration, which easily created a vocabulary for itself out of Marxist slogans . . . : liberation, revolution, alienation, etc. Apart from this, its ideology really has little in common with Marxism. It consists of "revolution" without the working class; hatred of modern technology as such; . . . the cult of primitive societies . . . as the source of progress; hatred of education and specialized knowledge.

Sound familiar?

ANY STUDENT of Marxism is perforce a student of intellectual and political pathology, and *Main Currents of Marxism*, in addition to its other accomplishments, is a pathologist's scrapbook, a catalogue of brutal, often phantasmagoric, deformations. Kolakowski's approach is generally more descriptive and diagnostic than polemical, but he can wax polemical to deadly effect when the occasion arises. The title essay of *My Correct Views on Everything* (2005) is Kolakowski's devastating response to a 100-page "Open Letter to Leszek Kolakowski" published by E. P. Thompson in the *Socialist Review* in 1973. Thompson is the author of *The Making of the English Working Class* (1963), an object of pious veneration among the Marxist and socialist brotherhood. His "Letter" is an expression, by turns righteously indignant and cloyingly sentimental, of his feelings of "injury and betrayal" at Kolakowski's criticisms of Communism. "We were both voices of the Communist revisionism of 1956," Thompson lamented, "we both sought to rehabilitate the utopian energies within the socialist tradition." What happened?

Kolakowski's response is a salvo that would have made Cato the Elder proud. Recalling Thompson's refusal to sit down at a table with Robert Cecil because he once worked in the British diplomatic service: "O blessed Innocence! You and I, we were both active in our respective Communist Parties in the '40s and '50s, which means that, whatever our noble intentions and our charming ignorance (or refusal to get rid of ignorance) were, we supported, within our modest means, a regime based on mass slave labor and police terror of the worst kind in human history. Do you think that there are many people who could refuse to sit at the same table with us on these grounds?" Kolakowski quotes this effusion, reminiscent of the more utopian passages of Marx's *German Ideology*: "My own utopia," Thompson wrote,

> two hundred years ahead, would not be like Morris's "epoch of rest." It would be a world (as D. H. Lawrence would have it) where the "money values" give way before the "life values," or (as Blake would have it) "corporeal" will give way to "mental" war. With sources of power easily available, some men and women might choose to live in unified communities, sited, like Cistercian monasteries, in centres of great natural beauty, where agricultural, industrial and intellectual pursuits might be combined. Others might prefer the variety and pace of an urban life which rediscovers some

of the qualities of the city-state. Others will prefer a life of seclusion, and many will pass between all three. Scholars would follow the disputes of different schools, in Paris, Jakarta or Bogota.

As Kolakowski notes, "This is a very good sample of socialist writing. It amounts to saying that the world should be good, and not bad." Nice work if you can get it! But of course, Thompson cannot get it, and neither can anyone else. It is just unadulterated hokum, nauseating in its sentimentality, dangerous in its appeal to the credulous. Thompson dreams of a world in which "corporeal" war gives way to merely "mental" war (Lawrence and Blake would be among his heroes), but Kolakowski is right that this dream is thoroughly utopian: "We do not know how to harmonize the contradictory tasks contemporary society imposes upon us. We can only try to reach an uncertain balance between these tasks because we have no blueprint for a conflictless and secure society."

To be an anatomist of totalitarianism is also to be a connoisseur of freedom, its many beguiling counterfeits as well as its genuine aspirations. The question—the lure, the never fulfilled but inescapable promise—of freedom stands at the center of much of Kolakowski's work. In "The Self-Poisoning of the Open Society," reprinted in *Modernity on Endless Trial*, Kolakowski dilates on an antinomy of liberalism that beset Western societies during the Cold War and is, if anything, even more pressing today as we negotiate what amounts to a moral war with fundamentalist Islam.

The antinomy is this: liberalism implies openness to other points of view, even (it would seem) those points of view whose success would destroy liberalism. Tolerance to those points of view is a prescription for suicide. Intolerance betrays the fundamental premise of liberalism, i.e. openness.

Kolakowski is surely right that our liberal, pluralist democracy depends for its survival not only on the continued
existence of its institutions, but also "on a belief in their
value and a widespread will to defend them."

Do we, as a society, enjoy that belief? Do we possess the
requisite will? The jury is still out on those questions. A
good test is the extent to which we can resolve the antinomy
of liberalism. And a good start on that problem is the extent
to which we realize that the antinomy is, in the business of
everyday life, illusory. The "openness" that liberal society
rightly cherishes is not a vacuous openness to all points of
view: it is not "value neutral." It need not, indeed it cannot,
say Yes to all comers. American democracy, for example,
affords its citizens great latitude, but great latitude is not
synonymous with the proposition that "anything goes." Our
society, like every society, is founded on particular positive
values—the rule of law, for example, respect for the individual, religious freedom, the separation of church and state.
Western democratic society, that is to say, is rooted in what
Kolakowski calls a "vision of the world." Part of that vision
is a commitment to openness, but openness is not the same
as indifference.

In my chapter on G. K. Chesterton above, I quote this
memorable line from his book *Orthodoxy:* Chesterton
championed freedom of thought, but wisely noted that
"There is a thought that stops thought. That is the only
thought that ought to be stopped." We saw a similar sentiment above in the writing of James Burnham. Our society is
extraordinarily accommodating of diverse points of view—
especially, it sometimes seems, to those that are hostile to
the ideal of diversity. In order to continue to enjoy the luxury of freedom, we must say No to those movements that
would exploit freedom only to abolish it. "In order to defend itself," Kolakowski writes, "the pluralist order should

voice [its fundamental] values ceaselessly and loudly. There is nothing astonishing or outrageous about the fact that within the pluralist society, the defenders and enemies of its basic principles are not treated with exactly the same indifference."

PART OF WHAT makes Kolakowski's reflections on freedom and its vicissitudes so fruitful is his understanding that human freedom is inextricably tied to a recognition of limits, which in the end involves a recognition of the sacred. This has been a leitmotif of his work from the beginning. In *The Alienation of Reason* (1966), he criticizes positivism as "an attempt to consolidate science as a self-sufficient activity, which exhausts all the possible ways of appropriating the world intellectually."

In "Man Does Not Live by Reason Alone" (1991), Kolakowski argues that "mankind can never get rid of the need for religious self-identification: who am I, where did I come from, where do I fit in, why am I responsible, what does my life mean, how will I face death? Religion is a paramount aspect of human culture. Religious need cannot be ex-communicated from culture by rationalist incantation. Man does not live by reason alone." He shows how the tendency to believe that all human problems have a technical solution is an unfortunate inheritance from the Enlightenment—"even," he notes, "from the best aspects of the Enlightenment: from its struggle against intolerance, self-complacency, superstitions, and uncritical worship of tradition." There is much about human life that is not susceptible to human remedy or intervention. Our allegiance to the ideal of unlimited progress is, paradoxically, a dangerous moral limitation that is closely bound up with what Kolakowski calls the loss of the sacred. "With the disappearance of the sacred," he writes, which imposed limits to the perfection that could be attained by the profane, arises one of the most dangerous illusions of our civilization—the illusion that there are no limits to the changes that human life can undergo, that society is "in principle" an endlessly flexible thing, and that to deny this flexibility and this perfectibility is to deny man's total autonomy and thus to deny man himself.

These are wise words, grippingly pertinent to an age conjuring with the immense technological novelties of cloning, genetic engineering, and other Promethean temptations. We pride ourselves today on our "openness" and commitment to liberal ideals, our empathy for other cultures, and our sophisticated understanding that our way of viewing the world is, after all, only our way of viewing the world. But Kolakowski reminds us that, without a prior commitment to substantive values—to an ideal of the good and (just as important) an acknowledgment of evil—openness threatens to degenerate into vacuousness. Given the shape of our post-Soviet, technologically infatuated world, perhaps it is that admonition, even more than his heroic demolition of Marxism, for which Leszek Kolakowski will be honored in the decades to come.

Hayek & the Intellectuals

*An ignorant man, who is not fool enough to meddle with
his clock, is however sufficiently confident to think he
can safely take to pieces, and put together at his pleasure,
a moral machine of another guise, importance and
complexity, composed of far other wheels, and springs,
and balances, and counteracting and co-operating powers.
Men little think how immorally they act in rashly meddling
with what they do not understand. Their delusive good
intention is no sort of excuse for their presumption. They
who truly mean well must be fearful of acting ill.*
—Edmund Burke, "Appeal from the New Whigs" (1791)

*We were the first to assert that the more complicated the
forms assumed by civilization, the more restricted the
freedom of the individual must become.*
—Benito Mussolini, 1929

IN FACT, BENITO, you weren't the first. The palm for first
promulgating that principle in all its modern awfulness
must go to V. I. Lenin, who back in 1917 boasted that when
he finished building his workers' paradise "the whole of
society will have become a single office and a single factory with equality of work and equality of pay." What Lenin

didn't know about restricting the freedom of the individual wasn't worth knowing. Granted, things didn't work out quite as Lenin hoped—or said that he hoped—since as the Soviet Union lumbered on there was less and less work and mostly worthless pay. ("They pretend to pay us," one wag said, "and we pretend to work.") Really, the only equality Lenin and his heirs achieved was an equality of misery and impoverishment for all but a shifting fraction of the nomenklatura. Trotsky got right to the practical nub of the issue, observing that when the state is the sole employer the old adage "he who does not work does not eat" is replaced by "he who does not obey does not eat." Nevertheless, a long line of Western intellectuals came, saw, and were conquered: how many *bien pensant* writers, journalists, artists, and commentators swooned as did Lincoln Steffens: "I have been over into the future," he said of his visit to the USSR in 1921, "and it works."

Of course, you can't make an omelet without breaking eggs. But it is remarkable what a large accumulation of eggshells we have piled up over the last century. (And then there is always Orwell's embarrassing question: "Where's the omelet?") I forget the sage who described hope as the last evil in Pandora's box. Unfair to hope, perhaps, but not inapplicable to that adamantine "faith in a better world" that has always been at the heart of the socialist enterprise. Talk about a hardy perennial! The socialist experiment has *never* worked out as advertised. But it continually blooms afresh in the human heart—those portions of it, anyway, colonized by intellectuals, that palpitating tribe Julien Benda memorably denominated "*clercs*," as in "*trahison de.*" But why? What is it about intellectuals that makes them so profligately susceptible to the catnip of socialism?

In his last book, *The Fatal Conceit: The Errors of Socialism* (1988), Friedrich Hayek drily underscored the oddity:

The intellectuals' vain search for a truly socialist community, which results in the idealisation of, and then disillusionment with, a seemingly endless string of "utopias"—the
Soviet Union, then Cuba, China, Yugoslavia, Vietnam, Tanzania, Nicaragua—should suggest that there might be something about socialism that does not conform to certain facts.

It should, but it hasn't. And the reason, Hayek suggests,
lies in the peculiar rationalism to which a certain species of
intellectual is addicted. The "fatal conceit" lay in believing
that, by exercising reason, mankind could recast society in a
way that was at once equitable and prosperous, orderly and
conducive to political liberty.

I say "mankind," but of course the fatal conceit is always
pursued by a tiny elite who believe that the imposition of
their reason can effect the desired revolution in society.
The rest of us are the raw material for the exercise of their
fantasy.

Hayek traced this ambition back through Rousseau to
Descartes. If man is born free but is everywhere in chains,
Rousseau argued, why does he not simply cast off his fet-
ters, beginning with the inconvenient baggage of traditional
social restraint? Whether Descartes deserves this paternity
suit is perhaps disputable. But I see what Hayek means. It
was a small step from Descartes's dream of making man
the "master and possessor of nature" through science and
technology to making him the master and possessor of
man's *second* nature, society. How much that was recalcitrant about human experience and the world had suddenly
to be rendered negotiable even to embark upon that path!
All that was summed up in words like "manners," "morals,"
"custom," "tradition," "taboo," and "sacred" is suddenly
up for grabs. But it was part of the intoxicating nature of
the fatal conceit—for those, again, who were susceptible to

its charms—that no barrier seemed strong enough to withstand the blandishments of mankind's ingenious tinkerings.
"Everything solid," as Marx famously said, "melts into air."

John Maynard Keynes—himself a conspicuous victim of
the fatal conceit—summed up its psychological metabolism
in his description (quoted earlier in this book) of Bertrand
Russell and his Bloomsbury friends:

> Bertie in particular sustained simultaneously a pair of opin-
> ions ludicrously incompatible. He held that in fact human
> affairs were carried on after a most irrational fashion, but
> that the remedy was quite simple and easy, since all we had
> to do was to carry them on rationally.

What prodigies of existential legerdemain lay compacted in
that phrase "all we had to do." F. Scott Fitzgerald once said
that the test of "a first-rate intelligence" was "the ability to
hold two opposed ideas in the mind at the same time" and
still be able to function. In fact, that ability is as common as
dirt. Look around.

FRIEDRICH HAYEK (he dropped the aristocratic "von" to
which he was born) was a supreme anatomist of this species of intellectual or intellectualist folly. Born to a prosperous family in Vienna in 1899, Hayek had already made a
modest name for himself as an economist when he departed
for England and the London School of Economics in 1931.
Over the next decade, he published half a dozen technical
books in economics (sample title: *Monetary Theory and the
Trade Cycle*). Life changed in 1944 when *The Road to Serfdom*—published first in England, then a few months later in
the United States—catapulted him to fame.

The University of Chicago's ongoing "definitive," twenty-
volume collected works of Hayek reminds us both of the

power of Hayek's criticism and the intractable persistence of the attitudes he argued against. It takes courage, or something like it, to declare one's offering "The Definitive Edition." "Definitive" is a shifting and elusive trophy in such matters. I have no hesitation, though, in describing this as an excellent edition. The longer lines make the type slightly less readable than Chicago's handsome Fiftieth Anniversary Edition of *The Road to Serfdom*, but the new edition corrects a handful of typographical errors and adds useful supplementary material, including notes identifying the figures Hayek cites.

The story of this short but extraordinary book—which is less a treatise in economics that an existential *cri de coeur*—is well known. Three publishers turned it down in the U.S.—one reader declared it "unfit for publication by a reputable house"—before Chicago, not without misgivings, took it on. One of Chicago's readers, while recommending publication, cautioned that the book was unlikely to "have a very wide market in this country" or "change the position of many readers." In the event, Chicago could hardly keep up with demand. Within months, some 50,000 copies were in print. Then *Reader's Digest* published a condensed version, which brought the book to some 600,000 additional readers. A *Look* picture-book version a few years later further extended its reach.

Translated into more than twenty languages, *The Road to Serfdom* transformed Hayek from a retiring academic into an international celebrity. In succeeding years, his influence waxed and waned, but by the time he died, six weeks shy of his ninety-third birthday, in 1992, Hayek had at last become a darling of the academic establishment. He'd been a professor at the London School of Economics, the University of Chicago, and the University of Freiburg, and was the recipient of numerous honorary degrees. In 1974, he was awarded the Nobel Prize for Economics—the first free-market economist to be so honored—and his theories helped lay the intellectual groundwork for the economic revitalizations that Margaret Thatcher and Ronald Reagan undertook in the 1980s.

In a deeper sense, however, Hayek remained a maverick, outside the intellectual or at least the academic mainstream. The message of *The Road to Serfdom* shows why. The book had two purposes. On the one hand, it was a paean to individual liberty. On the other, it was an impassioned attack on central economic planning and the diminution of individual liberty such planning requires.

It might seem odd, in the wake of the Reagan and Thatcher revolutions, to describe an attack on central planning or a defense of individual liberty as "maverick." But in fact, although Hayek's theories won some major skirmishes "on the ground," in the world of elite intellectual opinion his views are as contentious now as they were in the 1940s. Even today, there is widespread resistance to Hayek's guiding insight that socialism is a nursery for the growth of totalitarian policies. With the example of Nazi Germany before him, Hayek saw how naturally national socialism, leaching more and more initiative away from the individual in order to invest it in the state, shaded into totalitarianism. A major theme of the book is that the rise of fascism was not a reaction *against* the socialist trends of the 1920s, as is often contended, but on the contrary was a natural *outcome* of those trends.

What began as a conviction that, if planning were to be "efficient," it must be "taken out of politics" and placed in the hands of experts, ended with the failure of politics and the embrace of tyranny. "Hitler did not have to destroy democracy," Hayek noted; "he merely took advantage of the decay of democracy and at the critical moment obtained the support of many to whom, though they detested Hitler, he yet seemed the only man strong enough to get things done."

Britain, Hayek warned, had already traveled far down the road of socialist abdication. "The unforeseen but inevitable consequences of socialist planning," he wrote, "create a state of affairs in which . . . totalitarian forces will get the upper hand." Hayek quotes numerous influential commentators who cheerfully advocate not only wholesale economic planning but the outright rejection of freedom. In 1932, for example, the influential political theorist Harold Laski argued that "defeat at the polls" must not be allowed to derail the glorious progress of socialism. Voting is all well and good—so long as people vote for the right, i.e., the left, things. In 1942, the historian E. H. Carr blithely argued that "The result which we desire can be won only by a deliberate reorganization of European life such as Hitler has undertaken."

The eminent biologist and commentator C. H. Waddington also proposed handing society over to the experts, noting that freedom "is a very troublesome concept for the scientist to discuss, partly because he is not convinced that, in the last analysis, there is such a thing." Sir Richard Ackland, architect of the "Commonwealth movement," wrote with bluff chumminess that the community says to the individual "don't *you* bother about getting your *own* living." The "community" as a whole will take care of that, determining how, where, and in what manner an individual will be employed. It will also, he added, run camps for shirkers, but don't worry, "the community" will insist on "very tolerable conditions." Like Carr, Ackland found a good deal to admire in Hitler, who, he said, had "stumbled across . . . a small part of, or perhaps one should say one particular aspect of, what will ultimately be required of humanity." This, incidentally, was written in 1941, a moment when the world discovered that following Hitler required a very great deal of humanity indeed.

THE TWO GREAT presiding influences on *The Road to Serf-dom* were Alexis de Tocqueville and Adam Smith. Toc-queville has played a recurring role in this book. From him, Hayek took both his title and his sensitivity to what Tocqueville, in a famous section of *Democracy in America*, called "democratic despotism." Hayek, like Tocqueville, saw that in modern bureaucratic societies threats to liberty often come disguised as humanitarian benefits. If old-fashioned despotism tyrannizes, democratic despotism infantilizes. "It would," Tocqueville writes,

> resemble paternal power if, like that, it had for its object to prepare men for manhood; but on the contrary, it seeks only to keep them fixed irrevocably in childhood; it likes citizens to enjoy themselves provided that they think only of enjoying themselves. . . . It willingly works for their happiness; but it wants to be the unique agent and sole arbiter of that; it provides for their security, foresees and secures their needs, facilitates their pleasures, conducts their principal affairs, directs their industry, regulates their estates, divides their inheritances; can it not take away from them entirely the trouble of thinking and the pain of living? . . . [This power] extends its arms over society as a whole; it covers its surface with a network of small, complicated, painstaking, uniform rules through which the most original minds and the most vigorous souls cannot clear a way to surpass the crowd; . . . it does not tyrannize, it hinders, compromises, enervates, extinguishes, dazes, and finally reduces each nation to being nothing more than a herd of timid and industrious animals of which the government is the shepherd.

Echoing and extending Tocqueville, Hayek argued that one of the most important effects of extensive government control was psychological, "an alteration of the character of the people." We are the creatures as well as the creators of the institutions we inhabit. "The important point," he concluded, "is that the political ideals of a people and its attitude toward authority are as much the effect as the cause of the political institutions under which it lives."

A major part of *The Road to Serfdom* is negative or critical. Its task is to expose, describe, and analyze the socialist threat to freedom. But there is also a positive side to Hayek's argument. The road *away* from serfdom was to be found by embracing what Hayek called "the extended order of cooperation," AKA capitalism. In *The Wealth of Nations*, Adam Smith noted the paradox, or seeming paradox, of capitalism: that the more individuals were left free to follow their own ends, the more their activities were "led by an invisible hand to promote" ends that aided the common good. Thomas Malthus, as we've seen, had a similar insight: "we are indebted," Malthus wrote, "for all the noblest exertions of human genius, for everything that distinguishes the civilized from the savage state," to "the laws of property and marriage, and to the apparently narrow principle of self-interest which prompts each individual to exert himself in bettering his condition." In other words, private pursuits conduced to public goods: that is the beneficent alchemy of capitalism. Hayek's fundamental insight, enlarging Smith's thought, is that the spontaneous order created and maintained by competitive market forces leads to greater prosperity than a planned economy.

The sentimentalist cannot wrap his mind, or his heart, around that datum. He cannot understand why we shouldn't favor "cooperation" (a pleasing-sounding arrangement) over "competition" (much harsher), since in any competition there are losers, which is bad, and winners, which may be even worse. It is at this juncture that advocates of a planned economy introduce the word "fairness" into the discussion: wouldn't it be *fairer* if we took money from person "A," who has a stack, and gave it to person "B," whose stack is smaller? ("That is," as W. S. Gilbert put it in *The Mikado*, "assuming I am 'B'.")

Socialism is a version of sentimentality. Even so hardheaded an observer as George Orwell was susceptible. In *The Road to Wigan Pier* (1937), Orwell argued that since the world "potentially at least, is immensely rich," if we developed it "as it might be developed . . . we could all live like princes, supposing that we wanted to." Never mind that part of what it means to be a prince is that others, most others, are *not* royalty.

The socialist, the sentimentalist, cannot understand why, if people have been able to "*generate* some system of rules coordinating their efforts," they cannot also consciously "*design* an even better and more gratifying system." Central to Hayek's teaching is the unyielding fact that human ingenuity is limited, that the elasticity of freedom requires the agency of forces beyond our supervision, that, finally, the ambitions of socialism are an expression of rationalistic hubris. As David Hume, another of Hayek's intellecutal heros, put it, "a rule, which, in speculation, may seem the most advantageous to society, may yet be found, in practice, totally pernicious and destructive."

A spontaneous order generated by market forces may be as beneficial to humanity as you like; it may have greatly extended life and produced wealth so staggering that, only a few generations ago, it was unimaginable. Still, it is not perfect. The poor are still with us. Not every social problem has been solved. In the end, though, the really galling thing about the spontaneous order that free markets produce is not its imperfection but its spontaneity: the fact that it is a creation not our own. It transcends the conscious direction of human will and is therefore an affront to human pride.

The urgency with which Hayek condemns socialism is a function of the importance of the stakes involved. As he puts it in *The Fatal Conceit*, the "dispute between the market order and socialism is no less than a matter of survival" because "to follow socialist morality would destroy much of present humankind and impoverish much of the rest." We get a foretaste of what Hayek means whenever the forces of socialism triumph. There follows, as the night the day, an increase in poverty and a diminution of individual freedom.

The curious thing is that this fact has had so little effect on the attitudes of intellectuals. No merely empirical development, it seems—let it be repeated innumerable times— can spoil the pleasures of socialist sentimentality. This unworldliness is tied to another common trait of intellectuals: their contempt for money and the world of commerce. The socialist intellectual eschews the "profit motive" and recommends increased government control of the economy. He feels, Hayek notes, that "to employ a hundred people is . . . exploitation but to command the same number [is] honorable."

NOT THAT INTELLECTUALS, as a class, do not like possessing money as much as the rest of us. They do. But they also look upon the whole machinery of commerce as something separate from, something indescribably less worthy than, their innermost hearts' desires. Of course, there is a sense in which this is true. But many intellectuals fail to appreciate two things. First, the extent to which money, as Hayek put it, is "one of the great instruments of freedom ever invented," opening "an astounding range of choice to the poor man—a range greater than that which not many generations ago was open to the wealthy."

Second, intellectuals tend to ignore the extent to which the organization of commerce affects the organization of our aspirations. As Hilaire Belloc put it in *The Servile State*, "The control of the production of wealth is the control of human life itself." The really frightening question whole-sale economic planning raises is not whether we are free to pursue our most important ends but who determines what those "most important ends" are to be. "Whoever," Hayek notes, "has sole control of the means must also determine which ends are to be served, which values are to be rated higher and which lower—in short, what men should believe and strive for." Thus it is that while it "may sound noble to say, 'Damn economics, let us build up a decent world,' . . . it is, in fact, merely irresponsible."

Ultimately, the appeal of socialism is an emotional appeal. And because one of the primary vehicles of our emotions is language, the perversions of socialism have their correlative in a perversion of language. "While wisdom is often hidden in the meaning of words," Hayek notes, "so is error." Consequently, the task of reclaiming liberty involves the task of reclaiming language. Throughout his work, Hayek devotes a great deal of attention to "our poisoned language," showing how socialist sentimentality has distorted almost beyond recognition basic terms like "liberty," "freedom," and "equality." Quite apart from any definite meaning they convey, such words are *eulogistic*: they automatically solicit our allegiance even when they have been conscripted to serve realities different from or even opposed to the things they originally named.

As Hayek notes, the "most efficient technique" to achieve the requisite semantic transformation is "to use the old words but change their meaning." The phrase "People's Republic" epitomizes the process, but look at what has happened to words like "liberal," "justice," and "social." In *The Fatal Conceit*, Hayek made a quick list of 160 nouns to which the word "social" had been affixed, from "accounting," "administration," "age," and "awareness" to "thinker," "usefulness," "views," "waste," and "work."

A weasel was once said to be able to empty an egg without leaving a mark, and "social" is in this sense a "weasel word": a phonetic husk with only an echo of meaning. It is, Hayek writes, "increasingly turned into an exhortation, a sort of guide-word for rationalistic morals intended to displace traditional morals, and now increasingly supplants the word 'good' as a designation of what is morally right." Think only of the odious phrase "social justice." What it means, in practice, is *de facto* injustice, since it operates by enlisting the legal machinery of justice in order to support certain predetermined ends. Partisans of "social justice" eschew "merely formal" justice; in so doing they replace the rule of law—which was traditionally represented as blind precisely because it was "no respecter of persons"—with the rule of (pseudo) "fairness."

It is not surprising that Hayek is often described as "conservative." In fact, though, he was right to object that his position is better described as "liberal," understanding that term not in its contemporary deformation (i.e., leftist, statist) but in the nineteenth-century English sense in which Burke, for example, was a liberal. There is an important sense in which genuine liberals are (in Russell Kirk's phrase) conservative precisely *because* they are liberals: they understand that the best chance for preserving freedom is through preserving the institutions and traditional practices that have, so to speak, housed freedom. Although cautious when it came to political innovation, Hayek thought traditional Tory conservatism too wedded to the *status quo*. "The decisive objection" to conservatism, Hayek wrote in "Why I Am Not a Conservative," a postscript to *The Constitution of Liberty*, is that it is by nature *reactive* and hence unable to offer alternatives to the "progressive" program. It can retard our progress down the socialist path; it cannot, Hayek though, forge a different path.

Hayek's "liberalism" was in this sense an activist or experimental liberalism. This was a feature of Hayek's thought that the philosopher Michael Oakeshott coolly discerned when he observed that the "main significance" of *The Road to Serfdom* was not the cogency of Hayek's doctrine but "the fact that it is a doctrine." "A plan to resist all planning may be better than its opposite," Oakeshott continued, "but it belongs to the same style of politics." Perhaps so. But Hayek's inestimable value is to have dramatized the subtle and seductive insidiousness of the socialist enterprise. "It is seldom that liberty of any kind is lost all at once": that sentence from Hume stands as an epigraph to *The Road to Serfdom*. It is as pertinent today as when Hayek set it down in 1944.

Coda: *The Anglosphere & the Future of Liberty*

If we are together nothing is impossible. If we are divided all will fail.
—Winston Churchill, 1943

The future is unknowable, but the past should give us hope.
—Winston Churchill, A *History of the English-Speaking Peoples*

Be assured, my young friend, that there's a great deal of ruin in a nation.
—Adam Smith, 1782

"ESPECIALLY THIS NATION." That's what the cultural critic John O'Sullivan replied when I quoted Smith's line to him a couple of years back. The economy had suddenly turned very interesting, in the dismaying way that your doctor finds your latest symptoms "interesting," and a sentiment of gloomy inertia, a heavy, energy-sapping miasma, lay upon the land. Back in the 1940s, Cyril Connolly announced that "It is closing time in the gardens of the West." Was he right at last? Or was Smith–O'Sullivan closer to the mark? Adam Smith had written to calm a young correspondent who contemplated with alarm British losses in the American War of Independence. As it happened, Britain absorbed the parturition of the United States with aplomb, growing ever stronger for more than a century. Where are we now? There's lots of ruin about: no one disputes that. But how are we—we, the English-speaking peoples of the world—how are we faring?

I am not sure who coined the term "Anglosphere," but James Bennett gave it currency in his book *The Anglosphere Challenge: Why the English-Speaking Nations Will Lead the Way in the Twenty-first Century*. Bennett's book was published in 2004. A paperback edition, with a new Afterword, appeared in 2007, just before the world economy got wobbly. *The Anglosphere Challenge* endeavored to make good on its optimistic subtitle. The nineteenth century had been the British century. The twentieth century belonged to America. The twenty-first, Bennett argued, might well be a third, more capacious Anglo century. "If the English-speaking nations grasp the opportunity," he wrote at the end of his book, "the twenty-first century will be the Anglosphere century."

"If." A tiny word that prompts large questions. What were those opportunities that needed grasping? How sure was our grip? And who, by the way, were "we"? What was this Anglosphere that Bennett apostrophized? Churchill's opus on the English-speaking peoples, published in four-volumes in the mid-1950s, principally included Britain, Canada, the United States, Australia, and New Zealand. He commenced his story in 55 B.C., when Julius Caesar first "turned his gaze" upon Britain, and concluded as Victoria's long reign ended. By the time Andrew Roberts extended Churchill's work in his magisterial *History of the English-Speaking Peoples Since 1900* (2006), the Anglosphere had expanded to include Commonwealth Caribbean countries and, more to the point, India with its 1.1 billion people and the burgeoning capitalist dynamo that is its econo-my. The inclusion of India shows, as Roberts argues, that the defining quality of the Anglosphere is not shared race or ethnicity but shared values. It is a unity, as the Indian scholar Madhav Das Nalapat put it, of ideas, "the blood of the mind" rather than "the blood of the body." Its force is more intangible than physical—set forth primarily in argu-ments rather than armies—but no less powerful for that. The ideas in play are so potent, in fact, that they allow In-dia, exotic India, to emerge as an equal partner with Britain and the United States at "the core of a twenty-first-century Anglosphere."

I'LL SAY SOMETHING about the substance of those ideas in a moment. First, it is worth pausing to register the medium in which the ideas unfold: English. Nalapat remarks that "The English language is . . . a very effective counter-terrorist, counter-insurgency weapon." I think he is right about that, but why? Why English? In a remarkable essay called "What Is Wrong with Our Thoughts?," the Australian philoso-pher David Stove, whom we've met several times in these pages, analyzes several outlandish, yet typical, specimens of philosophical-theological linguistic catastrophe. He draws his examples not from the underside of intellectual life—spiritualism, voodoo, Marxism, Freudianism, etc.—but from some of the brightest jewels in the diadem of Western thought: from the work of Plotinus, for example, and Hegel, and Michel Foucault. He quoted his examples in transla-tion, he acknowledges, but notes that "it is a very striking fact . . . that I had to go to translations. . . . Nothing which was ever expressed originally in the English language resem-bles, except in the most distant way, the thought of Plotinus, or Hegel, or Foucault. I take this," Stove concludes, "to be enormously to the credit of our language."

Indeed. But why? What is it about English? I do not have an answer, but I note the fact that there seems to be some deep connection between the English language and that most uncommon virtue, common sense. I do not mean that English speakers act any less extravagantly than speakers of other tongues, but rather that English generally acts to tether thought to the empirical world. This is something Bishop Thomas Sprat dilated on in his *History of the Royal Society* (1667): "The general constitution of the minds of the English," he wrote, embraces frankness and simplicity of diction, "the middle qualities, between the reserv'd subtle southern, and the rough unhewn Northern people."

English, Bishop Sprat thought, is conspicuously the friend of empirical truth. It is also conspicuously the friend of liberty. Andrew Roberts, reflecting on the pedigree of certain ideas in the lexicon of freedom, notes that such key phrases as "liberty of conscience" (1580), "civil liberty" (1644, a Miltonic coinage), and "liberty of the press" (1769) were first expressed in English. Why is it that English-speaking countries produced Adam Smith and John Locke, David Hume and James Madison, but not Hegel, Marx, or Foucault? "The tongue and the philosophy are not unrelated," the philologist Robert Claiborne writes in *The Life and Times of the English Language*. "Both reflect the ingrained Anglo-American distrust of unlimited authority, whether in language or in life."

Andrew Roberts stresses the element of pragmatic skepticism that speaks English as its native language. "The unimaginative, bourgeois, earth-bound English-speaking peoples," he writes, "refuse to dream dreams, see visions and follow fanatics and demagogues, from whom they are protected by their liberal constitutions, free press, rationalist philosophy, and representative institutions. They are temperamentally less inclined towards fanaticism, high-flown rhetoric and

Bonapartism than many other peoples in history. They respect what is tangible and, in politics at least, suspect what is not."

I have nothing by way of an explanation for this filiation between the English language and the habit of liberty. I merely note its existence. Alan Macfarlane, in his classic *Origins of English Individualism* (1978), shows that the habit is far older than we have been taught to believe. According to the Marxist narrative, individualism is a "bourgeois construct" whose motor belongs to the eighteenth-century. Macfarlane shows that, on the contrary, "since at least the thirteenth century England has been a country where the individual has been more important than the group." "Peasant" was a term the English used about others but not themselves. Why? Macfarlane locates the answer in the presence of a market economy, an "individualistic pattern of ownership," and strong recourse to local initiative that were prominent features of English life at least since 1250. "In many respects," he writes, "England had probably long been different from almost every other major agrarian society we know."

Different in origins and different also in outcomes. Consider Britain's record as a colonial power. "Thanks to English law," the historian Keith Windschuttle has pointed out, "most British colonial officials delivered good government." And the positive effects are not merely historical artifacts. They are patent everywhere in the world today. "The key regional powers in almost every corner of the globe," Mark Steyn reminds us, "are British-derived—from Australia to South Africa to India—and, even among the lesser players, as a general rule you're better off for having been exposed to British rule than not: Why is Haiti Haiti and Barbados Barbados?"

"English institutions" you might say, "the rule of law, and all that." Well, yes, but why were the English peculiarly prominent among the bearers of that beneficence? Again, I do not have an explanation. It has something to do, I feel sure, with the habit of liberty, the contagious temperament of freedom. It's a trait that has been widely noticed. The Czech writer Karel Capek visited England in the 1920s. Writing about the country a few years later, he observed that the Englishman "stays in England all the time even when he happens to be somewhere else, say, Naples or Tibet. . . . England is not just a certain territory; England is a particular environment habitually surrounding Englishmen." Santayana registered something similar in his essay on "The British Character" in *Soliloquies in England* (1922). I quoted a bit of this passage above in "Rereading John Buchan." It bears quoting at greater length here. "What governs the Englishman is his inner atmosphere, the weather in his soul," Santayana wrote.

> Instinctively the Englishman is no missionary, no conqueror. He prefers the country to the town, and home to foreign parts. He is rather glad and relieved if only natives will remain natives and strangers strangers, and at a comfortable distance from himself. Yet outwardly he is most hospitable and accepts almost anybody for the time being; he travels and conquers without a settled design, because he has the instinct of exploration. His adventures are all external; they change him so little that he is not afraid of them. He carries his English weather in his heart wherever he goes, and it becomes a cool spot in the desert, and a steady and sane oracle amongst all the deliriums of mankind. Never since the heroic days of Greece has the world had such a sweet, just, boyish master. It will be a black day for the human race when scientific blackguards, conspirators, churls, and fanatics manage to supplant him.

The question is whether these mostly agreeable observations should be filed under the rubric "As We Were," like

A. C. Benson's nostalgic look back at a vanished Victorian heyday. The alarming possibility that recent history has presented us with is that the assault of Santayana's "scientific blackguards, conspirators, churls, and fanatics" may come as much from within the Anglosphere as from outside it. "Civilizations," observed the political philosopher James Burnham "die, in truth, only by suicide." What have we been doing to ourselves?

Two themes predominant in the question of the future of the Anglosphere. One is backward-looking and concerns the tonic relationship between the Anglosphere and political liberty. The second is forward-looking and stresses the extent to which the epicenters of the Anglosphere—Britain, North America, Australia—have abandoned their allegiance to the core values Alan Macfarlane descried in English society three-quarters of a millennium past: individual liberty and its political correlative, limited government. In a melancholy passage, the English writer Anthony Daniels, reflecting about contemporary British society, notes that

> The huge change in British society, from a free and orderly but very unequal society to a highly regulated but disorderly and rather more equal society, came about because the ruling political passions and desiderata, particularly among the ever-more important intelligentsia, changed from freedom and equality before the law to equality of outcome and physical well-being and comfort. If freedom failed to result in the latter, so much the worse for freedom: very few people in Britain now give a fig for it. The loss of their double-glazing would mean more to them than the loss of their right to say what they like.

A sobering contingency. Is it really as bad as that?

A growing influence of elites brings with it an erosion of local initiative as the blandishments of security are dispensed in exchange for a tithe on freedom. Tocqueville noted the perennial tension between the demand for freedom and the demand for equality in democratic regimes. And as we saw in the last chapter, his great disciple Friedrich Hayek described the process by which "extensive government control" produced "a psychological change, an alteration of the character of the people." "The important point," wrote Hayek, "is that the political ideals of a people and its attitude toward authority are as much the effect as the cause of the political institutions under which it lives. This means, among other things, that even a strong tradition of political liberty is no safeguard if the danger is precisely that new institutions and policies will gradually undermine and destroy that spirit." Evidence for the collapse of the spirit is not far to seek. In a characteristically penetrating observation, Mark Steyn cites the deliciously awful spectacle of former Prime Minister Gordon Brown endeavoring to come up with a patriotic British equivalent of Independence Day for Americans. What did his government turn up? July 5, the anniversary of the inauguration of National Health Service, a fitting symbol of British surrender of personal freedom for the sake of a spurious security. "They can call it," Steyn writes, "Dependence Day."

The anatomy of servitude, which has formed an important leitmotif in this book, tells a depressing story. But it is not all of the story. Even the "apocalyptic" Mark Steyn points to the way out. He is quite right that "you cannot wage a sustained ideological assault on your own civilization without profound consequence." We've had the assault and we are living with the consequences. He is also right that "without serious course correction, we will see the end of the Anglo-American era, and the eclipse of the powers that built the modern world." The hopeful part of that prediction comes in the apodosis: the course may still be corrected. As Hayek noted about his own dire diagnosis: "The consequences can of course be averted if that spirit reasserts itself in time." There are, I believe, two main sources of hope. One lies in the past, in the depth and strength of the Anglosphere's traditional commitment to individual freedom and local initiative against the meddlesome intrusion of any central authority. "The future is unknowable," said Churchill, "but the past should give us hope." The Anglosphere, James Bennett writes, "is not a fragile hothouse flower that can be easily uprooted and disappear forever."

The second main ground for hope lies in the present and immediate future. In the United States, anyway, we have lately witnessed a new "revolt of the masses," different from, in fact more or less the opposite of, the socialistic eruption José Ortega y Gasset limned in his famous essay on the subject. A specter is haunting America, the specter of freedom. It travels under different names, but its core motivation centers around the rejection of the business as usual: the big-government, top-down, elitist egalitarianism practiced by both major parties in the United States. In the aftermath of the November 2010 mid-term elections, I spoke on a cruise sponsored by *National Review* at which the pollster Scott Rasmussen observed that one thing the election demonstrated was that Americans do not want to be governed by Democrats or by Republicans: they want to govern themselves. If he is right—there's that little word "if" again—the Anglosphere has a lot more mileage in it. Are things bad? Is it late? Yes, and yes again. But as Lord D'Abernon memorably put it, "An Englishman's mind works best when it is almost too late."

Index

Index

Parks, Rosa, 52
Partisan Review, The, 23, 265, 273
Pascal, Blaise, 145, 284, 295, 298
Péguy, Charles, 75, 87
Peloponnesian War, 74, 79
Pepys, Samuel, 143
Pericles, 43, 73–91
Phidias, 81
The Pilgrim's Progress, 102, 104
Pindar, Wilhelm, 193
Pinter, Harold, 85
Piranesi, Giovanni, 216
Plato, *Phaedrus*, 33–34
Plotinus, 303, 332
Poirier, Richard, 23
Pol Pot, 8, 255, 280
Porter, Cole, 7
Potter, Stephen, 136, 160
Pound, Ezra, 263
Prescott, William Hickling, 227
Princeton University, 60, 261–262
Protagoras, 2
Proust, Marcel, 76, 110
Pryce-Jones, David, 41
Punch, 287
Putin, Vladimir, 36
Puvis de Chavannes, Pierre, 208

Rabkin, Jeremy, *Law Without Nations?*, 10
Rahv, Philip, 273
Ransom, John Crowe, 174–175
Rasmussen, Scott, 338
Ratzinger, Cardinal Joseph, *see* Benedict XVI
Rauch, Jonathan, 87
Ravitch, Diane, 32
Read, Herbert, 263, 271
Reader's Digest, 320
Reagan, Ronald, 89, 278, 282, 321
Regnery, Henry, 176–177, 188
Relativism, 1–11
Revel, Jean-François, 70; *The Flight from Truth*, 23
Revolutionary War, 52, 71
Rhodes, Cecil, 106
Richards, I. A., *Practical Criticism*, 262–263
Riegl, Alois, 186
Roberts, Andrew, *History of the English-Speaking Peoples Since 1900*, 331–333

Robespierre, Maximilien, 8, 191, 232, 247, 251, 280, 307
Rockefeller, John D., 176
Roosevelt, Franklin Delano, 55, 264
Roosevelt, Theodore, 57; *Autobiography*, 46
Rorty, Richard, 22, 301
Rosenberg, Harold, 263
Rousseau, Jean-Jacques, 8–9, 240, 245–247, 267, 278, 318
Rowe, Colin, 219
Royal Academy, 31
Rudolph, Paul, 225
Rush, Benjamin, 68
Ruskin, John, 152, 226
Russell, Bertrand, 231, 271, 319

Said, Edward, 85
Santayana, George, 95; *Soliloquies in England*, 115, 335–336
Sartre, Jean-Paul, 302
Saturday Evening Post, The, 287
Saudi Arabia, bombing of U.S. barracks in, 89
Sayers, Dorothy L., 142
Schapiro, Meyer, "The New Viennese School," 186–187
Schlesinger, Arthur, 272; *The Disuniting of America*, 51
Schorr, Daniel, 86
Schumann, Robert, 23
Schumpeter, Joseph, 183
Scopes trial, 181
Scotchie, Joseph, *Barbarians in the Saddle*, 177, 182
Scott, Geoffrey, *The Architecture of Humanism*, 207, 222–225
Scott, Robert, 124–125
Scott, Sir Walter, 99; *Ivanhoe*, 147
Scruton, Roger, *A Political Philosophy*, 10–11; 226
Sedlmayer, Hans, *Art in Crisis*, 185–198
Sennett, Richard, 60
September 11, 42–43, 48–50, 73–91, 97, 218
Sexual plasticity 30–31
Shakespeare, William, 13, 22, 26–27, 33, 35, 123, 137; *Hamlet*, 40, 90; *Macbeth*, 180
Sharia law, 70, 90
Shaw, George Bernard, 147–148, 286

Roger Kimball is Editor and Publisher of *The New Criterion* and Publisher of Encounter Books. Among his earlier books are *Tenured Radicals: How Politics Has Corrupted Our Higher Education*; *The Long March: How the Cultural Revolution of the 1960s Changed America*; *Experiments Against Reality: The Fate of Culture in the Postmodern Age*; *Art's Prospect: The Challenge of Tradition in an Age of Celebrity*; *Lives of the Mind: The Use and Abuse of Intelligence from Hegel to Wodehouse*; and *The Rape of the Masters: How Political Correctness Sabotages Art*. He lives in Connecticut.